STUDIES IN ROMANCE LANGUAGES: 9

A POET AT THE FOUNTAIN

A POET AT THE FOUNTAIN

ESSAYS ON THE NARRATIVE VERSE
OF GUILLAUME DE MACHAUT

BY

WILLIAM CALIN

THE UNIVERSITY PRESS OF KENTUCKY

LEXINGTON

I.S.B.N. 0-8131-1297-4

LIBRARY OF CONGRESS CATALOG CARD NUMBER 72-91663

*A statewide cooperative publishing agency serving
Berea College, Centre College of Kentucky, Eastern
Kentucky University, Georgetown College, Kentucky
Historical Society, Kentucky State University,
Morehead State University, Murray State University,
Northern Kentucky State College, Transylvania
University, University of Kentucky, University of
Louisville, and Western Kentucky University*

EDITORIAL AND SALES OFFICES: LEXINGTON, KENTUCKY 40506

PRINTED IN SPAIN

IMPRESO EN ESPAÑA

I.S.B.N. 84-399-2078-4

DEPÓSITO LEGAL: V. 1.719 - 1974

ARTES GRÁFICAS SOLER, S. A. — JÁVEA, 28 — VALENCIA (8) — 1974 *à Françoise*

CONTENTS

ACKNOWLEDGMENTS 11

ABBREVIATIONS 13

INTRODUCTION 15

1. *Le Dit dou Vergier* 23

2. *Le Jugement dou Roy de Behaingne* 39

3. *Remede de Fortune* 55

4. *Le Dit dou Lyon* 75

5. *Le Dit de l'Alerion* 92

6. *Le Jugement dou Roy de Navarre* 110

7. *Le Confort d'Ami* 130

8. *La Fonteinne amoureuse* 146

9. *Le Livre du Voir-Dit* 167

10. *La Prise d'Alexandrie* 203

Excursus: Machaut's Short *Dits* 227

CONCLUSION 239

BIBLIOGRAPHY 249

INDEX 255

ACKNOWLEDGMENTS

I wish to acknowledge grants-in-aid from the American Council of Learned Societies (1968) and the American Philosophical Society (1970), which enabled me to travel abroad in quest of old Machaut manuscripts. Without these grants my work would have suffered.

ABBREVIATIONS

CA	*Le Confort d'Ami*
DA	*Le Dit de l'Alerion*
DH	*Le Dit de la Harpe*
DL	*Le Dit dou Lyon*
DM	*Le Dit de la Marguerite*
DR	*Le Dit de la Rose*
DV	*Le Dit dou Vergier*
FA	*La Fonteinne amoureuse*
FLM	*Le Dit de la fleur de lis et de la Marguerite*
JRB	*Le Jugement dou Roy de Behaingne*
JRN	*Le Jugement dou Roy de Navarre*
P	*Le Prologue*
PA	*La Prise d'Alexandrie*
RF	*Remede de Fortune*
VD	*Le Voir-Dit*

INTRODUCTION

GUILLAUME DE MACHAUT, France's greatest poet and musician of the fourteenth century, was born around 1300, most likely in the village of Machault in Champagne (the Ardennes). He studied probably at Reims and Paris, receiving a Master of Arts degree, but never took Holy Orders. From around 1323 on he served John of Luxembourg, king of Bohemia, as *domesticus* and *familiaris, notarius,* and finally *secretarius.* He followed King John's campaigns in Poland and Silesia (1327, 1329, and 1331), Lithuania (1328-1329, 1336-1337), and probably Lombardy (1330). The king's favor exerted on Popes John XXII and Benedict XII won for Machaut a number of benefices. In 1337 the poet was awarded a canonicate at Reims and sometime between that date and 1340 left King John to settle down in the cathedral city. There, but for occasional trips to the courts of his protectors, he dwelt for the remainder of his life. He died in 1377. The corpus of his narrative poetry includes ten long *dits—Le Dit dou Vergier, Le Jugement dou Roy de Behaingne, Remede de Fortune, Le Dit dou Lyon, Le Dit de l'Alerion, Le Jugement dou Roy de Navarre, Le Confort d'Ami, La Fonteinne amoureuse, Le Voir-Dit,* and *La Prise d'Alexandrie*—and four shorter ones—*Le Dit de la Harpe, Le Dit de la Marguerite, Le Dit de la fleur de lis et de la Marguerite,* and *Le Dit de la Rose*—plus a *Prologue.* Machaut's lyric production was equally immense. He also composed *La Messe de Nostre Dame* (the first complete polyphonic setting of the Ordinary of the Mass by one man), a hoquet, and twenty-three motets, and set to music a good portion of his lyrics: nineteen *lais,* one *complainte,* thirty-three *virelais,* one *chanson royale,* forty-two *ballades,* and twenty-one *rondeaux.* His opus is preserved in several elaborate manuscripts, some apparently constituted under the master's personal supervision. [1]

A chronology for Machaut's *dits* has not yet been determined with any certainty. The following list indicates the order in which his long narrative poems are to be found in the best manuscripts, which include most of those prepared during the author's lifetime. After each poem, whenever possible, I place the date of composition or *terminus a quo*.

Le Dit dou Vergier	
Le Jugement dou Roy de Behaingne	
Le Jugement dou Roy de Navarre	1349
Remede de Fortune	
Le Dit dou Lyon	1342
Le Dit de l'Alerion	
Le Confort d'Ami	1356-1357
La Fonteinne amoureuse	1360-1362
Le Voir-Dit	1363-1365
La Prise d'Alexandrie	1369-1371

With excellent arguments, Ernest Hoepffner proposed that Machaut himself had arranged his *dits* according to the order of composition. Machaut would have made an exception only for *Le Jugement dou Roy de Navarre*. Although the *Roy de Navarre* was probably composed after *Le Dit de l'Alerion*, Machaut placed it directly after *Le Jugement dou Roy de Behaingne* because the two *Jugements* treat the same theme, and *Navarre* appears to be a reply to *Behaingne*, a kind of anti-Behaingne. [2]

The vast majority of specialists have accepted Hoepffner's theory. Gilbert Reaney and Leo Schrade suggest that the musical works were also arranged in the manuscripts for the most part chronologically, after having been sorted out by categories according to genre. [3] Although some scholars, including Armand Machabey, do

---

[1] The best life of Machaut is by Armand Machabey, *Guillaume de Machault, 130?-1377: La Vie et l'Œuvre musical* (Paris, 1955), 1: 13-83.

[2] Ernest Hoepffner, ed., *Œuvres de Guillaume de Machaut*, 3 vols. (Paris, 1908, 1911, 1921), in the introduction to each volume.

[3] Gilbert Reaney, "A Chronology of the Ballades, Rondeaux and Virelais Set to Music by Guillaume de Machaut," *Musica Disciplina* 6 (1952): 33-38,

not agree, in my opinion they do not submit convincing reasons for doubting the manuscript evidence nor do they suggest an alternate order of composition. Nonetheless, the arguments on both sides are far from conclusive. Therefore, I shall examine each of Machaut's *dits* in order, following Hoepffner's reconstitution of their chronology (the *Roy de Navarre* comes after the *Alerion*) but always bearing in mind that this reconstitution is but a hypothesis and that decisive critical judgments cannot be based on it.

On the whole, Machaut has fared well at the hands of philologists. His musical works have been edited twice in a most scrupulous fashion by distinguished scholars (Friedrich Ludwig, 1926, 1928, 1929, 1954; Schrade, 1956).[4] In addition, *La Messe de Nostre Dame* has been published separately five times since the Second World War by Guillaume de Van, Jacques Chailley, Machabey, H. Hübsch, and Friedrich Gennrich. Vladimir Chichmaref published a complete edition of the lyric poetry in 1909, which can still be used for scholarly purposes. However, for the lyrics set to music, the reader should consult Ludwig or Schrade and, for *La Louange des Dames,* the excellent forthcoming edition by Nigel Wilkins. Also still useful is Louis de Mas Latrie's old but competent edition of *La Prise d'Alexandrie* (1877). On the other hand, Paulin Paris's version of *Le Voir-Dit* (1875), prepared for the Société des Bibliophiles, does not measure up to contemporary standards of scholarship. Paris not only omitted a 265 line sequence—Polyphemus's song to Galatea, later published by Antoine Thomas (1912)—but left out other passages of a descriptive or allegorical nature, without telling the reader. Although Paris's deletions do not affect the plot in a significant way, I have consulted Ms 1584, fond français, of the Bibliothèque Nationale and will quote from it when appropriate. In the meantime, we must await Paul Imbs's promised critical edition of *Le Voir-Dit*

---

and "Towards a Chronology of Machaut's Musical Works," *Musica Disciplina* 21 (1967): 87-96; Leo Schrade, ed., *Polyphonic Music of the Fourteenth Century: Commentary to Volumes II & III* (Monaco, 1956), p. 20; also Ursula Günther, "Chronologie und Stil der Kompositionen Guillaume de Machauts," *Acta Musicologica* 35 (1963): 96-114; Sarah Jane Williams, "An Author's Role in Fourteenth Century Book Production: Guillaume de Machaut's 'livre où je met toutes mes choses,' " *Romania* 90 (1969): 433-54.

[4] For precise references to the various editions of Machaut and critical studies on his work, see the Bibliography in this study.

and the philological and literary commentary it will surely contain. Apart from *Le Voir-Dit* and *La Prise d'Alexandrie*, Machaut's other long narrative *dits* were edited in splendid fashion by Hoepffner for the Société des Anciens Textes Français (1908, 1911, 1921). Two of the short *dits* were published in America, *Le Dit de la Harpe* by Karl Young (1943) and *Le Dit de la fleur de lis et de la Marguerite* by James Wimsatt (1970). *Le Dit de la Rose* and *Le Dit de la Marguerite* still await a modern edition. Prosper Tarbé included both poems in his selection of Machaut's verse (1849), accurately enough in the case of the *Marguerite,* but without informing the reader he left out scattered fragments of *Le Dit de la Rose* adding up to twenty-eight lines. For the *Rose,* as for *Le Voir-Dit,* I have consulted Bibliothèque Nationale, fond français, 1584. I should also like to mention Wilkins's fine recent anthology of the late medieval French lyric (1969), meticulously presented and with a place of honor reserved to Machaut.

Fifty years ago the Sorbonne's great Du Bellay specialist, Henri Chamard, wrote:

Cette longue période de transition, cette période de deux siècles où le Moyen Age agonise, où se prépare la Renaissance, on l'a très longtemps dédaignée comme dépourvue d'intérêt. Les purs romanistes ne descendaient pas aussi bas, et les historiens de la littérature moderne ne remontaient pas aussi haut. A mesure qu'on l'a plus étudiée, on s'est rendu compte qu'il était facile d'y ressaisir les fils de la tradition que l'on croyait rompue, d'y retrouver les anneaux de la chaîne. Ainsi un voyageur aperçoit de loin deux montagnes qui lui semblent séparées par un immense précipice; qu'il s'approche seulement, il finira par reconnaître que ce qu'il a pris pour un abîme infranchissable n'est qu'une suite de déclivités, et, pour peu qu'il ait des jambes, il pourra, s'il lui plaît, aller d'un sommet à l'autre en passant par la vallée. Eh bien! le Moyen Age, c'est un sommet, la Renaissance en est un autre, et l'on peut aller de l'un à l'autre en passant par la vallée; la vallée ici, c'est précisément cette littérature si peu connue des XIVe et XVe siècles. [5]

Although Chamard displayed traces of condescension toward the late Middle Ages and considered the "valley" a means of communication between the two "mountains" rather than as a feature

---

[5] Henri Chamard, *Les Origines de la poésie française de la Renaissance* (Paris, 1920), p. 43.

of interest in its own right, his metaphor was apt, his analysis of the
scholarly *état présent* accurate, his solution to the problem fair.
Unfortunately, until very recent times students did not follow his
advice, so that the valley of the late Middle Ages, avoided both by
philologists and literary critics, remained unexplored. In the last few
years, however, this state of affairs has changed radically. Scholars
have come to look on the valley with new eyes. Chamard would
no doubt have been pleased at the high quality of studies devoted
to the period which is now considered a regular, full-fledged
province of the French literary domain. [6]

Four great musicologists, Ludwig, Machabey, Schrade, and
Reaney, have studied Guillaume de Machaut's musical works
exhaustively. Although his lyrics had not been properly examined
from a literary perspective, since 1958 we have two very fine articles
by Reaney, Daniel Poirion's thesis, and Wilkins's excellent editions.
Poirion's book now represents the definitive study on Machaut the
lyricist and his place in the evolution of French court poetry from
1330 to 1465.

On the other hand, Machaut's narrative verse has been largely
neglected, even to this day. The early critics (Tarbé, Louis Petit de
Julleville) were concerned with whether his opus paints an accurate
picture of fourteenth-century manners, yet at the same time they
condemned it for not conforming to late nineteenth-century sexual
mores, that is, those held by the scholars in question. In the first
half of the twentieth century, the best work on the *dits* is to be
found in the introductions to the three-volume Hoepffner edition and
in a few foreign dissertations, by Georg Hanf, Jakob Geiselhardt,
and Johanna Schilperoort. More recently, the distinguished Anglicist
D. W. Robertson alluded to the Canon of Reims, and James
Wimsatt has attempted to place Machaut in the tradition of the
pre-Chaucerian French *dit amoreus* and to trace the evolution of

---

[6] For example, among many other works, four important Sorbonne
doctoral dissertations: Daniel Poirion, *Le Poète et le Prince: L'évolution du
lyrisme courtois de Guillaume de Machaut à Charles d'Orléans* (Paris, 1965);
Jean Dufournet, *La destruction des Mythes dans les Mémoires de Ph. de
Commynes* (Geneva, 1966); David Kuhn, *La Poétique de François Villon*
(Paris, 1967); Jacques Ribard, *Un ménestrel du XIVe siècle: Jean de Condé*
(Geneva, 1969). Ribard's introduction contains a choice anthology of hostile
comments by scholars on the fourteenth century.

the Marguerite poem in French and English. Robertson's and
Wimsatt's studies are useful but, written with the purpose of
illuminating Chaucer, do not claim to be exhaustive. Finally, Poirion
has made very perceptive remarks on Machaut in his general study
of the fourteenth and fifteenth centuries in the Claude Pichois *Littérature française* series. Nor should we forget excellent brief discussions of Machaut by Stefan Hofer and Georges Becker in literary
manuals which deserve more attention than they usually receive.

In sum, although Guillaume de Machaut's musical and lyrical
works have now been examined by the best contemporary specialists,
his narrative *dits* still await a serious book-length treatment. Both
for their historical importance (their influence on Chaucer and on
later French narrative poets) and intrinsic artistic merit, I believe
the *dits* deserve much better. I wrote the present study with this in
mind. Each chapter of this book contains an essay devoted to one
dit (preceded by a brief plot résumé of the *dit* in question). An
excursus treats the four smaller *dits* and the *Prologue*. My concern,
apart from explication, is to explore Machaut's work for archetypal
patterns, comic modes, parody, levels of meaning, realism, narrative
point of view, and aesthetic values. A concluding chapter aims at
a more synthetic view of Machaut's work, traces his development
as an artist, and discusses his place in the history of French literature.

At the end of an earlier volume on the *chanson de geste* I wrote
approximately the following, which will define accurately enough
my purpose here too: Medieval texts were created in a particular
place and time; the trouvère earns a living under very different
conditions than apply to Valéry and Eluard. However, once uniquely
historical considerations have been taken into account, and providing
that the critic makes use of whatever aid historical scholarship can
give, he then has a right to approach a text from within, seeking
to determine what makes it a work of art—its structure, imagination,
world, and tone. This is the principle on which so much of modern
criticism rests. Although the external, superficial aspects of literary
creation vary from age to age (though not necessarily more for the
trouvère than for the Greek tragedian, the Roman satirist, and the
Renaissance sonneteer), internally the work of art remains essentially
the same over the ages. If it is worth reading as literature, it can
stand up under the most searching critical analysis. The Middle Ages
is no privileged domain, exempt from the rules of literature and

criticism, nor does it need to benefit from such exemption. The best medieval French poetry, like all great poetry, is beautiful; no tools that can help us to explain its beauty ought to be disdained. The final justification for our work is that we help render all poetry more accessible and more vital to the reader of today.

1. LE DIT DOU VERGIER

On an April morning the Narrator walks through
a beautiful garden and into a grove. Within the grove
he dreams that the God of Love appears to him
accompanied by twelve youths and maidens. When
requested by the Narrator, the God identifies himself
and his followers and delivers a lecture on the nature
of love. He promises to help the Narrator in his
amours if the latter behaves properly. Upon the
God's departure the Narrator wakes up.

ERNEST HOEPFFNER CONDEMNED MACHAUT'S first long narrative
poem, *Le Dit dou Vergier*.[1] According to Hoepffner, the poem
proves to be a servile, mediocre imitation of Guillaume de Lorris
and Jean de Meun (Hoepffner, 1: lvi-lvii). *Le Roman de la Rose,* one
of the summits of medieval literature, exerted a powerful influence
for almost three hundred years. In the first half of the fourteenth
century it was customary for an author to cast his poem as a
dream-vision narrated in the first person, recounting an interview
with the God of Love or some other mythico-allegorical character
in a beautiful garden (replete with birds, trees, and a fountain) on
an April or May morning. The weight of tradition is never an easy
burden for a young writer: it took Lesage, Marivaux, Balzac, and
Flaubert many years to find their way in the novel. That an author
fails to liberate himself from the prevalent conventions of his age
may indicate, however, that he has not properly assimilated them.
Imitating *Le Roman de la Rose* will not suffice to produce a mediocre
poem; one must imitate it badly. The failure of *DV* as a work of
art may derive from the fact that the central portion of the narrative

---

[1] 1.293 lines; ed. Hoepffner, 1: 13-56 (cited hereafter as *DV*).

is almost entirely made up of three speeches delivered by the God of Love (247-376, 401-1070, 1151-94) plus an indirect discourse (1105-50). A large part of *DV*, some 890 lines, are devoted to relatively static moralizing. The poem is concerned with a young Narrator; he is the hero, and the story is told from his point of view. Yet the God of Love speaks of passion in the abstract and of an abstract Lover and love-situation. Since these two focuses are not connected in any direct, meaningful way, the erotic experience, filtered through the God of Love's consciousness, appears too remote. As a result, his Lover and attendant allegorical figures rarely manifest any vitality. Because the Narrator learns about love but never experiences it directly, he too remains for the most part a static literary creation.

In Guillaume de Lorris, too, the God of Love explains the erotic experience to a young lover; his two speeches take up 674 lines. But 3,354 lines, five times as much, are devoted to other matters. Lorris elaborates an *Ars amandi* but at the same time recounts the young protagonist's quest. The story concerns a lover and his beloved. *Oiseuse, Dangier, Bel Acueil,* and *Honte* exist as universal abstract qualities, as character traits within the individual, and as lovable, charming, credible literary characters in their own right. The focus of the story remains clear; our attention is fixed on the protagonist, on his discovery of love and his development as a lover— conceived as one process. Machaut, on the other hand, by concentrating on the God of Love's speech and neglecting the narrative elements in his source, upsets the delicate balance which makes Lorris's poem a masterpiece.

Guillaume de Machaut's first *dit* is by no means without interest or aesthetic value, however. Since Machaut sacrifices narrative interest in favor of the didactic, the Narrator does not progress or develop in psychological terms as a lover. But he learns about love and at the end of the story will seek to put his learning to use and win the Rose. Admittedly, we do not see this happen. The God of Love's tale is not the Narrator's. An archetypal Lover, whose story is told by the God of Love, undergoes certain experiences, which the Narrator will emulate. He hopes to actualize the potentiality for loving that he bears within himself by conforming to a pattern set forth by the God of Love. Machaut has written an anatomy of love, not the story of an individual lover, and a poem about education. As

the Narrator learns, so does the reader. In fact, the reader is taught
more than the Narrator, since he profits not only from the God of
Love's speeches but also from the Narrator's own speeches and
actions. Only after having assembled this not-always-consistent data
can we understand the poet's views on love in *DV*.

In general, Machaut adheres to the orthodox notion of courtly
love as it had evolved by the fourteenth century. [2] The God of Love
claims his sway is all-powerful and universal. He resembles Death
in that no man can escape him but seizes his prey before Death, thus
enjoying the victim's firstfruits, and brings him joy not pain. He
refutes the physical and moral laws of nature—physically, by separating hearts from their bodies; morally, by upsetting man's social
hierarchy. For, insists Machaut (repeating a medieval commonplace),
love can render a wise man foolish or bring wisdom to a fool, make
a rich man poor or a pauper wealthy, and a good man evil or a
scoundrel kind and generous. Since love is blind, people do not fall
in love according to the dictates of reason or ways of the world.
Passion may blossom between rich and poor or between gentlefolk
and commoners. Guillaume de Machaut, poet of the court and
secretary to kings, is in no sense an egalitarian leveler. The God
of Love protests that he does not wish to denigrate the rich or
well-born, but rather to show that all men, of whatever class, are
subject to him and will commit folly for his sake: "Je vueil chascun
mon serf clamer, / Quel qu'il soit, soit contes ou rois" (462-63). The
social hierarchy is reversed, however, in that the rich, the well-born,
and the able (wise men) do not necessarily make the best lovers.
Grace and *douceur* are more important than beauty; *loiauté* and
debonnaireté more important than wealth, connections, and learning.
In fact, the God prefers a poor man to a rich one, for the former
knows that he can owe his success with women only to love. He
serves the God of Love best, for he takes the greatest risk in loving
above his station, and he is ennobled by love, thus raised above his
natural place in society. Machaut pleads for a spiritual aristocracy
of the heart, based upon good qualities in the individual. A lover's
heart must contain *Franc Voloir* and *Dous Penser* before he catches

---

2 Of course, there is no one doctrine of *fin' amor;* each major courtly
poet treats the erotic in his own way. Nevertheless, certain common traits
are shared by the troubadours, the trouvères, and the romancers. A consensus
of some kind can be reached, especially for the late Middle Ages.

sight of the lady; gazing upon her then causes him to fall in love. Whether or not a lover is rewarded by the God depends on how much *Franchise* he possesses. With these notions Machaut follows Ovid, the troubadours, Andreas Capellanus, *Le Roman de la Rose*, and the *Stilnovisti*. It is even possible that the ethos of *fin' amor* owes its existence to a struggle by petty nobility in the South of France, landless young squires of good family, to arrive at a better social position. [3] In most of the Northern romances, however, the squire of low degree turns out to be a prince in disguise, temporarily exiled from his own kingdom *(Amadas et Ydoine, Gliglois, Gui de Warewic, Jehan et Blonde)*.

Be this as it may, love is, in Andreas Capellanus's terms, the source of all good in the world: "Omnis ergo boni erit amor origo et causa" *(Trattato d'amore*, ed. S. Battaglia [Rome, 1947], p. 32). It makes men better and is the spur to knowledge, wisdom, and good deeds. By adoring the God of Love, our Narrator parodies worship that men accord to the one true deity. Two forces cause a youth to fall into the grip of passion: an attitude receptive to love (the will to love in his heart) and his lady's physical presence. Thereafter he lives both in joy and pain, the *dolce-amar* of the troubadours, the trouvères, and Petrarch. Physical desire renders him ill and brings him to the point of death; nevertheless, he delights in suffering, for the memory of his lady's beauty and the hope of one day winning her love neutralize his pain. However, the thought that she does not love him, is not yet aware of his passion, and, in fact, smiles impartially on all her suitors, even preferring one of the others, drives our young man to distraction. Joy returns when he remembers that she is the finest lady in the world. Because she is the best, he will be faithful no matter how she treats him. Indeed, he prefers to die of a broken heart rather than succeed with another. He would like to declare his passion but is so entranced by her beauty and afraid of angering her that for a long time his lips remain closed. This timidity is a good sign, however, for it shows he is not just a fancy talker who pays court to all the ladies and loves none. Eventually desire will elicit a *requête d'amour*. Although the girl at first refuses adamantly, she will one day grant his suit if the lover has proved

---

[3] This is Erich Köhler's thesis, which he defends in a series of articles reprinted in *Trobadorlyrik und höfischer Roman* (Berlin, 1962) and *Esprit und arkadische Freiheit* (Frankfurt am Main-Bonn, 1966).

himself humble, loyal, gentle, and debonair. According to the God of Love, 1) it is better to love him than a false, disloyal man; 2) he should have the boon of her affection, since he merits it; 3) love is good, and the joy of love is meant to be given, not refused; 4) if the youth is not rewarded, he will die of a broken heart. In a nonviolent, subdued version of *bellum intestinum, Dangier, Cruauté, Durté, Doubtance de meffaire, Honte,* and *Paour* give way to *Grace, Pitié, Franchise, Attemprance, Hardement, Loiauté,* and *Celer, Loiauté* and *Celer* convince *Honte* and *Paour* that the Lover has acted with exemplary discretion; therefore, the lady need not fear granting his request. The God of Love tells the Narrator that he will aid him only if he proves to be faithful and discreet. Loyalty and discretion are the most valuable traits a suitor can possess. With them and with the God of Love's assistance the ideal Lover succeeds in his quest, as the Narrator can one day also.

Finally, the God of Love will ease the suitor's pain, cease his woes, bring him joy (1049, 1052, 1138, 1196), and grant him the promised *don* (1287). What is the nature of this *don?* Does it imply physical possession or a profound, passionate, but chaste love (Andreas's *amor purus*) in which consummation is thwarted to maintain desire in its most intense state? Some scholars insist that adultery was an essential characteristic of *fin' amor,* others deny it; some urge us to take Andreas Capellanus's *De Amore* literally, others as satire. We are by no means certain whether Guillaume de Lorris meant to have the flower plucked in the incompleted portion of his *Roman de la Rose* and, if so, whether it symbolizes the girl or just her love. In my opinion, there are no ready answers to these questions. Differing attitudes toward the erotic coexisted in the Middle Ages—clerical, feudal, courtly, anticourtly—with variety within each category. Although courtly poets have elaborated what sometimes appears to be a common tradition, they differ among themselves as much as do Sartre, Camus, Marcel, Ponge, Char, and the other existentialists in the twentieth century. Love is sometimes more, sometimes less, sensual within the opus of a single writer (William of Aquitaine, Chrétien de Troyes). William, Marcabrun, Jaufré Rudel, Bernart de Ventadorn, and Montanhagol each treats erotic matters in his own manner. The relationship of love to marriage is by no means the same in Béroul and Chrétien, in *Le Châtelain de Couci* and *Jehan et Blonde.* To the extent generalizations can be

made, the earliest love poets of France usually stated as their goal
physical possession of the lady. Only later (and only in occasional
passages) did a few writers intentionally renounce all hope of
attaining their ends, often as a tribute to the lady's honor or to
themselves ("Thus can I prove how much I love you!"). To accept
nonfulfillment and respect the lady's wishes in everything did
become a literary cliché in the late Middle Ages. However, with
Guillaume de Lorris and Jean de Meun both serving as models, a
poet could adopt widely contrasting attitudes toward sex and still
work within the tradition. The different points of view in *Les Cent
Ballades,* the poetry of Alain Chartier and Charles d'Orléans, and
the quarrels over *Le Roman de la Rose* and *La Belle Dame sans
Merci* prove this well enough. Several times in *DV* the God of Love
promises the Lover and Narrator joy, but not if it will result in a
lady's dishonor (1053-62). Unfortunately, we cannot be certain what
the poet means by *honor* any more than by *joy.* Is a lady dishonored
if she sleeps with a man, if people discover she has slept with him,
or only if her love for him is made the talk of the town? Is honor
to be conceived in the context of a shame or a guilt culture? We
do not know, and Guillaume de Machaut does not tell us. The
semantic range of courtly vocabulary is sufficiently wide, especially
in the late Middle Ages, to allow for a sensual or a chaste interpretation of *joie* and *don.* I believe that readers or listeners were free
to interpret such words each in his own way, according to his own
temperament; today's reader should be allowed the same freedom.

Machaut's erotic imagery falls roughly into two categories: the
military and the idyllic. The God of Love appears to the Narrator,
an arrow in one hand, a torch in the other. As in Ovid, Guillaume
de Lorris, and so many courtly lyrics and romances, the Lover suffers from a wound in the heart; an arrow has entered his body
without leaving a visible trace. Desire lays siege to the youth, who
burns with flames of passion. He then falls sick, manifesting traditional Ovidian pathology: high temperature, sighing, trembling,
pallor, tears, fainting spells, hunger, and loss of sleep. He has become
a slave to Eros and is incarcerated in a *prison joieuse* (344-45, 529).
Although the Lover is assaulted by Love or by his lady, he then
attacks the lady in turn. The beloved is a castle or fortress, to be
seized and held. Jean de Meun pictured the sexual act itself as a
military operation: in this he followed Ovid, William of Aquitaine,

and his other predecessors, who also mounted unbroken mares, tilted at lances, and stormed castles.

However, Machaut, like Guillaume de Lorris, also conceived of love as peace and joy. The Narrator tells of awakening on a spring morning, strolling through a garden, listening to the song of birds, and finally entering a grove where he experiences the dream-vision. This passage recalls Ernst Robert Curtius's *locus amoenus*, a topic which dates back to Homer, Virgil, the biblical earthly paradise, and the gardens of the Song of Songs and the Apocalypse. [4] Following Guillaume de Lorris's example, the Narrator compares his grove to the *paradis terrestre* (66). Spring is a time of rebirth, when the old year dies and is born anew and when Christ died and was resurrected. It is also, according to medieval science, the sanguine season, warm and moist, favorable to the young. Late April and much of May lie under the astrological sign of Taurus, in the House of Venus. An evocation of spring is a standard *Eingangsmotiv* in epic, romance and the lyric.

The Narrator enjoys the flowers growing both outside and within the grove, and the God of Love appears with a chaplet of flowers on his head. Flowers are an image of youth, purity, and the perishable beauty associated with love. They also evoke springtime, nature's benevolence, the natural origin of love, fertility, and finally the woman herself (cf. 869, 872, and 880 where *Doubtance de meffaire, Honte,* and *Paour* urge the beloved not to grant the Lover any portion of Joy, for, if she does, her *flour* will decline). Flowers are assimilated to beautiful girls because they contain qualities men also ascribe to their women: freshness, beauty, purity—and for obvious erotic reasons. The woman-flower archetype is one of the richest in world literature, manifest in Horace, Ovid, Ausonius, Poliziano, Garcilaso, Ronsard, Apollinaire, Jouve, and Aragon, as well as in medieval allegory. [5]

---

[4] Ernst Robert Curtius, *Europäische Literatur und lateinisches Mittelalter* (Berne, 1948), chapt. 10.

[5] See William Calin, "Flower Imagery in *Floire et Blancheflor*," *French Studies* 18 (1964): 103-11; and Erhard Lommatzch, "Blumen und Früchte im altfranzösischen Schrifttum (12. 13. 14. Jahrhundert)," in *Akademie der Wissenschaften und der Literatur [in Mainz]: Abhandlungen der Geistes- und Sozialwissenschaftlichen Klasse* (1966), pp. 471-97.

Our protagonist is equally impressed by the number and variety of exotic trees in his grove. We associate the mixed forest with the *locus amoenus,* discussed above. But one small tree *(arbrissel)* stands out from the others. As the dream begins, the God of Love is perched on it; and the poet wakes up when the God shakes it at his departure. Similar trees are to be found in *Le Roman de la Rose, Le Roman de la Poire, La Messe des Oiseaux,* and *Le Dit de l'Arbre royal.* A single tree is an epic marker (in Curtius's phrase), under or near which speeches are made and battles fought. In the biblical earthly paradise a good tree of life is contrasted to the bad tree of the knowledge of good and evil. God plants good trees (virtues) while Satan plants bad ones (vices); in the garden of virtues, man is planted by God and grafted by Christ, his roots are love, etc. Christ is pictured iconographically as the last branch in the tree of Jesse, as a good tree in the garden of life, from which sprout the twelve apostles, or descending upon the tree of life, in the same way that the God of Love presumably lands on Machaut's tree. In *DV* especially the tree is a symbol of virility and perhaps also of flowering Nature, which provides a haven for birds, gods (Love), and men (the Narrator). [6]

Trees provide security for sweet-singing birds. The Narrator enters the grove to observe them more closely; he is attracted by one nightingale in particular. Then the God of Love appears upon the tree. Until line 376, where Machaut informs us of his identity, we know only that he is a creature with wings. Toward the end of *DV* the God of Love, by flying, away, shakes off dew which awakens the Narrator, thus ending his dream. Of course, the winged Eros was well known in the Middle Ages; he is to be found in *Le Roman de la Rose, La Vita Nuova, l'Ovide moralisé,* and elsewhere. The Narrator, intrigued and at the same time afraid of this phantasmal creature, speaks to him largely out of curiosity. He asks about Amor's wings in the same breath as about the torch and arrow Amor carries and why he is blind. The God tells him that they symbolize love's universality and omnipotence. Flying, according to depth psychology, is an image of sexual excitement both in dreams

---

[6] On *Le Roman de la Rose,* see Erich Köhler, "Narcisse, la Fontaine d'Amour et Guillaume de Lorris," in *L'humanisme médiéval dans les littératures romanes du XIIe au XIVe siècle* (Paris, 1964), pp. 147-64.

and daytime reverie. The bird manifests grace, charm, liberty, and triumph over physical obstacles associated with young love. It appears unafflicted by the gross material concerns of everyday life, hence the wings bestowed traditionally on angels and on representations of the freed human soul. This ubiquitous, omnipotent, birdlike god incarnates the Narrator's own desire for freedom and happiness.

The scene in the grove is purported to be a dream-vision. [7] By Machaut's time, a dream in the first person had become the standard convention for narrating amorous and didactic poetry. On the one hand, the dream convention was to be taken seriously. The Narrator, speaking in the poet's own voice, guarantees its authenticity. Furthermore, medieval and classical *auctores* taught that dreams often contain elements of wisdom, perhaps of divine origin. Guillaume de Lorris, citing Macrobius, defends the truthfulness of the dream-experience:

> 1 Aucunes genz dient qu'en songes
> n'a se fables non et mençonges;
> mes l'en puet tex songes songier
> qui ne sont mie mençongier,
> ainz sont aprés bien aparant,
> si en puis bien traire a garant
> un auctor qui ot non Macrobes,
> qui ne tint pas songes a lobes,
> ançois escrit l'avision
> qui avint au roi Scypion.
> 15 ... quar endroit moi ai ge fiance
> que songes est senefiance
> des biens as genz et des anuiz,
> que li plusor songent de nuiz

---

[7] On medieval dream theory, see Walter Clyde Curry, *Chaucer and the Mediaeval Sciences,* rev. and enl. ed. (New York, 1960); Constance B. Hieatt, *The Realism of Dream Visions* (The Hague-Paris, 1967); Richard Mentz, "Die Träume in den altfranzösischen Karls und Artus-epen," in *Ausgaben und Abhandlungen aus dem Gebiete der romanischen Philologie* 73 (Marburg, 1888); Karl-Josef Steinmeyer, *Untersuchungen zur allegorischen Bedeutung der Träume im altfranzösischen Rolandslied* (Munich, 1963); and Walther Suchier, "Altfranzösische Traumbücher," *Zeitschrift für französische Sprache und Literatur* 67 (1957): 129-67. I found helpful two American doctoral dissertations: Francis Xavier Newman, *Somnium: Medieval Theories of Dreaming and the Form of Vision Poetry* (Princeton University, 1962), and Ralph Howard Bloch, *A Study of the Dream Motif in Old French Narrative* (Stanford University, 1970).

maintes choses covertement
que l'en voit puis apertement.

According to Macrobius's *Commentarii in Somnium Scipionis*, dreams can be divided into five categories: *somnium, visio, oraculum, insomnium,* and *visum.* Of these, the first three were assumed to be legitimate manifestations of the supernatural. An objective, authentic dream could therefore take the form of *somnium* (an enigmatic experience often requiring allegorical interpretation), *visio* (a revelation of future events or eternal truths, which come to pass precisely as they appeared to the dreamer), or *oraculum* (the appearance of God, one of his angels, or a sacred personage making a prophecy or giving an order). Scipio's dream partook of all three forms. "Dream-books," which enjoyed great vogue in the Middle Ages, were written to help people interpret enigmatic *somnia.* Charlemagne's first four dreams in *La Chanson de Roland* are *somnia;* the last one, in which Gabriel orders him to aid King Vivien at Imphe, is an *oraculum.* In *chansons de geste* the author and his public assume that such dreams be taken seriously. If a hero declines to heed a dream-warning (as in *Renaud de Montauban* or *Huon de Bordeaux*), the public is expected to applaud his courage and pity his foolhardiness, which will lead inevitably to disaster. *Le Roman de la Rose* and many of the *dits amoreux* in its train should also be included under the heading of *somnium.* Some poets, however, prefer to treat their experiences as a genuine love-vision, comparable to a religious one; the God of Love or Venus comes to them in person and initiates them into the mysteries of Eros, much as the Christian God or one of his angels in a genuinely religious poem. Machaut employs this technique in *DV,* where the Narrator never says he dozed off or had a dream, but that in his misery he fell into a trance (146, 149), experienced a vision (152), then came out of the trance when dew fell onto his face (1205-16). Thus Machaut uses the love-vision as an authenticating device to guarantee the accuracy of the story he tells. Highly abstract or mystical principles are given realistic proportions; through the dream-device the public learns to accept these figures as belonging to reality. The waking frameworld encompasses a dream world, no less credible, no less problematic than itself, which brings the unknown into human perspective.

A literary convention which has survived for over a century will probably lose some of the impact it had in the formative period. A parody on the religious vision is likely to elicit a sophisticated response from some readers, who will recognize it for what it is—a convention. Also, in the late Middle Ages people paid more attention to dreams of subjective, human origin which give expression to day-to-day psychological problems: Macrobius's *insomnium* and *visum* as opposed to the *somnium, oraculum,* and *visio; somnium animale* and *somnium naturale* as opposed to the *somnium coeleste.* Jean de Meun expressly opposes Guillaume de Lorris when he claims that dreams often distort the truth just as mirrors distort light and that they lie: "E ce n'est fors trufle e mençonge" (18363). Homer and Virgil identified a Gate of Ivory as well as a Gate of Horn. Anticipating Freud, the ancients and medievals recognized that some dreams develop aspects of presleeping consciousness, the "day residue." According to Macrobius, a dream may be caused by the dreamer's having eaten or drunk too much, or having wept copiously before falling asleep, or by his recent waking thoughts. Comparable statements (and examples) are to be found in scripture as well as in Plato, Aristotle, Galen, Cicero, Lucretius, Petronius, Claudian, the Church Fathers, John of Salisbury, Aquinas, and Jean de Meun. However, Machaut gives the old thesis renewed vitality by integrating the Narrator's vision into the frame-story. The Narrator walks in a beautiful garden with lovely flowers, is moved by the singing of birds, and perceives a particularly beautiful flowering tree. In his dream he meets a winged god perched on the tree who wears a chaplet of flowers and refers to a lady as a flower. Before falling asleep the Narrator had wept profusely bewailing the unhappy course of his love affair. Irritated by weeping, he then dreams of the love affair of another. Finally, when the God flies away, shaking dew onto the sleeping Narrator, he awakes to discover none of the dream figures present but their memory still fresh in his mind.

Freud's *Traumdeutung* states that all dreams contain an element of wish-fulfillment. Again he was anticipated by Plato, Plotinus, and many others who declared that dreams may either be the result of divine revelation or the expression of a submerged wish. In *DV* an unhappy lover, at a loss how to proceed with his amours, dreams that an all-powerful authority-figure comes to him as by magic. The Narrator, who turns to the authority-figure for guidance, acts like a child, demonstrating an almost comic impatience and enthusiasm to learn and, more important still, demanding personal intercession in his own case. Due to his youthful inexperience, the Narrator appears as a conventional lover-learner, hero of so many romances and allegories, while the God of Love as teacher parodies the Divine Teacher and Maker of Parables, archetypal father, teacher, lawgiver, and judge. [8] A vertical relationship is established between lord and vassal, father and son, god and devotee. In his dream the Narrator receives the instruction which will permit him to win his lady; regressing to childhood, he finds security in the parent-child relationship. An omnipotent, protective father mediates between him and his sought-after goal. The God of Love tells the story of another suitor, who also appears to be unsuccessful but in the long run attains his ends. Of course, this Any Lover or Every Lover also stands for the Narrator's double. The Narrator projects his anxiety onto the Lover and then enjoys the latter's triumph as he would his own.

In his dream Machaut's protagonist repudiates loneliness, ignorance, and failure. The dream transports him into a realm of enchantment. The Narrator who, awake, received no comfort from singing birds, is aided by a flying god, who soars away in freedom. He undergoes an initiation experience and penetrates into a closed space (from the outside world to the garden to the grove) where time stops. Here, during an ecstatic vision, he receives the boon of knowledge. No longer miserable, he attains the talisman which will bring him joy.

The *DV* is an allegory; all the characters, with the exception of the Narrator, are personified abstractions. Significantly, of all Machaut's long narrative *dits,* it is this first one (along with *Le Dit de l'Alerion*) which adheres most firmly to the dominant literary mode of the age. [9] The God of Love, who stands for love in the abstract, appears as half-divine, half-human, a *daemon* of exceptional

---

[8] See Alan M. F. Gunn, "Teacher and Student in the *Roman de la Rose:* A Study in Archetypal Figures and Patterns," *L'Esprit Créateur* 2 (1962): 126-34.

[9] C. S. Lewis, *The Allegory of Love: A Study in Medieval Tradition* (London, 1936), and Rosemond Tuve, *Allegorical Imagery: Some Mediaeval Books and Their Posterity* (Princeton, N. J., 1966).

power and beauty. Part of the story's charm consists in the fact that the reader recognizes him long before his identity is revealed to the Narrator. Machaut also creates satellite figures, extensions of the God representing distinct facets of love. These characters also define the psychology of the Lover and of the Beloved. Six personifications embody traits that foment passion in a young man, either for pleasure *(Plaisance, Dous Penser)* or pain *(Desir),* that console him *(Souvenir, Esperance)* and compel him to make a declaration to the beloved *(Desir, Voloir).* The girl's psychology is conceived more in terms of a *bellum intestinum* between aspects of her personality which oppose granting the Lover's suit *(Dangier, Cruauté, Durté, Doubtance, Honte, Paour)* and those which favor it *(Grace, Pitié, Franchise, Attemprance, Hardement, Loiauté, Celer).* The traits favorable to love, both in man and woman, make up the God of Love's court: six youths *(Voloir, Penser, Plaisance, Loiauté, Celer, Desir)* and six maidens *(Grace, Pitié, Esperance, Souvenir, Franchise, Attemprance).* Machaut does not insist that the youths be associated with the Lover and the maidens with the beloved. Two maidens, *Esperance* and *Souvenir,* "belong" to the man, and two youths, *Celer* and *Loiauté,* to the woman. Machaut also claims that *Celer* and *Loiauté* are maidens (899, 1037). Furthermore, some figures do double duty. *Voloir,* who represents an intangible quality of goodness and aptness for love without which *fin' amor* is impossible, also spurs the Lover to declare his suit. The God of Love recommends *Celer* and *Loiauté,* feminine traits encouraging the lady to yield, as qualities the Narrator must acquire also. Finally, two figures, *Hardement* and *Dous Regard,* never appear in the God of Love's suite at all, but help the Lover in his trials.

These disparities may be the result of clumsiness or oversight on Machaut's part. The *DV* is his first long poem, written in a mode with which he may have felt ill at ease. It is also true, however, that Machaut's conception of allegory differs somewhat from his source, Guillaume de Lorris. Never in *Le Roman de la Rose* is the allegorical figure merely a personified abstraction, an idea which has been given human trappings. The God of Love and his assistants exist first of all as credible representations of human beings; second, as characteristics of the individual Lover and Lady; and third, as universal traits to be found in all lovers, aspects of love subsumed under the heading *Amor* much as in treatises on ethics where magnificence is subsumed under *Fortitudo* and chastity under *Temperantia*. Guillaume de Lorris emphasizes the dramatic and psychological: his rose-plot serves as a battleground between youth and maiden and as the décor for their mental anguish. We observe the lover yielding to passion, then watch his progress. We witness the maiden swaying back and forth, struggling with herself and with him as to whether she will grant his suit. In *DV* the Narrator fell in love before entering the grove. He meets allegorical figures who act in a particular way toward all people in love. They have no immediate relationship to him nor to his lady. Admittedly, these personages refer to one Lover, who is, in a certain sense, the Narrator's double; and *Celer* and *Loiauté* are recommended to the Narrator with particular warmth: they are or will become part of him. But on the whole Machaut presents general rather than particular manifestations of Eros. This may explain why certain personifications serve equally well for the Lover, the lady, and the Narrator, and why Machaut's *Honte, Paour,* and *Dangier* appear so much less vital than comparable figures in *Le Roman de la Rose*. Whether for reasons of doctrine or simply because Machaut lacked inspiration, it cannot be denied that the strictly allegorical passages are, aesthetically speaking, the least successful part of *DV*.

Machaut achieved success in a different area of characterization, however: with the Narrator, the one nonallegorical figure in the poem. The naive, blundering, comic hero is a literary convention, largely developed by Machaut himself (though it existed already in *Le Roman de la Rose*), then imitated by Froissart, Christine de Pisan, Chaucer, Alain Chartier, Pierre de Nesson, and others. The Narrator is depicted as a young, innocent boy who has just fallen in love and seeks instruction. Although, as a child he possesses the purity and enthusiasm required of a perfect lover, he also suffers from physical weakness and intellectual immaturity and is revealed to be timid, foolish, and ignorant. When the Narrator first perceives the God of Love, he shies from the latter's torch, lest it be thrown at him, and dares neither to advance nor retreat. Still afraid, yet driven by insatiable curiosity, he advances toward the dream-figures slowly, "le petit pas / Tout couvertement" (208-9). The Narrator asks the God of Love to reveal his identity and that of his court as well as for an explanation of his blindness, his torch, and arrow. The God replies in two parallel discourses. However, before the second speech and, therefore, before all the questions have been answered, the Narrator interrupts, begging tearfully for intercession in his personal affairs, a request he repeats more than once. The God replies kindly but firmly that further queries must wait till later; he will continue his lecture in proper order. When, finally, his tears metamorphosed into joy, the dreamer wakes up quite suddenly to discover that the dream figures have disappeared, he is "esperdus" and "en moult grant effroy" (1212, 1213). Viewed from a Bergsonian perspective, the Narrator's curiosity, fear, and egocentric personal concerns become fixations. He reacts mechanically to his environment, shows excessive fear when none is called for, and later demonstrates foolhardiness and bad manners equally at the wrong moment. This particular individual's emotional needs are thwarted by the exigencies of social decorum. He is neither all good nor all bad, simply inept; he cannot adapt to the ways of the court.

At the end of the poem, the Narrator has acquired knowledge which, together with the good qualities he already possesses, should enable him to succeed in his love-quest. We use the term *should* advisedly. Machaut's first long poem manifests more than a little ambiguity. The Narrator cannot be identified with the archetypal Lover, of whom the God of Love speaks, even though the latter is, in a sense, a projection of the former. The Lover meets a lady, desires her, declares his passion, and is rewarded all in the course of the God's speech. Such is not the case with the Narrator. He fell in love before the poem began; what will happen to him after line 1293 is left open to conjecture. The God of Love promises success to all *vrais amis;* he will help the Narrator provided the latter is faithful and discreet. We have reason to believe in the Narrator's loyalty: before ever meeting the God and again at the poem's end he proclaims how faithful he is. Concerning his discretion, we are not directly informed at all. True, he does refer to the lady in the vaguest possible terms; but, on the other hand, he also tells the story of *DV*. Within the grove the Narrator is instructed in the traits required of a good lover, traits he may or may not already possess. The *dit* ends on a note of expectancy. We do not see the Narrator leave the grove nor are we told whether he will succeed. He has been lifted out of time into an eternal present, a moment of revelation; at the end of the poem, having returned to temporal reality, his eyes are cast upon the future.

In the central section of *DV* we are told of love objectively, as in a university lecture, by a god, from his distant point of view. At the beginning and end, however, we concentrate on the Narrator and see the world filtered through his consciousness. He praises his lady, claims to have created the poem with her uniquely in mind, and has written down the God's lesson for his own purposes. Thus an abstract doctrine is to some extent made vital when assimilated to the Narrator's personal life. We react to love through his eyes.

I must insist, however, that the Narrator is not a self-portrait of Guillaume de Machaut the poet and that his experiences belong to the realm of fiction not autobiography. The I-narrator is a literary convention. He brings to fiction a sense of immediacy and personal involvement as well as authenticity. In medieval allegory especially the I-narrator assumes a quality of universality, becomes a figure for Every Man or Any Man. [10] Although, because of the long-standing medieval practice of oral recitation, the narrator will always to some extent be identified with an author or author-surrogate telling his tale before the court, the nameless, unidentified Narrator of *DV* also refers to any and all young lovers and to young love in the abstract. Thus does an old convention retain vitality in the fourteenth century, as an inspiration to writers, a lesson for gracious, refined conduct, and an elegant, nostalgic escape from the sordidness of everyday reality into the garden of love and beauty.

---

[10] Leo Spitzer, "Note on the Poetic and the Empirical 'I' in Medieval Authors," *Traditio* 4 (1946): 414-22.

2. LE JUGEMENT DOU ROY DE BEHAINGNE

> While taking a walk one morning, the Narrator
> overhears a conversation between a Knight and a
> Lady. Both are unhappy, each claiming to be more
> wretched than the other. The Lady tells how her
> Lover died, the Knight how his Beloved left him
> for another man. Eventually the Narrator comes out
> of hiding and proposes John of Luxembourg, king
> of Bohemia, to judge their disagreement. They go to
> Durbuy Castle where John, counseled by *Raison,
> Amour, Loiauté,* and *Juenesse,* decides in favor of
> the Knight, then entertains his guests for a week
> before permitting them to go home.

WITH *Le Jugement dou Roy de Behaingne* [1] Guillaume de Machaut
sets out in a new direction. Whereas his first tale was a dream
allegory in the tradition of *Le Roman de la Rose, JRB* recounts
a dispute over a point of love casuistry: who suffers more, a lady
whose lover has died or a knight whose beloved has left him?
Machaut was probably inspired by either the original Latin or a
vernacular adaptation of Andreas Capellanus's *De Amore,* by the
débat and *jeu parti* of the trouvères (who themselves imitated
the Provençal *tenso* and *partimen,* and by judgment poems *(Altercatio Phillidis et Florae, Romaricimontis Concilium, Le Jugement
d'Amors, Florence et Blancheflor, Hueline et Aiglantine, Melior et
Ydoine),* which had played an important role in the elaboration of
the courtly ethos and were prime sources for *Le Roman de la Rose,*
itself a grand debate or symposium treating all facets of love. [2] In

---

[1] 2,079 lines; ed. Hoepffner, 1: 57-135 (cited hereafter as *JRB*).

[2] Hoepffner, 1: lx-lxi; Charles Oulmont, *Les débats du clerc et du
chevalier dans la littérature poétique du moyen-âge* (Paris, 1911); Edmond

the *Recueil général des jeux-partis français* (ed. Arthur Långfors, 2 vols. [Paris, 1926], we find the following (editor's résumé): LVII *... Vous avez une amie demeurant à Abbeville. En allant la voir, préféreriez-vous la trouver morte, ou qu'elle vous eût trompé avec un homme de bien, et s'en repentît?...*; LXXII *... Supposé que vous aimiez une demoiselle, qu'est-ce qui vous causerait plus de chagrin ou qu'elle se mariât, ou qu'elle mourût?...*; XCVI *... Vous aimez une dame et elle vous paye de retour. S'il vous fallait choisir, préféreriez-vous qu'elle mourût ou qu'elle vous quittât pour en aimer un autre?...* Machaut renewed an old literary convention by making it the subject of a relatively long narrative *dit*.

The ideological content of *JRB* would seem to present no unusual features of interest. Love casuistry was highly popular in the elegant, sophisticated courts of the Middle Ages, and *fin' amor* a social game, a pastime for courtiers as well as an ecstatic personal experience. Such literature can quite properly be categorized as *précieux*, if *préciosité* is not limited to the seventeenth century but considered a universal literary trend or style to be found throughout world literature and in France one link in a chain extending from the trouvères to Giraudoux.[3] The *JRB* certainly manifests those traits generally ascribed to the *précieux*: vivacity, psychological penetration, wit, play, and concern for social relationships. Furthermore, the Knight and the Lady conform to the most rigorous standards of *fin' amor* laid down by Guillaume de Lorris and by Machaut himself in *DV*. Their long speeches in the garden breathe a spirit of pathos, melancholy, and ecstatic commitment to love which as poetry surpasses anything in the earlier *dit*.

Nonetheless, it appears that *JRB* was criticized by certain members of the court, especially the ladies (Hoeppfner, 1:lxix). They presumably objected to Machaut's decision, rendered in King

Faral, *Recherches sur les sources latines des contes et romans courtois du moyen âge* (Paris, 1913); Giuseppe Tavani, "Il dibattito sul chierico e il cavaliere nella tradizione mediolatina e volgare," *Romanistisches Jahrbuch* 15 (1964): 51-84; Paul Remy, "Jeu parti et roman breton," in *Mélanges de linguistique romane et de philologie médiévale offerts a M. Maurice Delbouille* (Gembloux, 1964), 2: 545-61; Ernest Langlois, *Origines et sources du Roman de la Rose* (Paris, 1891); Alan M. F. Gunn, *The Mirror of Love: A Reinterpretation of "The Romance of the Rose"* (Lubbock, Texas, 1952).

[3] See René Bray, *La préciosité et les précieux de Thibaut de Champagne à Jean Giraudoux* (Paris, 1948).

John's name, that the Knight was more to be pitied than the Lady. This controversy was sufficiently important that years later, c. 1350, Machaut wrote *Le Jugement dou Roy de Navarre,* reversing his original verdict. Unfortunately, the only evidence we have for the controversy comes from the second *Jugement.* If poetry was written by Machaut's adversaries, it has not survived. To the extent we can accept a romancer's word, and without committing the "intentional fallacy," it is probable that a minor literary furor was unleashed by the appearance of *JRB* in the middle or late 1330s and that Machaut was accused of having defamed the fair sex ("Vers les dames estes forfais," *Le Jugement dou Roy de Navarre,* 811), of having made a judgment in opposition to *fin' amor.*

Whether or not the ladies are correct, Machaut's verdict does play an important role in *JRB.* Four allegorical judges and King John decide unanimously for the Knight. Their decision is based on reasoning that might well shock the ladies: that love, born from desire, is physical rather than spiritual in nature. *Raison* declares in the strongest possible terms that all men love the body more than the soul and, when they love, are subject to sin:

> 1704   Mais il n'est ame,
> N'homme vivant qui aimme si sans blame,
> S'il est tapez de l'amoureuse flame,
> Qu'il n'aimme mieus assez le corps que l'ame.
>   Pour quel raison?
> Amour vient de charnel affection,
> Et si desir et sa condition
> Sont tuit enclin a delectation.
>   Si ne se puet
> Nuls, ne nulle garder qui amer vuet
> Qu'il n'i ait vice ou pechié; il l'estuet;
> Et c'est contraire a l'ame qui s'en duet.

This being the case, *Juenesse* will soon cause the Lady to forget her dead Lover. A purely spiritual affection, unreinforced by physical contact, cannot last one day, says *Raison.* Out of sight, out of mind! She supports the Knight's argument that when a man or woman dies he is soon forgotten. Such is the human condition, and only a fool will resist it.

The physical as such was never completely absent from *fin' amor.* Andreas Capellanus defines love as a passion whose goal is physical consummation: "Amor est passio quaedam innata procedens ex visione et immoderata cogitatione formae alterius sexus, ob quam aliquis super omnia cupit alterius potiri amplexibus et omnia de utriusque voluntate in ipsius amplexu amoris praecepta compleri" (p. 4). Although *amor purus* is to be preferred, Andreas permits *amor mixtus* as a legitimate alternative. Many romances terminate with a happy consummated marriage; others *(Tristan, Lancelot, La Châtelaine de Vergi, Le Châtelain de Couci, Flamenca)* tell a tale of adultery. However, we also noted that some lyric poets deemphasized the sensual in favor of a refined, purified, spiritual longing; some even renounced hope of physical possession altogether. Their attitude became more prevalent as *fin' amor* evolved into a literary cliché, a game to be enjoyed at court. By the second half of the thirteenth century, Jean de Meun portrayed a courtly lover outraged when Lady Reason calls the objects of regeneration by name. Like Machaut, he struck a blow against the unworkable, excessively "romantic" conception of *fin' amor* prevalent in his day.

The tradition, whether sensual or chaste, whether culminating in marriage or adultery, claimed that essential to *fin' amor* is the notion of obstacle. Love is enhanced by longing, frustration, uncertainty, and long periods of absence. Sometimes a couple achieves union only in death. Or the bereaved lover, unable to survive his mate, follows him immediately into the hereafter *(Pyramus et Tisbé, Tristan, Le Châtelain de Couci, La Châtelaine de Vergi)*. Machaut, on the other hand, declares that love is destroyed, not enhanced, by separation and death. Once her Lover has died, the Lady will neither perish of a broken heart nor maintain her passion forever. She will simply follow *la costume:* forget him and love anew. (A comparable problem is discussed in the *De Amore*, Dialogue VIII, where a Man of the Higher Nobility suggests that after a two-year period of mourning the Lady of the Same Class should be prepared to love once again; refusing to do so will be an act of defiance against God's will, pp. 196, 202.)

The Knight too is a sensual being who has loved in a sensual way. Since his Beloved is still alive and has left him, he is tortured by jealousy. He admits that the most exquisite moments of suffering occur when he imagines meeting her often in public (separation does not operate in his case), yet knowing she is with another. He wishes to die. In fact, the logical, symmetrical structure of the

Knight's second discourse is broken by repeated intrusions of this jealousy motif, which becomes an obsession. Andreas Capellanus proclaims jealousy to be a necessary constituent of love (Rule 2: Qui non zelat, amare non potest; Rule 21: Ex vera zelotypia affectus semper crescit amandi; Rule 22: De coamante suspicione percepta zelus et affectus crescit amandi). He makes it very clear that jealousy is a good trait in a lover, never in a husband. In general, however, the courtly tradition decreed that only ugly old husbands and guardians manifested jealousy. These were the *gilos*, a pejorative term in the courtly lexicon. With only a few exceptions (Tristan was one of them), a good lover rarely distrusted his lady or speculated on her conjugal life. If after having married her, however, he became a *gilos*, she was entitled to deceive him *(Flamenca)* or to replace him with a new husband *(Eracle)*. In *JRB*, on the other hand, jealousy is inherent in the erotic experience, more powerful than the Lady's chaste tenderness, more powerful than death.

After the four judges agree on the main point of contention, a second issue is raised: whether the Knight should remain faithful to his Beloved. This question too was treated in the *jeux-partis* (ed. Långfors; II and LXXXVIII). Although the judges cannot agree (*Amour* and *Juenesse* reply in the affirmative, *Raison* and *Loiauté* in the negative), Machaut grants *Raison* the longest, most eloquent speech and King John's approbation. He undoubtedly meant her view to prevail. According to *Raison*, anyone who serves Love and does not obtain his reward is mad (1818-19). The deceived Knight should give up a passion he can never hope to satisfy. By stating that the Lady will not and that the Knight ought not to remain faithful, Machaut modifies his own ultraorthodox exaltation of *Loiauté* in *DV*. He says in effect that everyday experience and the world of books are quite different entities. Lovers should maintain freedom of action and not, as in the romances, be slaves of passion unto death.

Although the notion of free choice was essential to the Provençal love ethos, and the development of *fin' amor* in the West has been construed as a movement in the direction of equality of the sexes, courtly literature merely substituted one form of servitude for another. In place of the adoring Saracen or Christian princess of *chanson de geste* and her proud, indifferent, masterful paladin, we often find an adoring lover at the feet of his proud, indifferent, masterful lady. The master-slave relationship has been reversed, but love is still envisaged from the man's perspective, with the woman treated as an object: to be enjoyed or adored. However, in the late Middle Ages, with Jean de Meun, Machaut, and Christine de Pisan, polite literature becomes oriented toward the woman, treating her own problems from her own point of view. By participating directly in the narrative, by partaking of love and expressing erotic sentiments, the Lady cannot hide the fact that she, like the man, is a creature of the senses. The *JRB* recounts two contrasting love-affairs. The one, told by the Knight, reflects the old courtly tradition of a timid lover and relatively inaccessible *domna*. Significantly, the Beloved is unworthy of the Knight's adoration and their affair is doomed to failure. The second relationship concerns the Lady. We hear nothing of frustration, anguish, and protracted love-service. Neglecting the details of courtship, the Lady concentrates almost exclusively on the happy period of her amours. She admits that she has been one of Love's serfs from earliest youth. For seven or eight years she loved her man, and he her; they were one heart and will, and she took all of life's pleasures from him. They loved as equals. Her relationship, though doomed, was more successful, honest, and genuine than the Knight's; it could be destroyed only by powers beyond human control.

In *Le Jugement dou Roy de Navarre, Bonneürté* accuses Guillaume de Machaut of having defamed ladies (cf. above, p. 41). The accusation appears at first sight ludicrous. Nowhere in *JRB* does Machaut indulge in the antifeminist diatribe rampant in the most orthodox courtly literature (*Erec et Enide, Lancelot, Yvain, L'Escoufle, Guillaume de Dole, Flamenca,* even Marie de France). But a fourteenth-century *Précieuse* might well take umbrage at Machaut's plot line. Of his four main characters, two are men and two are women. One man lives and dies a perfect lover; the other, no less a paragon, will suffer possibly for the rest of his days because his love is so pure. Of the two ladies, we are told a different story. One is disloyal, vicious, and a liar, has abandoned the Knight for no good reason, and will be forever dishonored; the other, despite good intentions, will forget her Lover. Machaut says nothing to indicate that his characters' actions are conditioned by their sex. On the contrary, he insists that both man and woman are wounded by love (5-6), that both will forget deceased loved ones (1109). Since nothing in the doctrinal content of *JRB* forbids a complete reversal of roles, the poem could just as easily have told of a lady abandoned by her lover and a man bemoaning his mistress's death. However, whether by chance or intention, Machaut wrote his story the way he did. His male characters adhere more closely to *fin' amor* than do the female. These are the only men and women Machaut permits us to see; in *JRB* the men love "better" than the women. And in a semiallegorical, didactic poem, the various characters attain greater universality than in most works of literature. So, too, Molière's *Dom Juan* and *Tartuffe* were condemned in the seventeenth century in part because, even though the dramatist himself never attacks the Church in so many words, he creates a "world" hostile to the Christian perspective. Those of his characters who defend Christian or clerical values are generally scoundrels (Tartuffe) or fools (Orgon, Sganarelle), whereas the more exciting, dynamic ones are indifferent to *la vie dévote* or attack it. Machaut presents ladies in a bad light (as he will in *Le Jugement dou Roy de Navarre* and *Le Dit de l'Alerion*), pokes fun at them, and, for whatever reason, allows a gentleman to defeat a lady in argument.

Finally, it is Lady Reason who gives the verdict in her name and declares herself and the court opposed to love-madness. In so many romances *(Enéas, Eracle, Cligès, Lancelot, L'Escoufle, Flamenca)* Reason or Sense debates Love or the Heart within the protagonist's psyche; a similar *conflictus* occurs in both parts of *Le Roman de la Rose*. But Reason always gives way before Love and is defeated in the course of the narrative: *Omnia vincit Amor, et nos cedamus Amori*. Not so in *JRB*. *Raison* reigns supreme in King John's court, mistress over all other allegorical figures, including *Amour* (1989-95). She speaks first in the deliberations, upon which the other judges, including *Amour*, conform to her opinion. She draws up the court's verdict (1958). And she and *Loiauté* both criticize *Amour*, blaming him for the Knight's having loved an unworthy girl, for the girl's having subsequently fallen in love with another man, and for wanting the Knight to remain loyal in spite of everything. Their criticism goes largely unanswered.

Love's supremacy in the courtly world is undermined. The *JRB* reflects late medieval interest in a more naturalistic, noncourtly erotic, the most illustrious example being Jean de Meun's portion

of *Le Roman de la Rose*. However, Machaut does not deny courtly
love altogether. Instead, he seeks a compromise, perhaps a synthesis,
between the courtly and anticourtly positions. From Machaut's
perspective, *fin' amor* is a lovely, ennobling, admirable way of life.
But it also is based upon physical desire. Because love is a natural
sentiment, derived from Nature, it is good in essence; therefore
the physical must not be entirely suppressed. Machaut asks only
that in erotic matters people avoid fanatical adherence to exaggerated
or false principles. *Fin' amor* is eminently valid but must be adapted
to the needs of everyday reality; then only can it permit realization
of happiness according to the dictates of wisdom and experience.

In addition to the love-doctrine, other conventions of the *dit
amoreus* are undermined in *JRB*. We mean allegory and the figure
of the narrator. It is true that the Knight, recounting how he had
fallen in love, names *Plaisance, Fine Amour, Dous Regart, Dous
Penser,* and *Dous Espoir,* who recall similar figures in *DV*. But
whereas an allegorical *bellum intestinum* is central to the structure
of *DV,* here the Knight evokes these figures only to proceed to other
matters. Similarly, *Fortune* and *Amour, Esperance* and *Desesperance,*
are alluded to briefly, then forgotten. In one quite moving speech,
the Knight seeks to discover the cause of his unhappiness; yet he
absolves from blame Fortune, the Beloved, Love, himself, Nature,
and God each in turn (725-860). Personifications are mentioned
in the same breath with physically tangible human beings and with
God; they serve but to underscore the Knight's anguish.

The only episode in which allegory predominates is the trial scene
at Durbuy. The king of Bohemia is surrounded by personifications
who assume the role of courtiers and palace domestics: *Prouesse*
carries King John's sword, *Hardiesse* escorts him, and *Largesse* is
his doorman. When the Knight, the Lady, and the Narrator arrive,
they are received by *Honneur* and *Courtoisie,* then ushered into the
king's presence. There they discover that he is attended by *Richesse,
Loiauté, Leësse, Volenté, Noblesse, Franchise,* sixteen such figures
in all, who had been "given" to him by God and Nature at birth
and have served him ever since.

Four councillors, *Raison, Amour, Loiauté* and *Juenesse,* decide
the litigation. Like her prototype in Jean de Meun, *Raison* talks
too much and is overbearing. She delivers an overly long discourse
(1665-1784), using a highly intellectual vocabulary in parody of

scholastic argumentation. She is also quite short-tempered, a woman as well as a goddess, who denigrates *Amour* and replies out of turn to the latter's speech (1812-19). *Amour* takes two and one-half lines to agree with *Raison* (1788-90), then devotes the remainder of his speech to a divisive point concerning the Knight's fidelity, disparaging *Raison* all the while. Following this, *Loiauté* castigates *Amour* and, in a delightfully ironic touch by Machaut, urges the Knight to be disloyal to his Beloved. Finally, *Juenesse* flings herself into they fray, attacking both *Raison* and *Loiauté;* of the four, she is the most impetuous. She would be content to have the Knight die of a broken heart, because, "s'il y muert, chascuns le clamera / Martir d'amours, et honneur li sera" (1918-19). King John laughs at *Juenesse,* though without rancor, for he recognizes that she speaks in character. He then gently rebukes all his judges for having wandered from the matter at hand.

Machaut flatters the king of Bohemia by attributing to his court all chivalric virtues. Some of these virtues are depicted not just as personified abstractions but as if they were real people. A humorous disparity is created between the role these figures usually play in literature and their deeds in *JRB,* between how we expect them to act and how Machaut makes them act, between the somewhat stilted virtues they represent and the very human traits they display at John's court. That their human failings (*Raison's* pomposity, *Juenesse's* brashness) conform to their given emblematic nature only adds to the fun. The result is a tension between humor and sentimental rhetoric; the judgment scene partakes both of formal ritual and the high art of comedy.

In *DV* we noticed a blurring of focus between the Narrator conceived as a participant in the action (a hero telling his own story) and the same person portrayed as an unobtrusive, neutral recorder of speeches delivered by the God of Love. Machaut resolves the problem in *JRB* by splitting his protagonist in two. The Knight appears as the subjective, passionate, emotionally involved lover; characteristics of the fumbling, eavesdropping onlooker are delegated to the Narrator-witness. True, the Narrator declares that he also is a lover (11-12, 2067-79) and speaks of his passion for a lady, which, though unrequited, brings him joy. Since he and the Knight both suffer from frustrated passion, the Narrator is especially qualified to console his friend. In a sense too the Knight is the Narrator's double, an alter ego or surrogate. The parallelism corresponds to the one in *DV*. However, we are told of the Narrator's sentimental problems only at the very beginning and end of the story; elsewhere he acts in antithesis to the Knight: uninvolved, passive, seemingly independent, in contrast to the Knight's spontaneous commitment to passion. A spectator, he remains outside the action. It is the Knight who manifests traits of the good courtly lover we would normally expect to find in the Narrator. The Narrator has projected onto the love-sick Knight and then, in a burst of wish-fulfillment, finds a solution to the Knight's problems by introducing him to King John.

Machaut's originality lies in the creation of an I-narrator who witnesses the story but does not himself play a leading role in it. On the one hand, he maintains an illusion of personal involvement and authenticity present in all good first-person narratives (*Le Roman de la Rose, La Vie de Marianne, A la recherche du temps perdu*). Thus, for example, the Narrator intervenes after the Lady's first speech to assure us that he personally saw her fall down as if dead (206-8). Yet, by depicting the Narrator as a spectator, not an actor, viewing love from outside, from almost the same perspective as his public, Machaut also creates distance and a greater sense of objectivity, the hallmark of good third-person narratives. The Narrator's obtrusive intervention and the fact that his story is filtered through more than one consciousness remind us that *JRB* is fiction and not confession or reportage, that the Knight and the Narrator exist for us as characters in a work of imagination. Such is the case when the various characters refer to *JRB* as a book, telling us that certain material has already been written down and is to be found earlier in the story (1595-96, 1782).

Having conceived the Narrator as a witness enables Machaut to solve a problem which often obtrudes in *Ich-erzählungen:* how a nonomniscient narrator can be expected to know all the events he recounts. However, the author must create a plausible witnessing-scene. This Machaut does with some skill. The Narrator tells us how he lay down in the garden to listen to a bird sing, hiding lest the bird take fright. Hence he was in a position to observe the Knight and Lady without damaging his own moral character, and they talk freely, unaware of his presence. Machaut even answers the question why, once the Knight and Lady appeared on the scene, the bird now presumably having flown away, the Narrator remained hidden: because he thought they were lovers come to a rendezvous and, discreet court poet that he is, pressed into the underbrush so as not to embarrass them (53-55).

Finally, splitting the protagonist gives Machaut an opportunity to emphasize humorous traits in the Narrator while maintaining the Knight as a figure of tragic disappointed love. Machaut's narrator-witness is placed in the humiliating situation of an eavesdropper overhearing secrets of the heart; at key moments in the story he reminds us that he lies half-buried in the leaves and grass. Once the Knight and Lady have told their stories, he would like to make his presence known but dreads embarrassing the litigants, revealing that he had been spying on them, and making himself importunate. Even when the Narrator decides to act, his problem is resolved by an outside agent. The Lady's *petit chien,* which had accompanied her into the grove, leaps at the intruder, barking furiously and biting at his robe. Pleased at this accident which gives him a conversational opening, the Narrator brings the animal back to her. This *chiennés* recalls, of course, Petit-crû and Husdent in the *Tristan* romances as well as the Châtelaine de Vergi's *chienet afetié.* [4] Petit-crû and the Châtelaine's pet were both ladies' lapdogs; the latter acted as a go-between in his mistress's love affairs. The ringing of the bell around Petit-crû's neck abolished pain in those who heard it, while Husdent had been trained to hunt and the Châtelaine's dog to make its rounds without making noise. In humorous contrast, the dog in *JRB* barks gleefully, tears people's robes, leaves his mistress's side, and offers no consolation to her grief. Although he apparently plays no role in her amours, he does serve as an intermediary, not for her lover but for a perfect stranger, an eavesdropper who will, incidentally, bring about her condemnation. The archetypal friendly beast who leads the hero into the Other World is transformed into the merest trifle of a domestic pet and the romance hero into a bumbling busybody, good only to advise others.

---

[4] Jean Frappier, "*La Chastelaine de Vergi,* Marguerite de Navarre et Bandello," in *Publications de la Faculté des Lettres de l'Université de Strasbourg, No. 105: Mélanges 1945. II. Etudes littéraires* (Paris, 1946), pp. 89-150; Pál Lakits, *La Châtelaine de Vergi et l'évolution de la nouvelle courtoise* (Debrecen, 1966).

Machaut comments ironically on poets and lovers, regards the nonparticipating poet with good-humored deprecation and the anguished lover with equally good-humored sympathy. He shows us the strengths and foibles of both poets and lovers. Nor are we given a simple happy ending. A week after the trial is over, the Knight and the Lady return each to his own home. Although they both accept King John's trial judgment, they do not necessarily follow his advice to mend their ways. Machaut leaves it an open question whether they can readapt to everyday reality. The lovers are criticized for their failure in the experiential world, and the Narrator for his in the realm of courtly convention. Machaut presents opposing but not necessarily incompatible perspectives on love: those of youth and of maturity. With an unusual degree of sophistication, he asks questions and gives answers, which the characters themselves and presumably the public are free to disregard.

Machaut wishes neither to exalt nor to destroy courtly orthodoxy. He urges that *fin' amor* be tempered with common sense. Although his characters are plunged into suffering, *JRB* does proclaim that man has a right to cast off despair, to take comfort in whatever way he can.

Already in the grove, the Knight beseeches the Lady to tell him her story, then offers to recount his own (79-80, 87-92, 248-50, 253-56). With amazing insight, he realizes that he can help console her by giving her an opportunity to unburden herself and by distracting her with his own problems. Her narcissistic self-absorption will be broken, and some of her grief with it. This consolation-theme was later taken up by Chaucer in *The Book of the Duchess*.

The encounter between Knight and Lady takes place *au temps pascour* within a lovely garden, one among a thousand evocations of the *locus amoenus*. As in *DV* but with even greater felicity, Machaut evokes dew on the grass shimmering in the sunlight, the sweet smell of flowers, a stream flowing near a lovely bower, a fountain, and the song of birds. The beauty of the décor contrasts with the pitiful human situation of the two lovers. However, since a pleasance is, by definition, the only setting where love can flourish, this *locus amoenus* tones down the pathos of *JRB* and provides, for the reader if not for the characters, a glimmer of hope. Nature's beauty in all its splendor persists no matter how men direct their lives; human grief is inevitable, but life goes on. Perhaps Nature even *causes* the two forlorn lovers to meditate on (and seek to regain) lost happiness. After all, Guillaume de Lorris banished *Tristesce* from the Garden of Delight. It is then perhaps not irrelevant that the greater part of the Knight's and Lady's speeches are devoted to moments of loving rather than to subsequent loss. We remember the Beloved less as a traitor than as the sweet coquettish girl of fourteen and a half the Knight fell in love with the first day he saw her. She is praised with traditional courtly imagery: her beauty compared to the light of the sun, her complexion redder than the rose and whiter than snow, tender and shimmering, reflecting light like a mirror, her shining blonde hair richer than gold. We also see her singing and dancing in the full joy of youth as her laughing eyes bewitch the Knight. Her physical beauty reminds us that the bleakest tragedy, also dependent on the senses, cannot endure forever. Life and love have been beautiful; the perfection of their past beauty dampens present misery and also points the way to future joy.

Machaut states his doctrine of consolation most strongly in the scene at King John's court. Durbuy Castle, with its birds, fountain, and river, is a parallel locus to the *hortus deliciarum,* retaining some characteristics of the Other World motif in romance, and provides a worthy backdrop for so great a potentate as John of Luxembourg. The *JRB* follows a long tradition of panegyric. If, however, Machaut sings his patron's praises, the presence of King John contributes to the poem as a total work of art.

John of Luxembourg, king of Bohemia, was perhaps the most prestigious monarch in the first half of the fourteenth century. Although modern historians have characterized him as a foolish spendthrift who wasted his life and his people's revenues in Quixotic pursuits, to his contemporaries he cut a magnificent figure. His father, Henry VII, was Holy Roman Emperor. His son, Charles IV, became Holy Roman Emperor and perhaps the greatest ruler in the history of Bohemia. He himself epitomized Froissart's ideal of chivalry: a great knight, master of the arts of war and diplomacy, the very archetype of largess, and a *miles Christi* who defended the pope's interests as leader of the Guelf coalition in Lombardy and brought Christian culture to the Pagan East during his many campaigns in Poland, Prussia, and Lithuania. His reputation was such that people could say, "Sine rege Bohemiae, nemo valet expedire."

Machaut served John from 1323 to approximately 1340. He and his brother, Jean de Machaut, were rewarded materially due to the king's good offices. Guillaume is referred to in a papal bull as "clerico, elemosinario et familiari suo domestico" (1330), "domestico, familiari, notario suo" (1332), and "familiari et domestico, notario, secretario suo" (1333). [5] Furthermore, it was almost certainly through John, himself allied to the Valois and Bourbons, that Machaut entered into contact with those members of the royal family who protected him during the last three decades or so of his active career. He alludes to King John often in his work, always with enthusiasm.

The king of Bohemia appears in *JRB* as the epitome of courtly honor and decorum. Although Machaut invests him with the false modesty of one who claims no experience in love's doings, a "Juge ignorant et de sens desgarni" (1614), in reality he is presumed to be more learned than Ovid and to surpass Hector and Alexander. The allegorical figures who serve him all display good manners, breeding, and the virtues of *Jovens*.

To sympathize with the wretched, to console the unconsolable, are tasks worthy of the wisest, most gracious of monarchs. John does not live just for himself but to serve others. He is king, law-giver, and judge, a father figure who protects the weak and rights wrongs. The Narrator's trip to Durbuy represents an archetypal return to the Father's house. John's courtliness is bestowed quite properly on two young people of the most elegant taste and breeding, fully capable of responding to it, as they demonstrated in the grove. And his prestige gives Machaut's doctrinal line a weight it otherwise would not have. The court is a focus for the aspirations of a whole society; it provides example as well as precept for how men should live. The feast, the eight-days rejoicing, the departure with gifts, are a tribute to King John's vaunted largess and a tangible manifestation of a way of life open to the fourteenth-century French aristocracy and to all true lovers of noble heart.

---

[5] Antoine Thomas, "Extraits des archives du Vatican pour servir à l'histoire littéraire. III. Guillaume de Machaut," *Romania* 10 (1881): 325-33.

Machaut elaborates *JRB* at an appropriately slow, majestic pace. Formal presentation of argument at court and the Knight's second discourse in the grove—divided into prologue, *narratio, partitio, confirmatio, reprehensio,* and *conclusio,* though not in that order— give the impression of a calm, patterned existence, ordered according to fixed rules of decorum. The story contains a number of contrasts: between the Knight and the Narrator, the Knight and the Lady, the Lover and the Beloved, *Raison* and *Amour,* and the four judges and King John. Like much of fourteenth-century allegory, *JRB* does not rely upon sprightly narrative. The plot, whether in grove or castle, is largely static; the major characters make speeches which often recapitulate earlier speeches. Our emotions are engaged primarily by the Knight's first discourse, which tells how he fell in love. The rest of the action mostly concerns the Narrator. Machaut's tale is centered upon two closed, stationary worlds, where time is to some extent abolished and men fixed in intense emotional problems they cannot resolve.

Spatially, the characters are set in movement: the Narrator enters the garden, then proceeds with the Knight and Lady to Durbuy, whence they return each to his own home. The plot can be divided into two sections: the dispute in the garden; and the resolution of the dispute at court. In the garden we witness a pair of lovers, but not in love with each other, alone, unhappy, secretive, enslaved to their passions. In the castle we observe a dynamic community, working together in relative harmony. The story does build to a climax: from conflict through resolution to celebration. The protagonists themselves do not particularly grow in the course of the poem, but the Narrator and to some extent his readers progress from the garden to the castle, from ignorance to knowledge, from illusion to reality, from spying to public display, from youth to maturity, from isolation to the community. The Knight and Lady once knew Joy, then lost it; at King John's court, whether or not they accept it, they are given consolation for loss of Joy, and in this refined, civilized world perhaps the closest replica of Joy man can hope to conserve.

Chaucer treated the theme of *JRB* in *The Book of the Duchess.* *The Duchess* is a beautiful poem, but, in my opinion, Machaut was more successful in depicting the complexity and ambiguity of life and the eternal tension between fiction and reality. Well might Machaut take pride in his work and sign his name in an anagram; [6] *JRB* is his first major literary triumph.

---

[6] See Ernest Hoepffner, "Anagramme und Rätselgedichte bei Guillaume de Machaut," *Zeitschrift für romanische Philologie* 30 (1906): 401-13.

3. REMEDE DE FORTUNE

The Narrator has fallen in love but dreads an avowal to the Lady in question. Instead he gives expression to his sentiments in a *lay*. Unfortunately, the *lay* falls into the Lady's hands. When she has the Narrator read it to her and then asks him who wrote it, he runs away in tears to the *Parc de Hesdin,* where he delivers a *complainte* against Love and Fortune. Suddenly Lady Hope *(Esperence)* appears by his side. After she has comforted him, the Narrator proceeds from the garden to his Lady's residence. There he confesses his love, and she declares she will accept him as her *ami*. When, upon returning to the Lady's home sometime later, the Narrator reproaches her for gazing upon others, she declares that she acted in that way to keep their relationship secret.

IN HIS THIRD NARRATIVE POEM, *Remede de Fortune,*[1] Machaut returns to the format of *DV*. Again he writes a didactic allegory, which is also a poem of education. The story begins with a general statement listing the twelve rules to be followed by anyone who would learn ("Cils qui vuet aucun art aprendre." l. 1). From the general, the Narrator proceeds to a concrete, individual case— himself. When he was but a lad, his mind corresponded to the *tabula rasa;* in those days, he tells us later, he was foolish, ignorant, fickle, lazy, and prone to bad habits (3573-78). Then he fell in love. Once he gave himself utterly to his Lady, she and *Amour* taught him everything he now knows. The Narrator first tells us of his early education; then, as the plot unfolds, we see him learn from

---

[1] 4,298 lines; ed. Hoepffner, 2: 1-157 (cited hereafter as *RF*).

Esperence and again from the Lady. *Esperence* berates him for being an ignorant ninny who has never been to school, has not lived long enough to know anything, is blind and as dense as a bird in a cage. But in the course of their dialogue, and later with the Lady, we observe the Narrator's blindness cured, his foolishness alleviated, and his stupidity transformed (albeit with relapses) into awareness and self-confidence. As in *DV,* the reader is informed of Machaut's doctrine both directly and indirectly: in speeches by the Narrator, Hope, and the Lady, and by observing the Narrator's active progress to manhood.

The *RF* is first of all an *Ars amandi,* a treatise on the nature of love, the psychology of lovers, and tactics which contribute to the attainment of Joy. Machaut's doctrine differs little from what he proposed in *DV.* We are again told that Love, created by Nature, is in essence good; Love may pour out joy to all people yet never deplete her treasure. Because *Amour* and the Lady are a source of inspiration to the Narrator, he is made a better man by loving, even though the Lady be unaware of his devotion. The *locus amoenus* where he meets *Esperence* is enclosed by high walls. Like the Garden of Delight in *Le Roman de la Rose* it is reserved for an elite, the Happy Few capable of *fin' amor.* Here, in solitude, the Narrator weeps; love is a personal experience of trial and ecstasy.

He falls in love easily. As in *DV,* he is set on fire, endures torture and imprisonment, and is ill unto death. Machaut develops the *dolce-amar* motif: his hero sways back and forth, from sadness to joy and from hope to despair, now laughing now weeping, now warm now cold. But joy wins out, and he relishes being in love like a fish in water. When content, the Narrator becomes a poet and expresses his delight in song.

Submission, loyalty, and discretion are virtues especially dear to the Lady. True, the Narrator dreads telling her of his love or that she should find out from a third party or by accident. Machaut approves his protagonist's timidity. Smooth talkers, capable of twisting a girl's will, are inevitably insincere, we discover. The Narrator and his Lady agree that a youth commits an unforgivable affront by making a formal love-request. Praising a girl alone will permit her to discern his wishes. A timid lover may find the way to joy long and full of obstacles, but any other approach must be rejected out of hand. Since the Narrator chose the right path, the Lady does return his love. She later says that they are joined together as one, each will serve the other's peace and honor, and neither will seek lordship (4037-52). Machaut, while adhering to the traditional precepts of *fin' amor*, introduces the theme of liberty and equality between the sexes, which he found in Jean de Meun and had already broached in *JRB*.

The *RF* ranges beyond courtly love to treat other, more serious questions. As the poem's title indicates, Machaut is concerned with Fortune: the mutability of secular affairs and man's apparent inability to control his destiny. His major source is Boethius's *De Consolatione Philosophiae*.[2] Not only are ideas and images taken from the Roman poet; Machaut to some extent follows Boethius in elaborating his plot. In both the *Consolatio* and *RF* the speaker declaims against Fortune. A female authority figure (Lady Philosophy in Boethius, Lady Hope in Machaut) comes to him, launches a philosophical dialogue (interspersed with lyrics), and ultimately provides consolation. The *De Consolatione Philosophiae* was available to Machaut in the original text and a wide variety of French translations and adaptations. Other medieval works in the Boethian tradition, both before and after Machaut, include Hildebert of Lavardin's *De Exilio Suo*, Simund de Freine's *Roman de Philosophie*, Alan of Lille's *De Planctu Naturae*, parts of *Le Roman de la Rose* and *Fauvel*, Albertano of Brescia's *Liber Consolationis et Consilii*, Petrarch's *De Remediis Utriusque Fortunae*, Boccaccio's *De Casibus Virorum Illustrium*, poems by Watriquet de Couvin and Jean de Condé, the *Liber Fortunae*, Gerson's *De Consolatione Theologiae*, Christine de Pisan's *Mutacion de Fortune* and *L'Avision Christine*, Alain Chartier's *Livre de l'Espérance*, Jean Régnier's *Fortunes et Adversités*, and Martin Le Franc's *L'Estrif de Fortune et de Vertu*.

---

[2] Hoepffner, 2: xvi-xxxii. Machaut mentions Boethius in line 982. For the Boethian heritage in the Middle Ages, see Howard Rollin Patch, "Fortuna in Old French Literature," in *Smith College Studies in Modern Languages* 4, no. 4 (July 1923); *The Goddess Fortuna in Mediaeval Literature* (Cambridge, Mass., 1927); and *The Tradition of Boethius: A Study of His Importance in Medieval Culture* (New York, 1935); Antoine Thomas & Mario Roques, "Traductions françaises de la *Consolatio Philosophiae* de Boèce," in *Histoire littéraire de la France* 37 (1938): 419-88, 543-47; Pierre Courcelle, *La Consolation de Philosophie dans la tradition littéraire: Antécédents et Postérité de Boèce* (Paris, 1967); and *The Middle French Liber Fortunae*, ed. John L. Grigsby (Berkeley-Los Angeles, 1967), chapts. 3 and 4.

In the second part of *Le Roman de la Rose,* Jean de Meun created a *Speculum amoris* treating all aspects of love: *fin' amor,* sensuality, friendship, the calls of money, reason, and God. Fortune's relation to Eros is discussed at length by the hero and *Raison,* another prototype for Machaut's *Esperence.* Although Machaut escapes the sterile didacticism found in so many of his contemporaries, he also fails to capture the magnificent Gargantuan splendor of Jean de Meun. He develops to its fullest potential only one major theme from Jean and Boethius. Like Guillaume de Lorris, Machaut is a poet of equilibrium; by limiting himself, he succeeds in balancing his story's doctrinal and narrative lines.

We have seen how the Narrator complains of his lot. His unhappiness is then given universal relevance when assimilated to the problem of Fortune. We are told that all worldly goods, success, and joy must wither away, for happiness cannot endure. Fortune, who skins her victims instead of shearing them, is castigated as a cruel jailer, an evil tree, and a biting serpent. As in *JRB,* man suffers most by remembering irrevocably lost past joy. Machaut has recourse to the imagery of Fortune's wheel, her two-sided face, and two buckets in a well. Quite properly, he also compares her to the moon and a stormy sea. The moon is a feminine image, gracious and lovely; its visual form changes each night of the month; it is subject to eclipse; and all the natural world, which exists under the circle of the moon, is subject to Fortune's sway. The sea too is an image of the eternal feminine. Man is free, says *Esperence.* His boat is equipped with a good sail; but when he sets out on the sea of Fortune, he tries to row or swim. People yield to Fortune when they do not have to. Above all, *Esperence* lashes out at misers who sacrifice peace of mind, honor, and their immortal souls for love of money. The more they have, the more they desire and thus can never be satisfied, whether Fortune smiles on them or not. From the Old Testament (Daniel 2:31-35) Machaut takes the story of Nebuchadnezzar's dream, a motif to which he will return in *Le Confort d'Ami.* Nebuchadnezzar dreams of a giant statue whose head is of gold, arms and chest of silver, belly and thighs of brass, legs of iron, and feet of iron and clay. The dream figure is then interpreted as an allegory of Fortune. The statue appears solid enough and resplendent but will collapse on top of anyone who puts faith in it.

James Wimsatt claims that Machaut contributed to the development of an important "sub-genre" of the *dit amoreus:* the Poem of
Complaint and Comfort. [3] Already in *JRB* we find the theme of consolation: King John gives the Knight and Lady sound advice on how
to avoid misery. A similar pattern is elaborated in *RF.* Following
Boethius and Jean de Meun, Machaut is not only concerned with
philosophical abstractions but seeks to teach men how to live. Lady
Philosophy in the *Consolatio* justifies Fortune's existence; so does
Machaut's Lady Hope. The Narrator should not blame the goddess
of mutability. By making him suffer she has done her duty, both to
him and to all men. We are told that Fortune was good to the Narrator in his early life: born naked from his mother's womb, he has
been granted the power of reason and has acquired riches and glory.
Fortune is compared to a nursemaid, giving the Narrator suck (2618-
27). Finally, the Narrator should take comfort from his present
predicament for the following reason: his affairs must eventually
take a turn for the better since they cannot possibly get worse.

Machaut's hero originally set value on Fortune's gifts by a conscious exercise of free will. Medieval Christian tragedy consists in
man's placing faith in the wrong values, then being overwhelmed
by the disparity between expectation and reward. Instead, he should
turn away from the vanity of human wishes. As in *JRB,* Machaut
counsels recourse to Reason and Nature, from whom true happiness
comes:

> 2467 La bonneürté souvereinne
> Et la felicité certeinne
> Sont souverein bien de Nature
> Qui use de Raison la pure;
> Et tels biens, on ne les puet perdre.

Raison teaches that *pacience* and *souffissance* will lead the Narrator
to *bonneürtez.* Admittedly, Reason in *RF* resembles much more
the idealistic philosophical principle found in Boethius and Jean de
Meun than the down-to-earth common sense of *JRB.* But the con-
tradiction, if any, is more apparent than real. In both of Machaut's

---

[3] James Wimsatt, *Chaucer and the French Love Poets* (Chapel Hill, N. C.,
1968), chapts. 6, 7, and 8.

poems *Raison* seeks to liberate man from false doctrine and his own pride.

For the love-remedy, Machaut takes a different tack. Since desire for a woman forms an integral part of nature and since the joy of love outweighs the pain, there is no point in renouncing one's amours. Making war on love is like warring against the self, says *Esperence. Amour* caused him to love the finest lady in the world; therefore, the Narrator has no right to complain. Were he a hundred times more accomplished, he still would not be worthy of her. She cannot but treat him better than he deserves. In an important *chanson roial* (1985-2032), the Narrator is told a true lover can never be miserable as long as he enjoys *Esperence, Dous Penser, Joie,* and *Plaisence.* He finds contentment in meditating on his beloved's perfections and will remain happy whether or not she grants his suit, no matter what happens to him or to her. Therefore, on the one hand, the Narrator should resign himself to the worst and keep his passion hidden, never demanding more tangible rewards than *Souvenir* and *Douce Pensée.* Yet, he ought not to lose hope either. Since his Lady is perfect, she will be sufficiently intelligent to divine his passion, sufficiently gracious not to hold his cowardice against him, and sufficiently merciful to reward his suit.

Although the *De Consolatione Philosophiae* is Machaut's principal source for *RF,* our poet diverges from the Boethian tradition. He avoids almost all reference to ideas expressed in the last two books of the *Consolatio.* Machaut is not in the least interested in relating happiness to the Good Life or to God. Nor does he expound Boethius's views on providence, free will, and predestination. He discusses love of money and of women, but does not allude to Fortune's other gifts: political rule, power, honors, fame, high position, and empire. Boethius's treatise is broadly philosophical and religious in a way Machaut's poem never claims to be.

Esperence consoles the Narrator by defending erotic love, not by attacking it. This is the greatest difference between the French poet and his source. Although Boethius scarcely mentions sexual love, he does say that man should not care for externals, those things which he has never really possessed in the first place. *Luxuria* is considered one of a number of false lures—along with riches, pride of birth, and fame—which distract man from the Final Good. Machaut skirts Boethius's prohibition by assimilating Eros to friendship. Boethius, Cicero *(De Amicitia),* and Jean de Meun place friendship on the highest possible spiritual plane, quite beyond Fortune's reach. One use of misfortune is to help a man distinguish true friends from false. In a catastrophe, when riches, honors, women, and other possessions have disappeared, only real friends will stick by him. Machaut declares that the Narrator should not hesitate to love, for his friend *(amie)* will remain faithful to him; such friendship, source of goodness and wisdom, is not subject to Fortune's sway. The French poet takes full advantage of the rich ambiguities inherent in words such as *ami, amie,* and *amistié.* Almost a century earlier, in *Li Livres dou Tresor* (ed. Francis J. Carmody [Berkeley & Los Angeles, 1948], pp. 212-13, 290), Brunetto Latini, following Aristotle, includes a man's love for family, wife, and lover under the rubric of friendship. And Jean de Meun discusses friendship in his grand *conflictus* on love. But in Latini as in Jean, friendship generally refers to an affectionate, nonsexual relationship between equals of the same sex. Indeed, Latini condemns love of women as a false friendship, false love, and false good which leads to slavery (p. 290); so does Reason in Jean de Meun's portion of *Le Roman de la Rose.*

In a sense, Machaut attempts to resolve conflicts exposed in *Le Roman de la Rose* between the Boethian and courtly philosophies. Like Jean de Meun's *Raison, Esperence* condemns the Narrator for having committed himself to Fortune, yet, unlike *Raison,* she also counsels him not to abandon love. She preaches a remedy against Fortune and, at the same time, how one can attain one's ends through Fortune. Howard Rollin Patch claims that, more than other French writers of his time, Machaut anticipates the Renaissance when he suggests that the ultimate remedy against ill fortune is success, that man has the power within himself to triumph even over externals. [4] Machaut admits that the Narrator's external courtship is subject to the mutability of all worldly things. However, the Narrator's misery derives neither from force of circumstance nor ill will on the Lady's part, but from an excess of melancholia within. If he will take heart and act, he can influence his fate. *Fin' amor,* not subject to Fortune, not of the same essence as Boethius's *luxuria,* is a sentiment without which no man can be truly noble or complete. And a perfect lady, endowed with Pity, cannot refuse mercy to a

---

[4] Patch, "Fortuna in Old French Literature," p. 21.

perfect lover. Their *amistié* will survive the ravages of time. The ecstatic, mystical state ascribed to rational man in his relationship to God is transferred by Machaut to the amorous man's relationship to the mirror and exemplar of all good things (171-72)—his lady. Fortune is transcended, not by God, but by Love.

As in *DV,* the Narrator is taught the secrets of life. The *RF* differs from Machaut's earlier poem, however, in that its protagonist does not learn passively. He develops dynamically in time. A static affirmation of principles is followed by a dramatic effort to put them into practice.

The Narrator appears first as a youth unable to adapt to a given situation. When the Lady asks him to read the *lay* which has fallen into her hands, he is thunderstruck. He recites the poem, though with fear and trembling, but has the courage neither to affirm nor deny that he is the author. Instead, he runs away weeping, to indulge in a temper tantrum directed against Love and Fortune and remains in this state until the appearance of *Esperence,* who minces no words concerning her pupil's failings. Then, in the course of his discussions with *Esperence* the young man is slowly transformed. He opens his eyes, one at a time, asks questions, and finally participates actively in the dialogue. He breaks out of the despondent stupor in which he had been wallowing to become a vibrant, more active human being. At the end of his "course of study" the Narrator has even learned joy. Then he leaves the garden to return to his Lady's manor. Although still suffering from timidity, with the help of *Amour* and *Esperence* he joins in a dance and sings a *virelay*. His next ordeal is an interview with the Lady. Without Hope's instruction, says the Narrator, he would never have had the courage to approach her. But now he woos her eloquently, expressing the previously inexpressible and avowing the unavowable. As a reward, the Lady grants him her love. In the end, after a brief relapse into jealousy, the Narrator questions his lady as to why she smiles at others. We may criticize him for lack of confidence, but at least he is not afraid to protest. He plans his complaint and carries it out with professional aplomb.

As in *JRB,* the protagonist leaves a garden (where he wished to be alone) and returns to society. He sees a group of people singing and dancing. He joins them. After the interview with the Lady, he participates with the others in community activities: religious services, a magnificent banquet, drinking, games, and more singing and dancing. Machaut takes pleasure in describing preparations for the feast, the coming and going of servants, and the extraordinary variety of musical entertainment. Scholars have noted that this portion of the narrative provides material for the social historian; musicologists especially have been fascinated by Machaut's lists of musical instruments here (3961-86) and in *La Prise d'Alexandrie* (1140-68). [5] However, in terms of the narrative the feast above all celebrates the hero's integration into society. He now belongs to a sophisticated world of song, dance, poetry, and the pleasures of the table, the harmonious world of the court.

Machaut's protagonist develops in time. An inept, narcissistic, cowardly adolescent has been transformed into a relatively mature member of society. His inner development is paralleled by progress in space. The Narrator's retreat into solitude and subsequent return to the court correspond to the classic pattern of "withdrawal and return" found in so much literature of heroism and romance. After having communicated with one lady, he communicates with another and with her peers. This marks the hero's initiation into the community. The Narrator knew Joy for the first time in the *Parc de Hesdin*. Now, when he and the Lady avow their love, he revels in a second, much greater Joy. To consecrate his triumph he sings a *rondelet* (4107-14), his final burst of lyricism in *RF*.

The Narrator experiences parallel moments of joy: one in conjunction with *Esperence*, the other in the presence of his Lady. Whereas the archetypal guides in Machaut's first two *dits* are male (the God of Love, the king of Bohemia), the *RF* protagonist is inspired by female figures. The Lady is his first and last love, the mirror of all good things. He claims she is humble as a lamb or turtledove, her beauty more resplendent than solar gold, and that she is the most beautiful and sweet-smelling of flowers, "fleur souvereinne / Seur toute creature humeinne" (59-60). The Lady is man's ideal of womanhood, placed on a pedestal, object of the hero's

[5] See Armand Machabey, "Guillaume de Machault," *La Revue Musicale* 11 (1930): 425-52, and 12 (1931): 320-44, 402-16, esp. 409-11; and *Guillaume de Machault: La Vie et l'Œuvre musical*, 2: 135-57. For a bibliography, up to 1928, of works discussing musical instruments in *RF*, see *Guillaume de Machaut; Musikalische Werke*, ed. Friedrich Ludwig, 4 vols. (Leipzig, 1926, 1928, 1929; Wiesbaden, 1954), 2: 53a, n. 1.

adoration. However, like the Lady in *JRB,* she has a personality of her own. At first involuntarily, later of her own will, she teaches the Narrator. The divine goddess of his dreams, she is also an earthly *châtelaine* who presides over a banquet and entertains guests. In both roles, she is a source of plenty, a cause for joy, and, finally, one whom all obey (3510-12). Although the Lady remains superior to her suitor in every way, she too is transformed in the course of the narrative. Eventually, somewhat like the reader, she discovers the hero's devotion, good character, and poetic art.

Esperence personifies a universal abstract quality and one of the Narrator's own character traits, his capacity for hope. Thus is to be explained Machaut's insistence that Love and Lady Hope will sustain him even when they do not stand physically in his presence. Like Boethius's *Philosophia* and Jean de Meun's *Raison, Esperence* is conceived as a stately, regal figure who appears to the Narrator in the garden, a true *puella senex* possessing equally the beauty of youth and wisdom of old age. She is the dreamer's doctor, who cures his symbolic blindness, a light that dispels the shadows which surround him. *Esperence* is said to be a flower and a tree of goodness, a sweet odor and balm, and the star of the sea. In Machaut's most extended simile, as the sun warms, illuminates, and gladdens the earth, creating new life in springtime, so Hope shines in men's hearts, creates joy and laughter, and nourishes plants of love (2194-286). Hope corresponds to the traditional benign agent acting on the hero's behalf, a protective figure not unlike Pallas and Venus in classical epic. As divine intercessor and mediatrix, she permits the Narrator to win the Lady. As teacher, she grants him knowledge. A good mother, she replaces the terrible image of Fortune in his life. And once the apprentice lover-poet has mastered his lessons, he will pass on wisdom to us, having become a teacher in turn.

The Lady and *Esperence* closely resemble each other. They are both extraordinarily good, beautiful, and wise. They outshine the sun. They are teachers and healers, authority figures to be obeyed without question. Woman so conceived appears superhuman, a demigoddess revealing the best of man's inner nature and leading him to happiness or salvation. This archetype, the Jungian *Anima,* is found throughout world literature; some of the more striking manifestations are the troubadour *domna,* Guinevere in Chrétien de Troyes and the *Prose Lancelot,* Dante's Beatrice, Rousseau's

Julie, Stendhal's Mme de Rênal, and Proust's Duchesse de Guermantes. In courtly literature especially the woman appears as a mother figure: she is often older than the lover, married to someone else, of higher social class, and is, from his perspective, the unique source of all good. He submits masochistically to her will. Although the lover yearns for fulfillment in her arms, seldom or never is his passion consummated. Naturally, when the lady treats him harshly, he falls into a fit of depression. He suffers from guilt, pines for forbidden pleasures, yet is sworn to absolute secrecy, and his greatest fear is that she may reject or forget him. [6] The *RF* Narrator indeed adheres to the courtly pattern; Machaut underscores especially his dread of offending the Lady and anxiety over the possibility that she loves others as well as he.

Esperence is the Lady's double or surrogate. She not only helps the Narrator conquer the Lady; in the *Parc de Hesdin* she *is* the Lady, that is, the Lady's physical and moral traits have been transferred to her. Machaut elaborates a pattern of wish-fulfillment wherein the Narrator meets a gracious, motherly figure who forgives his faults and offers him love. As he has succeeded with *Esperence,* he will succeed with the Lady, just as Hope promised. His vision is prophetic as well as therapeutic.

Hope's assimilation to the Lady is underscored by ring imagery. Giving or taking a ring plays an important role in epic *(Girard de Roussillon, Les Enfances Guillaume, Gaydon)* and in romance *(Yvain, Perceval, Guillaume de Dole, Le Lai de l'ombre, Amadas et Ydoine, La Manekine, La Dame à la licorne).* In *RF* it serves as an authenticating device, a weapon in Love's wars, a pretext for humor, and a symbol of devotion. Approximately halfway through the poem *Esperence* gives the Narrator her ring. She places it on his finger as a sign that she loves and will protect him:

---

[6] For a Freudian interpretation of courtly love, explained in terms of the Oedipus complex, see Herbert Moller, "The Meaning of Courtly Love," *Journal of American Folklore* 73 (1960): 39-52; and Richard A. Koenigsberg, "Culture and Unconscious Fantasy: Observations on Courtly Love," *Psychoanalytic Review* 54 (1967): 36-50. According to Moller, the lover's obsessive fear of *losengiers* and rival suitors can be assimilated to post-Oedipal sibling rivalry. Koenigsberg underscores direct conflict with a husband-father rival. Neither scholar alludes to Machaut.

2083 Et je t'offre toute m'aïe,
Com ta bonne et parfaite amie.
2091 ... Mais je vueil bien que certeins soies
Que tes besongnes seront moies,
Car je t'aim et faire le doi.

The coolness of the metal shakes the Narrator out of his somnolence
and makes him listen more carefully to Hope's speech. Later, when
the Lady perceives the ring on her lover's finger, half-jealously she
demands to know whence it comes. He tells of his encounter with
Esperence, the Lady believes him, and they exchange rings. The
Lady places Hope's band on her own finger, taking back her surrogate's token, now that an understanding has been reached. The
Narrator recalled to *Esperence* that she had "married" him by giving
him her ring (2364-65); now Lady Hope suddenly appears to sanctify
his love for the Lady, also by an exchange of rings, a symbolic
marriage. In *Le Roman de la Rose* the lover spurns *Raison,* rival to
Amour and the Rose. In *RF* he accepts the love of *Esperence*
(*Amour's* friend), since their "marriage" anticipates success with the
Lady. The ring symbolizes both moments of joy or, rather, one joy
envisaged from two perspectives and twice given literary form.

Hope's placing her ring on the Narrator's finger marks his initiation into the mysteries of Love and Fortune. The initiation takes
place away from courtly society in a *locus amoenus,* which, as in
courtly romances, partakes of the Other World motif, a foreign,
perhaps supernatural realm into which the hero penetrates to commit
deeds reserved to him alone. The Narrator's passage into the *Parc
de Hesdin* through a narrow wicket between high walls (as in *Le
Roman de la Rose*) bears obvious Freudian overtones of sexual
initiation. Inside he falls into a trance, then awakens, i.e., is reborn,
full of hope. We are told that he wanted to die, his trance was that of
a man who thinks death is upon him, and he would have died but
for *Esperence,* who resuscitated him. Just as the sun rekindles nature
after winter's death, so too a sacred teacher brings the young man
to life after the symbolic death of despair. In an example of pathetic
fallacy, the birds, flowers, green grass, and fountain symbolize
Nature's renewal in spring, an external phenomenon which corresponds to the Narrator's inner state. Within the garden he finds
happiness, his ills are cured his sight restored, he undergoes initiation, and is rewarded by a sacred marriage.

The Narrator tells the Lady of his adventure in the garden as if it actually took place. *Esperence* promised that the Lady would reward him, the Narrator says; it is not right for her to deny Hope's wishes (3748-60). In fact, he courts her only because *Esperence* made him; she alone is responsible! The Lady replies that she gladly will love the young man in Hope's name. To what extent either the lover or his beloved takes the vision seriously is open to question. The Narrator speaks with tongue in cheek, using his story as a gambit in Love's wars, a witty sophisticated way of asking for his Lady's favors while remaining her devoted servant. She then claims to believe the story also with tongue in cheek. The vision provided an excuse for the Narrator to present his suit; it provides an equally valid excuse for the Lady to grant it. Both times an allegorical vision-experience serves as artifice, half reality-half illusion, permitting courtiers to love gracefully.

Just as we cannot help pitying the poor, humiliated suitor forced to read his *lay* in public, so too we cannot help smiling at his discomfiture, for running away serves only to increase his anguish and the impression of immaturity he makes on others. We may even question the validity of his dread in the first place, since he admits having written all his poems in the hope that the Lady will discover them and his love for her at the same time (413-18). Although the youth has learned some of love's theory and expressed his passion eloquently enough in the *lay,* he fails miserably when forced to act in the real world, indeed makes a total fool of himself. Machaut underscores the point by having courtiers play the game of *Le Roy qui ne ment* (justly celebrated in Adam de la Halle's *Jeu de Robin et Marion*) while the Narrator reads his poem. Since the Narrator dares not speak the truth, an ironic parallel is established between the truth of the game and falsehood in his life, between reality in fiction and the fiction of everyday existence.

He manifests similar humorous traits in the garden. The hyperbolic style of the *complainte* is indeed excessive, when we realize that the Narrator has no one to blame but himself. Machaut lightens the tone when, recovering slowly from his trance, the lover looks at *Esperence* with but one eye open, and during the first half of their colloquy manages only to sigh and groan. She berates him for his dullness, comparing him to a dog who barks at the man who made him learn to swim (1727-32). Furthermore, the Narrator's dozing off comments favorably on neither master nor disciple.

After *Esperence* has left him, our protagonist still dreads an immediate confrontation with his Lady. Upon catching sight of her residence, he falls into despair. Like the heroes of *JRB,* he will have his own way and neither listen to reason nor obey authority. *Esperence* returns to cheer him up but also to berate him, declaring he is afraid of his shadow and as stupid as a bird in a cage. She also points out that she cannot devote all her time to him alone. In this passage *Esperence* appears less the Mother Goddess than another figure, the old scolding crone, helpful friend and guide. The youth then proceeds on his way but not before having knelt in the middle of the road to deliver a prayer to *Amour.*

Significantly, when he does speak to the Lady, the Narrator discovers he has nothing to dread at all. His exacerbated fears rest on no serious foundation. The Lady knew all along that the Narrator loved her and why he ran away. We may assume that his ineptness, a manifestation of sincerity, helped rather than hindered his suit. Nevertheless, in spite of her avowal, the youth once again despairs. Believing that the Lady casts amorous glances on her other suitors, he suffers from jealousy until she explains herself, even though he suspected that she may have so acted as a ruse or to test him. The Narrator admits that she still causes him anguish, although he believes that, being perfect, she cannot lie, and prays to God that he do nothing to lose her good graces. "Non sans une pointe de malice" (Hoepffner, 2: xvi), he swears blind obedience no matter what she does.

A warm, gracious, compassionate human being, at all times Machaut's Lady acts benevolently to the Narrator. But he sees her in a different light: as the *domna,* an archetypal *belle dame sans merci* who destroys men who fall under her sway. He confuses convention with reality. In addition, the Narrator despairs at least four times: upon reading the *lay;* when in the garden; after *Esperence* has left him; and on his second return to the castle (after the feast). He is obsessed with the Lady's supposed pride and his own inadequacy. Repeated outbursts demonstrate that his concern has become, in Bergsonian terms, a mechanical fixation, at odds with the smooth functioning of a well-rounded, adaptable person in society. He reacts in identical fashion to different events occurring under different circumstances. These events, of no great importance in themselves, snowball in his mind, building up to a terrible crisis. Furthermore, the strict alternance of joy and depression in his psyche may be compared to the ups and downs of Fortune's wheel, for which he has sought a remedy all along. As the traditional hero of a *dit amoreus,* the Narrator cuts a sorry figure. His opposition, his "Shadow," are to be found neither in a father-husband surrogate nor in the Lady's pride. He is impeded only by himself, his own cowardice, indecision, and immaturity.

This singularly inept protagonist recalls, of course, the artificial fumbling narrators of *DV* and *JRB.* It is possible that for the fourteenth-century public part of the humor in *RF* came from identifying the Narrator as Guillaume de Machaut himself. Unfortunately, since we know practically nothing of the poet's personal life in the late 1330s, we can make only the most vague suppositions on this point. The Narrator is portrayed as a man in love, which Guillaume de Machaut may or may not have been; he is also shown to be a poet, which Machaut certainly was. Historically, all seven lyrics inserted in *RF* (eight, counting the prayer) were composed by Guillaume himself, as was the frame text. Following the story line, however, five poems are attributed to the Narrator and two to *Esperence.* On two occasions the Narrator deprecates his own talent (3444-45, 4290); and the Lady, who claims the *lay* to be a great work of art, expresses amazement that the Narrator could have written it all by himself. But then Lady Hope praises her own *chanson roial* in a humorous little speech:

> 2039 Comment t'est? Que me diras tu [?]
> Ay je ton chief bien debatu?
> Que te samble de ma chanson?
> Y a il noise ne tenson
> Qui te plaise ou qui te desplaise
> Ou dont tu soies plus äaise?
> Que c'est? Ne me diras tu rien,
> Se je say chanter mal ou bien?
> Se ce n'estoit pour moy vanter,
> Je diroie de mon chanter
> Que c'est bien dit...

Although the Narrator declines to answer, he praises her *baladelle* in the warmest possible terms and takes the trouble to learn it by heart. By having the Narrator pretend to modesty while the other characters laud his or their poems, Machaut praises himself obliquely, without appearing arrogant or vulgar. Yet such plaudits call attention to the fact that these are poems within a poem, thus literary artifacts. To the extent that the reader identifies the Narrator with Guillaume de Machaut, he will recognize that Machaut does praise his own work. A delightful tension between author and character, modesty and vanity, then results.

Jean Renart was the first French poet we know to insert songs in a long romance. A partial list of Old French narratives prior to *RF* containing lyrics would include, in addition to Jean Renart's *Guillaume de Dole* (1227-30), *Le Roman de la Violette, La Châtelaine de Vergi, Le Châtelain de Couci, Le Lai d'Aristote, Cléomadès,* the *Prose Tristan, Perceforest, Le Roman de la Poire, Le Dit de la Panthère d'Amours, La Prise amoureuse, La Dame à la licorne, Meliacin, Renart le Nouvel,* and *Fauvel.* Boethius too included lyric passages in the *De Consolatione Philosophiae.* Unlike his predecessors, Guillaume de Machaut took upon himself the role of legislator of the arts. Each of the seven *RF* songs belongs to a different literary kind, and each kind is represented by only one poem. Machaut presents a more or less complete tableau of the most important lyric genres in his day. The author's didactic purpose is underscored by the fact that the seven poems are arranged in a pattern, in order of decreasing difficulty and complexity: *lay, complainte, chanson roial, baladelle, balade, chanson baladée* or *virelay,* and *rondelet.* Machabey has suggested that these lyrics form the nucleus of an *Ars poetica* Machaut elaborated for the use of his students, including perhaps Eustache Deschamps. [7]

---

[7] Machabey, *Guillaume de Machault: La Vie et l'Œuvre musical* 1: 50-51. In a very perceptive passage, Poirion has compared Machaut to Malherbe: *Le Poète et le Prince,* pp. 203-4: "Le travail de mise en ordre et de classement répond d'abord à ce souci didactique qui caractérise la création littéraire de Machaut dans presque toutes ses manifestations: s'il est devenu comme l'initiateur d'un mouvement poétique, le chef d'une 'école', il faut bien dire qu'il a tout fait pour mériter ce titre .... Machaut fut-il donc, pour la littérature poétique, le Malherbe du XIVe siècle? Comme celui-ci, il liquide le passé, fixe les formes et la doctrine littéraire, forme des disciples." From a historical perspective, Poirion is perfectly correct. I suggest only that, in strictly aesthetic terms, Machaut is by far the greater poet. He speaks to the modern reader in a way Malherbe never can. And he towers over his contemporaries, whereas Malherbe's achievement pales before those of his

Certainly one goal of *RF* was to classify the genres of contemporary lyric poetry. We must never forget, however, that these poems, by providing relief from the more technically philosophic passages, vary the texture of *RF*. Each one echoes the author's doctrine and reveals in vivid, emotional tones the exact psychological state of the character supposed to have composed it. Thus, rather than say that the story of *RF* was written for the sake of the lyrics, I suggest the opposite: although these poems can exist as independent literary entities and perhaps were composed independently of *RF,* they form part of a larger narrative pattern, in which they are completely integrated. In this respect Machaut's *RF* emerges as a structure, not just a poetic anthology held together by pseudoautobiographical commentary.

The *lay* (431-680) is a crucial increment in the plot. Once it has fallen into the Lady's hands, she makes the Narrator read it and asks him who wrote it. Because he dares not answer her questions, he runs away to the garden, rails against Fortune, falls into a trance, and is consoled by Hope. But for having composed the *lay,* the youth would never have matured as an individual nor won the Lady's favor. This long poem launches the action; without it the narrative could not exist in its present form.

In the garden the Narrator delivers a *complainte* against Fortune (905-1480). Its very length and repetitiveness express perfectly his distraught state of mind, and its delivery, which no doubt also tired him, may be considered an immediate cause for his trance, but only after he has been prepared to meet *Esperence*. The *complainte* is central to the "complaint and comfort" pattern of *RF*. Without it, the Narrator would hardly have needed consolation at all.

Hope cheers up the Narrator with a *chanson roial* (1985-2032), which contains instruction he must learn before winning his Lady. A lovely piece of work on purely aesthetic grounds, it also contributes to the youth's intellectual development and prepares him psychologically for further progress in his amours.

Esperence sings to her disciple a second time: a *baladelle* (2857-92) delivered just before she leaves him. Again the song is in a happy mood, meant to cheer up the forlorn youth. Again it discusses traits

rivals, Théophile and Saint-Amant, not to speak of his immediate predecessors, D'Aubigné, Sponde, La Ceppède, and Chassignet.

of love which will help him in his quest. Hope succeeds so well that the Narrator memorizes her song for future recitation; he struggles so hard that her departure passes unnoticed, The *baladelle* thus marks the successful conclusion of Hope's teaching and provides a structural transition from the world of allegory to everyday reality.

The Narrator's conversion from despair to joy is commemorated by the *balade* (3013-36) he sings upon leaving the garden. This is a poem of hope. He has assimilated *Esperence*'s lessons. By contrasting this *balade* with his earlier *complainte* against *Amour,* Machaut shows us how the youth's psychological state has changed during his stay in the park.

At court the Narrator sings a *chanson baladée* or *virelay* (3451-97) in praise of the Lady. For the first time we find him singing of love in public. While he sings, the courtiers dance; his poem contributes to the diversions of a social group. Without fear he praises his Lady in her presence, thus performing *servitium amoris.* In fact, the Narrator later refers to this poem as evidence of the purity of his love:

> 3705 Et s'il vous plaist, ma dame chiere,
>   A resgarder la darreniere
>   Chansonnette que je chantay,
>   Que fait en dit et en chant ay,
>   Vous porrez de legier savoir
>   Se je mens ou se je di voir.

Finally, as the *balade* consecrated his joy with *Esperence,* the Narrator sings a *rondelet* (4107-14)—a song of triumph—to consecrate his joy with the Lady. More than the other lyric forms Machaut included in *RF,* the *rondeau* is constructed in a concentrated, circular, repetitive pattern, dependent on music for its full aesthetic effect. [8] At his moment of ecstasy, the Narrator expresses himself appropriately in the shortest, most purely lyrical of poems. The *rondelet* provides a flourish at this crucial point, the climax of the *dit.*

The Narrator, depicted as the traditional allegorical lover, is also an artist. His proclivity to write poems brings about a temporary setback in his love life, but later contributes to its successful outcome.

---

[8] For the aesthetic of the *rondeau,* with special attention to Machaut, see Poirion, *Le Poète et le Prince,* pp. 318-26, 333-43, 348-60.

The Lady appreciates his *lay* and *chanson baladée;* they are tangible proof of love-service. Perhaps the Lady returns her suitor's love in part because he is a poet and a good one. In the Middle Ages music contributed to social pastimes and was also believed to possess therapeutic value, hence *Esperence's* willingness to cheer up the Narrator by singing to him. The ability to compose love poetry was a standard accomplishment of the courtier; in romances music often is included in the young knight's education. And finally, the mathematical order which forms the basis of the musician's art also determines the structure of the universe as a whole. The poet sings of nature and reflects its majesty in his own work.

A didactic poem, *RF* instructs us in love, Fortune, ethics, and the art of poetry. It is also a fictional narrative of some complexity, treating a young man's development from childhood to maturity. And *RF* contains lyrical passages of great beauty that also tell much about the character who recites them. These didactic, narrative, and lyrical elements are carefully united to form a total work of art. The major theme is education: Machaut begins with general statements concerning the learning process and its relation to the human situation. Then the protagonist receives lessons in how to love; both he and the public learn to integrate erotic love into a Boethian *Weltanschauung*. We see the hero grow. He hesitates, argues, sways back and forth, and finally puts his new-found learning to good purpose: by progressing from precept to example, from theory to practice. The plot of *RF* is based upon the archetypal structure of romance: withdrawal and return. The Narrator leaves society, experiences a first triumph after having encountered *Esperence* (the potentiality of learning), then a second, greater one upon being readmitted to the community (the actuality of living). At the beginning and end the court provides a frame for the hero's adventures; Machaut's tale follows a circular pattern even though it tells a story of linear becoming. In the course of the narrative an opposition is set up between opposing forces: complaint and comfort, sickness and health, storm and calm, cold and heat, winter and spring, blindness and sight, darkness and light, death and life. In each case the second term of the antithesis wins out. An element of joy pervades much of *RF,* evoked by imagery of the garden (fountain, grass, birds, sweet odors), animals (lamb, dove, pigeon), treasure (gold, silver, the ring), light (the sun, stars), archetypal Woman (*Esperence,* the Lady), and the court (singing, dancing, the feast, the heraldry of love). The Narrator's capacity to adapt to light contributes to his successful initiation.

The *RF* is more complex than Machaut's first two *dits.* Our protagonist is a conventional figure in medieval allegory, whom we admire, pity, perhaps even identify with. He also partakes of the inept, obtuse I-narrator whom we laugh at from a distance. Machaut writes a light, playful satire on the overemotional, inexperienced young lover. The youth triumphs in his quest but cannot escape his failings as a man, for since he persists in suspecting the Lady, he is not capable of enjoying stable happiness at court. In the end we, Machaut's public, know more than his character, the Narrator, does. We are made aware of the ambiguous relationship between illusion and reality, between dreams and the world of men. Courtly society itself proves to be of a different essence, more concrete and down-to-earth, than books would make us believe. Joy is possible, but only in isolated moments of ecstasy, not as a permanent state. A man and a woman fall in love, but their love must evolve in the world, at court, among *losengiers,* in the presence of others. A shadow will inevitably fall because lovers are flesh-and-blood human beings, who struggle to maintain a relationship ever in a state of flux. However, although the court, the Lady, and love itself contain the possibility of flaw, for all their precariousness they enrich our lives. The hero who embodies the values of his culture is undermined, but Machaut's distortion does not destroy the courtly vision. A poet is admitted to revelry and is accepted into the courtly world, even though his "reformation" is perhaps never made complete.

4. LE DIT DOU LYON

> Awakened one morning by the chirping of birds,
> the Narrator takes a walk. He crosses to an island
> where he is assaulted by a Lion. The Lion turns out
> to be friendly, however, and leads the Narrator
> through a wasteland (where they must endure the
> snarling of wild beasts) to a *locus amoenus*. There
> they are received by a beautiful Lady and her re-
> tainers. The Lady and one of her knights explain
> the secrets of the island. The Narrator intercedes
> on the Lion's behalf: the poor animal adores the
> Lady but is rendered despondent by the envious wild
> beasts who torment him. The Narrator then returns
> to his own side of the river.

MACHAUT'S FOURTH POEM, *Le Dit dou Lyon*,[1] concentrates on an
aspect of *fin' amor* touched upon briefly toward the end of *RF*:
the lover's relationship to *losengiers*, talebearers who expose the
lover to public shame and sully him in his lady's or her husband's
eyes. The *losengier* motif is one of the most venerable in courtly
tradition; it appears in troubadour and trouvère lyrics, the Tristan
romances, *Guillaume de Dole*, and *La Mort Artu*. Machaut conceives this classic lover-*losengier* conflict in allegorical terms. Of
course, one danger inherent in allegory is that the bond between
tenor and vehicle may appear tenuous or artificial and that, as a
result, the reader will refuse either to accept the allegory's con-
ceptual relationship or to follow the story. However, I am convinced that he who comes to *DL* with an open mind will discover

---

[1] 2,204 lines; ed. Hoepffner, 2: 159-237 (cited hereafter as *DL*).

that its imagery is no more artificial than in Guillaume de Lorris or Dante, and that actions of Machaut's characters which appear bizarre when interpreted as "slice of life" can be justified in allegorical terms. In the reader's shock at these characters' strange antics and his thrill upon discovering their interpretation lie two of the many aesthetic pleasures which are to be found in literature of this mode.

Machaut's Lion, the protagonist and title figure, represents both a particular human courtly lover and, in more general terms, Every Lover or Any Lover, the ideal or typically good courtly lover as a universal. The Lady whom the Narrator meets on the island stands for the Lion's counterpart: a particular courtly lady, object of the lover's affections, or the ideal courtly lady in the abstract. That she is older than the Lion and has cared for him from his earliest days evokes the courtly lady's role in educating her suitors (as in *RF*). The Lady's ability to render the Lion happy merely by gazing upon him indicates that her slightest display of interest should suffice to dispel a lover's unhappiness; it also refers to the physiological role of eyes in the genesis of *fin' amor*. The Lion is persecuted by wild beasts, including dragons, snakes, scorpions, buffalo, camels, tigers, panthers, elephants, leopards, bears, lynxes, foxes, hunting dogs, German mastiffs, beavers, asps, unicorns, and "une autre beste a deus cornes" (390). They mock him, scratch him, and disturb him with their howling, which, worst of all, also distracts the Lady. Machaut thus depicts the *losengiers* of courtly convention. The Lady explains to the Narrator that they torment the Lion out of envy. It is this envy which renders *losengiers* the vile, bestial creatures they are (1955-66).

When, due to *losengiers,* the Lady ceases to gaze upon the Lion, he goes mad with despair, leaps about in rage, and at one point tries to commit suicide. He is about to die nine or ten times. Yet by merely looking at the animal or calling him to order, she subdues him at once. Love-madness and love-suicide (threatened or actual) are old courtly themes, commonplace in the early romances. As in his first three *dits,* Machaut assumes the lover to be in a state of *mutation* (706): that is, oscillating between extremes of joy and misery. By manifesting such violent contrasts in behavior, the Lion proves his sincerity. Machaut agrees with those lyric poets for whom the true lover is an innocent, natural man who cannot help revealing his inner feelings no matter how hard he tries to hide them. [2]

To alleviate his friend's suffering, the Narrator suggests building a fence which will isolate him from the other beasts. However, the Lady objects that no barriers are permitted on her island. Humility alone will succor the Lion: if he feigns indifference to the *losengiers'* taunts they will die of rage. Machaut tells us that his lonely desert island stands for the real world of men. The court is an open place, where both true lovers and *losengiers* congregate on a footing of equality. There an individual's reward depends upon his behavior under stress. Since neither narcissism nor flight from reality can save the lover, he must make his way in the company of others.

By depicting his ideal courtly lover as a lion, Machaut perhaps meant to surprise his public; nonetheless, the relationship between tenor and vehicle can be justified in a number of ways. In medieval bestiaries and in works of imaginative literature, such as Chrétien's *Yvain*, the lion was considered the King of Beasts, noblest of all animals, an ideal monarch, and symbol of trust. In *DL* the Lady herself praises his cleanness (1942-43), in implicit contrast to the *losengiers*. The best of animals is chosen to represent the best of lovers. Nonetheless, just like his enemies, the Lion is an animal, and the Knight points out that he knows of no infallible way to distinguish good lovers from bad. A lady can tell them apart only after long experience, by testing suitors empirically. She can readily distinguish a lion (or the protagonists of *JRB* and *RF*) from loud, self-assured boasters, but not from a wily hypocrite who apes the true lover's anguish. Even the most prudent ladies may be deceived, he says.

The Lion, who resembles the *losengiers,* is separated from his Lady by an unbridgeable chasm: they belong to totally different species. She maintains a natural sovereignty: that of a human over a beast, of reason over the flesh. Furthermore, since an animal cannot speak, verbal communication between the two is impossible. Although he would like to tell her of his love and the torments he

---

[2] See Roger Dragonetti, "Trois motifs de la lyrique courtoise confrontés avec les *Arts d'aimer* (Contribution à l'étude de la thématologie courtoise)," *Romanica Gandensia* 7 (1959): 5-48.

endures, he can only lie at her feet, nod his head, and weep. Machaut depicts in a very charming way two principles of *fin' amor* he had emphasized in *DV,* discretion and timidity. The Lover must not voice amorous sentiments, lest others discover his secret and lest the lady herself take umbrage at his audacity. In fact, the Lion's isolation points up the fundamental alienation of the courtly lover, thrust into an inferno of desire, with no resolution to his problem in sight.

Machaut's Lion is capable of ripping apart and devouring his enemies, the Lady tells us. However, out of regard for her he eats only from her own hands (1879-1916). She has tamed the King of Beasts; love and a mere woman have turned the fiercest of animals into a household puppy-dog. Not only is the courtly lover totally dependent upon his lady, he also regains the innocence of the animal world. The lover is his lady's lapdog, her pet. They are not joined as equals, nor in a legitimate feudal bond, lady to lover as lord to vassal, but in a cruel parody of vasselage: the master-slave relationship. The lover-lion is a slave to his mistress, but content with his state, and asks only to maintain it forever, without having to share her with others.

This master-slave relationship evolves in a magic grove on an island from which most people are excluded. Having crossed to the island on a magic bark, the Narrator must traverse a plain covered with briars and thorns. The Lion then guides him to a beautiful fountain and to a pavilion belonging to the Lady, seated nearby. It would indeed be imprudent for us to suggest hidden meanings for each part of the décor. Machaut's allegory is by no means as systematic as in *Le Roman de la Rose.* Although we can identify the various characters, the setting, typical of romance, quite possibly was never meant to be interpreted allegorically. Nonetheless, a medieval audience would assimilate this sacred island to the world of the court, reserved to a social, spiritual elite, expressly forbidden to *vilains, marits,* bad lovers, and other undesirables. The Narrator's bark is covered with green silk cloth and impervious to age. It will transport only true lovers to the island. Perhaps it represents the ever-renewed joy of young love, the birth of new love, or the virtue Hope (as in *RF*), without which no lover can hope to succeed. The thorns, of course, evoke the suffering which all suitors undergo before attaining their heart's desire. In *Le Dit de la Panthère d'Amours,* nettles, thorns, and brambles are allegories respectively for amorous thoughts, desire, and *losengiers'* malicious tattle. Like the narrator of *La Panthère d'Amours,* after undergoing the adventure of the thorns, Machaut's heroes arrive at the Lady's abode, a *locus amoenus,* the perfect setting for love. There they drink of a stream flowing from the fountain of love, sweet water which will neutralize the bitter water of their tears. The Lady herself is referred to as a fountain of joy (570-71). Machaut also tells us that all beasts and birds partake of love in springtime. And the song of birds lures the Narrator to the island. Love is universal: these animal characters —lark and nightingale, lion and panther, serpent and unicorn—serve as a bridge between man and nature. Love is part of nature, absolute, irresistible, at the center of the universe.

The main plot of *DL* must be interpreted in allegorical terms. The Lion's relationship to the Lady and to the other beasts reflects the dicta of *fin' amor.* However, *DL* also contains symbolism of a more general kind. Machaut's poem differs from *Le Roman de la Rose* in that this central, mainly allegorical element is inserted into a frame-story, whose protagonist is the Narrator. Although Machaut has integrated the two narrative lines with skill, it is apparent that the Narrator's portion of the story is much less allegorical and didactic than the Lion's. In fact, we cannot reduce it to allegory at all.

In my opinion, the Narrator's experiences recall the traditional plot of romance. Machaut quite probably patterned this section of *DL* on the twelfth- and thirteenth-century fiction available to him. These poems, and Machaut's as well, are made up of elements found throughout world literature, the archetypes of romance. Maud Bodkin defined archetypes as "themes having a particular form or pattern which persists amid variation from age to age, and which corresponds to a pattern or configuration of emotional tendencies in the minds of those who are stirred by the theme." [3] The archetypal structure of romance often resembles that of the folktale, fairy story, or popular ballad. This is to be expected, given the role of persistence or resemblance inherent in the notion of archetype. Above all, the general outline of the protagonist's life will adhere to a pattern

---

[3] *Archetypal Patterns in Poetry,* 2d ed. (London, 1948), p. 4; also Northrop Frye, *Anatomy of Criticism: Four Essays* (Princeton, N. J., 1957), pp. 95-115.

outlined by Lord Raglan, Joseph Campbell, and Jan de Vries, traditional to heroic-romantic literature everywhere.[4] True, Machaut's Narrator does not partake of all characteristics of the popular hero. He is not endowed with supernatural parents; he is not born in striking fashion; he is not separated from family during infancy or given an unusual upbringing. Machaut has disregarded his earliest deeds as well as his final apotheosis and/or death. But the events which befall the *DL* Narrator do correspond to the central element in the romance hero's career, a trip to the Other World. Campbell has summarized the Adventure or Quest in the following terms: "A hero ventures forth from the world of common day into a region of supernatural wonder: fabulous forces are there encountered and a decisive victory is won; the hero comes back from this mysterious adventure with the power to bestow boons on his fellow man" (p. 30).

Campbell's first increment is a Call to Adventure. The hero must be separated from his everyday environment. Only a tiny elite receive the call. Machaut's Narrator, who had heard of a marvelous garden, distant from his home, has come specifically to discover its mysteries. On an April morning in the year 1342 he is awakened by the song of birds, a traditional harbinger of adventure in folktales; these birds represent a benevolent force in nature sympathetic to the hero, eager to launch him on his quest. Alone, apart from the society of others, he sets out: "Mais je n'i trouvay creature / Fors moy seul; si pris l'aventure" (157-58).

In traditional literature the Other World is depicted as a lovely garden, a subterranean realm, or a kingdom beneath the sea.[5] A hero wishing to enter the forbidden area must first cross the threshold of the Other World, a dangerous enterprise reserved to a chosen few. Machaut evokes a marvelous grove on an island in the middle of a river, which separates the Other World from our own. The Narrator would have been unable to cross it without supernatural aid, in the form of a magic bark which he finds waiting for him on the shore. Of its own accord it comes to the Narrator when he

---

[4] Lord Raglan, *The Hero: A Study in Tradition, Myth, and Drama* (New York, 1937); Joseph Campbell, *The Hero with a Thousand Faces* (New York, 1956 [1st ed., 1949]); Jan de Vries, *Heroic Song and Heroic Legend* (London, 1963); William Calin, *The Epic Quest* (Baltimore, Md., 1966), chapt. 4.

[5] Howard Rollin Patch, *The Other World* (Cambridge, Mass., 1950).

is ready to go home. Similar barks are to be found in Marie's *Guigemar,* the Tristan stories, *Partonopeus de Blois, La Queste del Saint-Graal, La Vengeance Raguidel, La Manekine,* and other romances. In archetypal terms, crossing a water barrier alone in a small boat symbolizes death and rebirth, and has been named the Charon Complex. [6] Water represents the feminine principle, in this case a beneficent manifestation of Nature; the boat itself is an image of the womb. The Narrator returns to the Mother, dies to humdrum, everyday reality, and is born anew in the Other World, itself often depicted as an Inferno or Paradise.

Having crossed the threshold, the hero undergoes a series of ordeals, the purpose of which is to test his manhood. This road of trials or inner barrier may be purely physical in nature. Moses, Theseus, Lancelot, and Huon de Bordeaux traverse a Waste Land or forest, climb a mountain, cross a river, or penetrate to the center of a labyrinth. Although Machaut's Narrator is faced by a wasteland, covered with thorns and briars, torn and bleeding, he arrives at the goal.

First, however, he must overcome a more immediate obstacle: the living guardian of the Other World. So often in the old epics and romances a monster or dragon blocks the hero's path; Yvain, Lancelot, and Huon are obliged to fight the monster before proceeding on their way. The *DL* Narrator faces a lion, whose task is to prevent evil people from entering the island. A sympathetic martyr to love, the Lion will become the hero of the poem's central section; but we only discover this later. Upon first meeting him, the Narrator is terrified. According to typological exegesis of scripture, the lion may represent Christ *in sensu bono,* or Satan *in sensu malo.* In *chansons de geste* a lion generally represents the enemy or personifies wrath, pride, and heresy. Two such felines guard the sword bridge in Chrétien's *Lancelot;* they symbolize unbridled passion in Béroul's version of Iseut's dream; [7] and hostile lions are slain by Gawain in several romances.

After the Lion reveals himself to be a friend not an enemy, he and the Narrator then must stand up to an army of wild beasts. In

---

[6] Gaston Bachelard, *L'Eau et les Rêves* (Paris, 1942), chapt. 3.

[7] See Pierre Jonin, "Le songe d'Iseut dans la forêt du Morois," *Moyen Age* 64 (1958): 103-13.

chanson de geste and courtly romance the snake, buffalo, camel, tiger, elephant, leopard, bear, lynx, fox, and mastiff are often associated with the Saracen enemy or otherwise manifest ferociousness or treason. Although the bestiaries interpret some of Machaut's beasts in a favorable light, others (dragon, snake, scorpion, tiger, fox, asp) are figures either of Satan or of mortal sinners. And in the *Bestiaires d'Amours* dragon, snake, scorpion, and fox appear as images of the *losengier*. Furthermore, the medievals thought each of the seven deadly sins to be characteristic of certain animals. *Superbia* was sometimes attributed to the dromedary, elephant, and unicorn; *Invidia* to the dragon, snake, and dog; *Ira* to the dragon, snake, camel, bear, dog, and unicorn; *Acedia* to the buffalo, leopard, bear, and dog; *Avaritia* to the snake, camel, elephant, fox, and unicorn; *Gula* to the dragon, snake, wildcat, bear, fox, and dog; *Luxuria* to the snake, scorpion, leopard, bear, and dog. [8] In any case, these exotic beasts represent the archetypal enemy, the monster who guards both maiden and treasure. In Jungian terms they are the Shadow, the negative element in the hero's personality threatening his identity. Gilgamesh, Perseus, Theseus, and Hercules, Christ, Michael, and George, Beowulf, Siegfried, Tristan, Lancelot, and Gawain, Orlando, Ruggiero, Rinaldo, and Astolfo struggle against such monsters and defeat them. So too, in his own way, must the *DL* Narrator.

Like the traditional protagonist of romance, Machaut's Narrator could not have withstood his enemies but for supernatural aid more efficacious than the bark which conveyed him to the island in the

---

[8] I have consulted Friedrich Bangert, "Die Tiere im altfranzösischen Epos," in *Ausgaben und Abhandlungen aus dem Gebiete der romanischen Philologie* 34 (Marburg, 1885); Gustaf Wüster, *Die Tiere in der altfranzösischen Literatur* (Göttingen, 1916); Morton W. Bloomfield, *The Seven Deadly Sins* ([East Lansing, Mich.] 1952); Florence McCulloch, *Mediaeval Latin and French Bestiaries* (Chapel Hill, N. C., 1960); Emmanuel Walberg, ed., *Le Bestiaire de Philippe de Thaün* (Lund-Paris, 1900); P. Meyer, ed., "Le Bestiaire de Gervaise," *Romania* 1 (1872); 420-43; Robert Reinsch, ed., *Le Bestiaire: Das Thierbuch des normannischen Dichters Guillaume le Clerc* Leipzig, 1892); Charles Cahier, ed., "Le *Physiologus* ou *Bestiaire*" [Pierre de Beauvais], *Mélanges d'Archéologie, d'Histoire et de Littérature* 2 (1851): 85-100, 106-232; 3 (1853): 203-88; 4 (1856): 55-87; Cesare Segre, ed., *Li Bestiaires d'Amours di Maistre Richart de Fornival e li Response du Bestiaire* (Milan-Naples, 1957); Arvid Thordstein, ed., *Le Bestiaire d'amour rimé* (Lund-Copenhagen, 1941).

first place. Just as other fictional heroes are assisted in the nether regions by a sympathetic guide, a Hermes figure who at first may appear to be hostile (Gériaume or Auberon in *Huon de Bordeaux,* Morgain la Fée or Merlin in the *Lancelot-Grail Cycle*), in *DL* the hero is protected by a lion, who guides him through the road of thorns to the Lady's pavilion and, even though he cannot speak, serves as the Narrator's mentor. Machaut took the idea from *Yvain,* where the beast represents perhaps elemental prowess and forces of Nature intervening on the hero's behalf. In fact, at one point in both stories the feline tries to commit suicide. However, whereas Chrétien's lion adheres to the tradition of the grateful beast, who repays the hero for having saved his life, the *DL* animal's friendship is gratuitous. Other works of literature also may have contributed to the lion-friend archetype: the Bible, versions of the Androcles and Saint Jerome legends, a lion symbolizing the world tamed by Christ in *Perlesvaus,* and good lions in *Octavien, Gilles de Chin,* and *La Dame à la licorne.* By 1342 the struggle between a lion and a panther was allegorized to depict the Hundred Years War with, of course, the House of Valois represented by the king of beasts. And in the bestiaries he generally appears friendly to man and, for a variety of reasons, symbolizes Christ.

The Lion embodies a masculine element of the cosmos intervening on the hero's behalf. Feminine manifestations of the supernatural are not absent from *DL,* although Machaut does not exploit them to the same degree. On two occasions when the Narrator fears for his life—confronted by the Lion, and by the loathly beasts—his only defense is to invoke the lady he loves ("Chiere dame, a vous me commant!" 313, 376), a formula which works like magic; the Lion becomes his friend, and the beasts dare not attack. The Lion too is preserved from harm by his Lady, who, even though she refuses to build a fence isolating him from the others, will gaze upon him lovingly whenever they do insult him. Both ladies are to some extent patterned after the Fairy Queen of romance, who befriends the hero and delivers him from enchantment.

Having traversed a Waste Land, the Narrator and Lion arrive at a *locus amoenus,* which contains a fountain, image of Nature's renewal through water, the feminine element (cold and moist), and of nourishment from the Mother. Cushions and a pavilion, also feminine images, exude luxury, bounty, rest, and the formalism of the court. This scene recalls episodes in *Lanval, Jaufré,* and the *Lancelot Cycle,* where the hero meets a great lady for the first time in comparably idyllic surroundings. Machaut's décor is not realistic but decorative, not empirical but hieratic and symbolic. It has archetypal significance: the Narrator has penetrated to the center of the labyrinth, the goal of his quest.

Within the Other World the hero submits to various ordeals designed to test his manhood. And once he has penetrated to the inner sanctum, a final obstacle, the most dangerous of all, must be overcome before he can seize the treasure or marry the princess. Having left the court to defy a wicked *costume* instituted by an enemy of society, he succeeds in replacing the innovation by a good *costume* and thus restores a balanced, properly functioning, feudal community.[9] Such is the Joy of the Court in *Erec et Enide* and the freeing of the prisoners in *Lancelot.* In *DL,* although neither the Narrator nor the Lion ever engages in combat nor does the Narrator seek to overthrow an evil *costume,* his very presence on the island implies triumph over obstacles (the river, the thorns, the Lion, and other beasts) due to his outstanding qualities as a lover. He has succeeded in *L'Esprueve de fines amours* (1778), a good *costume* instituted by the sage who originally planned the garden. Furthermore, the Narrator intercedes with the Lady on the Lion's behalf. He encourages her to reveal her sentiments toward him, thus breaking a conspiracy of silence which had brought his friend to the verge of despair. By establishing communication between the lovers, arranging some sort of accommodation between them, and putting the Lion on the right path to success in his amours, the Narrator improves the lives of others. At least symbolically, he undergoes an adventure and delivers a friend from his enemies.

Seated on a carpet next to the pavilion the Narrator finds a great lady, the mistress of the grove. She wears a crown of gold (489-98); her name is *Tout passe* (759); he kneels before her as to a queen. Mistress, feudal lady, temptress, and goddess all in one, she holds power of life and death over the Lion. Although she can-

---

[9] See Erich Köhler, *Ideal und Wirklichkeit in der höfischen Epik* (Tübingen, 1956), and "Le rôle de la 'coutume' dans les romans de Chrétien de Troyes," *Romania* 81 (1960): 386-97. Also Alfred Adler, *Rückzug in epischer Parade* (Frankfurt am Main, 1963), pp. 266-68.

not also enter into an erotic relationship with the Narrator, from his perspective she plays the role of teacher and fairy queen. For him, as for so many heroes of romance, she is a goddess or mother, a *puella senex* resembling *Esperence* in *RF*.

The Lady is not the only authority figure to aid or counsel the Narrator. Although she will answer some of his questions, on several points she defers to one of her vassals, an old Knight. This personage, who apparently has no other function in the story, proceeds to lecture for almost a thousand lines (853-1800). He is the Lady's vassal, and she benefits from his service; a very great tribute to her comes from being served by such a man. Furthermore, although young and beautiful, she is, *puella senex,* as wise as he.

We are also told of the Lady's ancestor, who founded the island, a creator of wonders patterned after Merlin or the Fisher King. The old Knight, who continues the tradition of wisdom exemplified in the old king, the Lady's ancestor, thus appears symbolically as a father figure in his own right. Machaut's protagonist is helped by both male and female; he is united with a symbolic fairy queen (mother) and with an elderly Knight (father). Reunion with both figures forms the climax of much folk literature; Machaut's desire to follow a conventional narrative pattern may well explain why the two greybeards appear in *DL*.

The romance hero has left home to undertake adventures; his victory is then consecrated by a triumphant return to the point of departure. Crossing the return threshold and readmission into one's own society may be as difficult as the quest itself. Machaut's Narrator leaves the wicked animals on his left as he descends to the island's shore 2099-2100). There the magic bark comes to him of its own accord and transports him back to the main. Although we are told nothing of nighttime or sleep, it appears that the Narrator has been away from his friends for one and one-half days (2143). Bark, grove, lion, beasts, and fairy queen—these are natural to romance but contrast vividly with the gracious, charming, but mundane world of the frame-story. The Narrator begins his adventure alone, on the far side of the river. With some difficulty he penetrates to a marvelous court on the island. Then he returns to his own world, where he partakes of a feast, celebrating his return to society and successful completion of the quest.

Normally a hero returns from the Other World with a token of victory—treasure or a bride. In *DL* the Narrator returns with nothing, except for the secret of *L'Esprueve de fines amours*. Symbolically, he drank water originating from the magic fountain; in the most practical terms he is given the boon of knowledge. In this regard *DL* is a poem of education no less than *DV* and *RF*. The Knight not only explains the ways of the island but, in a spirited monologue, classifies all the world's lovers: fancy talkers, hypocrites, timid suitors, cynical seducers, playboys, soft-spoken warriors, fickle skirt-chasers, boasters, and uncouth peasants. He then discourses on the various types of ladies that correspond to each category of men. The Knight's diatribe contributes to the poem's doctrinal line by describing bad love *(afferre contrarium),* in contrast to the positive Eros represented by the Lady and the Lion. Although his speech has not been especially well integrated into the plot, it provides comic relief and satirical high spirits justifiable in their own right. His portraits are more striking than those on the outer wall of the Garden of Mirth in *Le Roman de la Rose*. The *DL* has the makings of an erotic *Narrenschiff;* indeed Hoepffner considered this section the most original in the entire *dit* (2:lvii).

Adventures in the Other World initiate the Narrator and the Lion. Both learn the way to happiness. The Narrator, in particular, sets out on a quest into the unknown; he crosses a threshold, explores a strange realm, submits to ordeals, proves his qualities as a lover, and is informed of the mysteries of the place. The Lion too undergoes a series of ordeals, suffers pangs of love, but then is accepted by his Lady. Through a symbolic act of mediation by the Narrator, the Lion's sufferings are curtailed, and he is forgiven. Communication is established between lover and beloved; the Lion understands that the Lady cherishes him and that he will ultimately win her total, undivided love.

Machaut's imagery can be interpreted in more immediately erotic terms. Symbolically, the Narrator returns to the womb by crossing the river alone in a magic bark, where he experiences death and rebirth. The road of thorns through a wasteland threatens both him and the Lion in a very particular way (castration complex) as do the exotic wild animals, who represent the Shadow, the Terrible Father, libido anxiety, and, as ever, an unconscious fear of castration (the two-horned beast). Yet at the end of the labyrinth they discover a lush green prairie adorned by tent, carpet, cushions, and fountain, a feminine world where they are protected from the beasts by an *Anima* figure, a loving, kind, gentle Mother Goddess. And the Lion's relationship to the Lady is sanctioned by an equally kind, gentle, and harmless father-surrogate, the old Knight. As in *RF,* a latent Oedipal situation develops between the Lion and the Lady. She is an older woman, who has raised him since he was a cub; he desperately fears her rejection and is fanatically jealous when she manifests favor to others (sibling rivalry). He remains speechless in the Lady's presence, terrified of her abandoning him. Yet any overt sexual contact between them is impossible. Indeed, their only physical intimacy occurs when the Lion lies down at her feet and places his head in her lap.

Lion and Narrator are both deeply, hopelessly in love. Their ladies protect them from harm. When the Narrator kneels before the Lion's Lady, he is rendered speechless by the memory of his own beloved, as if she were standing before him. From a psychological perspective, the Narrator and the Lion are doubles (cf. *JRB*). The Narrator's libidinal anxiety is projected onto the Lion, who suffers persecution and misunderstanding far greater than his own, yet who in the end is assured of happiness. If even in such a case love be not hopeless, the Narrator will surely succeed in his own amours. The Lion is content because the *losengiers* prove to be harmless and because the Lady will reward her suitor in time. The Narrator is content because of the wish-fulfillment experience which he himself, acting as mediator between Lion and Lady, helps to bring about. As in *RF,* the lover's enemy is within him, his greatest fear, fear itself. Once he learns to vanquish weakness, to communicate with his lady and trust in her good nature, hope is restored. The lover's alienation proves temporary, a state which can be overcome.

In *DL* Guillaume de Machaut brings questing, adventure, and the Other World into an allegorical romance. A *roman d'aventures* is interpreted as an *Ars amandi.* Although the two strands, adventure and allegory, exist side by side, they are not fused as in Spenser or Bunyan, for example. Machaut creates an aura of romance but only the aura, only a façade of symbols. Whereas Chrétien de Troyes and his most gifted successors are concerned equally with love and adventure, the one played off against the other, each indispensable to the other's flowering and to the development of the knight as a total person, in Guillaume de Machaut adventure always takes second place to love. The Lion triumphs as a lover because he manifests humility and obedience. Although his capacity for deeds of prowess is taken for granted, the Lady has no opportunity to witness them. What counts is the Lion's attitude, not his accomplishments. Perhaps Machaut's doctrine undermines the heroism present in older literary modes. Or perhaps, like his contemporaries Boccaccio, Juan Ruiz, and Chaucer, Machaut's own temperament turns more to humor, the delicate play of ironies, a graciously sophisticated treatment of conventional romance themes. A genuine spirit of adventure would have appeared as incongruous in Machaut's century as in Voltaire's.

This element of humor underlies the entire plot. The Narrator is not a knight errant or quest hero at all. Unlike Yvain, he has done nothing to merit the Lion's service. His ordeals are relatively insignificant and his enemies easily cowed, or they are transformed into friends. Merely invoking his beloved's name gets him out of trouble. And his greatest triumph consists in clearing up a lover's misunderstanding. Ultimately the Narrator only participates in the action from a distance, as witness to the Lion's plight and as his mediator. He is reduced to being the Lion's go-between, the *internuntium* Andreas Capellanus permits to every lover.

Although the Narrator is admitted to the island and successfully undergoes *L'Esprueve de fines amours,* Machaut deprecates him throughout. He is shown to be inept as a knight-adventurer in that he is totally incompetent to steer the bark. Furthermore, lacking weapons, he dreads the hostile animals, especially the two-horned beast, and wishes him back overseas where he comes from. And when the Narrator manifests fear in the Lady's presence, smilingly she tells him to sit down, for these beasts are after the Lion, not him:

> 1818   "N'aiés doubte, biau sire,
> Eins vous seës; car cilz courrous
> N'est pas encommenciés pour vous."

He is also shown to be inept as a narrator in that he forgets certain facts in the story and cannot avoid wandering from his subject. He digresses with a comparison between his beloved and the calendar lark, apologizes for having digressed and promises not to do so again (67-70), but then prattles on anyway about his beloved *ad nauseam* (201-84), fully aware that he should condense his remarks. He also falls into a reverie at the fountain and is ashamed at not having had the presence of mind to address the Lady properly. A timid, helpless fellow who cannot concentrate, the Narrator resembles that other timid, self-conscious lover: the Lion. He is portrayed as coward and adventurer, observer and actor, objective historian and obtrusive singer of his beloved's praises, mediator and lover. By juxtaposing the various roles he plays and by debunking him in light-hearted fashion (as in the three previous *dits*), Machaut generates an element of humor, which contributes to the elaboration of a complex, charming literary character.

Equally charming, and no less complex, is his faithful alter ego, the Lion. On the one hand, the Lion partakes of various heroic traditions: the ferocious guardian of the Other World or the benevolent supernatural agent who aids the hero to fulfill his quest. But the central feature of his *persona* is something quite different: a caricature of the timid, foolish, inexperienced lover. His violent, brusque shifts in temper, from laughter to tears and from joy to near-suicide, prove a point of erotic doctrine and also can be justified by medieval psychological theory, which holds that internal states of mind will always be embodied in external physical acts, their most natural manifestation in a more violent, emotive, "primitive" society. [10] Nonetheless, Machaut's public must have considered such behavior incongruous, not to say ridiculous. How else could it appreciate a young lover who reacts to *losengiers* in rigid, mechanical fashion, overresponding to relatively insignificant stimuli, and, obsessed by his lady's eyes, falls into ecstasy or despair depending on whether or not she gazes at him. These fixations prevent him from coping with external forces in a supple, resilient, normally human way.

The comic element in *DL* is further increased by the fact that Machaut's protagonist is not a human being but an animal. We may or may not smile at the foolishness of an adolescent in love; the same behavior from an amorous lion cannot be taken seriously. A comic tension exists between the human and the animal, the fact

---

[10] On these matters see Paul Rousset, "Recherches sur l'émotivité à l'époque romane," *Cahiers de Civilisation Médiévale* 2 (1959): 53-67; Lionel J. Friedman, "Occulta Cordis," *Romance Philology* 11 (1957-1958): 103-19; J. Huizinga, *The Waning of the Middle Ages* (London, 1924), chapt. 1.

that human behavior is depicted in animal terms and a wild beast succeeds in acting like a human courtly lover. Whenever we think of the refined, civilized courtly lover, we are reminded also of his animal exterior. As Bergson says, "Est comique tout incident qui appelle notre attention sur le physique d'une personne alors que le moral est en cause" (*Le Rire,* 97th ed. [Paris, 1950], p. 39).

Yet the Lion is depicted not only as the fierce king of beasts but also as a little dog or cat. The Narrator pets him on the head, while the Lion scampers about his new friend and rubs against him (325-40). Then, upon catching sight of his Lady, the Lion runs and jumps, scratches the earth, pricks up his ears, and does "marvels with his tail" (504). Finally, he approaches the Lady humbly, kneels, his tail between his legs, and lies down at her feet with his head in her lap. The qualities of a lion and of a house-pet are juxtaposed, as are those of an animal and a human. As a lion or a pet, he is ridiculous to be in the throes of an engrossing love affair; as a human or a lion, he is ridiculous to scamper about and wag his tail, manifesting the physical and psychological characteristics of a *petit chiennet* (327, 1941), which impinge upon the more noble, spiritual *servitium amoris.* Narrator and Lion, each a comic character in his own right, each dependent on the other, interact to form a perfect comic team. It is fitting that the Narrator's sojourn on the island ends with a farewell: the two of them, human and animal, the Narrator in his bark and his guide on shore, bow and gaze at each other as long as the return voyage lasts (2128-35).

The *DL* is a subtle, complex poem. It contains elements of allegory, adventure, and humor, successfully integrated to form a total work of art. On the one hand, Machaut smiles at the traditional knight-errant metamorphosed into a prattling chronicler, and the passionate lover become a house-pet. That precarious synthesis of *chevalerie* and *clergie,* of *fortitudo* and *sapientia,* which had been sought after for so many generations, no longer commands the absolute faith of poets. On all fronts, heroism and adventure have given way to love, and love itself, become a tyrannical, jealous god, is subject to the barbs of a sometimes heretical priest. Yet the spirit of love and romance is manifest in *DL,* more perhaps than in any other of Machaut's tales. This story, which contains no dreams, trances, or visions, nonetheless generates a dream-aura unmatched in French poetry since Guillaume de Lorris. The secret grove, exotic beasts, and fairylike décor, the suspension of everyday problems, even to the suspension of time, create a sense of evanescent mystery unique in Machaut's century. The Narrator, the poet, and his public all participate in a world of displacement and wish-fulfillment. The *DL* radiates humor and a delicate melancholy, but even more the joy of children in a fairy world, a vision which recovers, if only for a short time, the innocence of childhood and purity of Eden.

5. LE DIT DE L'ALERION

> The Narrator is a devotee of falconry. He tells
> us how he acquires, enjoys, but loses four birds of
> prey: a sparrow hawk, an allerion, an eagle, and a
> gerfalcon. Then the allerion returns to him. Never
> again will they be parted. This falconry romance is
> to be interpreted as an allegory of love, and the
> various raptores stand for ladies the Narrator has
> known. The entire poem presents analogies between
> hawking and *fin' amor.*

Le Dit de l'Alerion[1] begins with a statement that four, and only
four, "poins" tell us how to lead the good life: "Bien penser, bien
dire, bien faire / Et eschuer tout le contraire" (13-14). Machaut then
investigates the implications of a second notion, that all actions occur
in three closely interrelated times: beginning, middle, and end. If
you wish to do something, he says, you should begin at once and
proceed through to completion. Furthermore, you can always tell a
man's character from the way he acted as a boy; the inclinations
a person manifests in childhood (the beginning) will continue
throughout his lifetime (middle and end). Only after this preamble
does the Narrator tell of his own childhood experiences, the starting
point for his tale. To begin a story with one or more *sententiae* is
a mode of composition authorized by the *Artes poeticae.* Equally
significant is the presence for the first time in Machaut's *dits* of
exempla, another element esteemed in medieval rhetoric. All this
points to the fact that in *DA* the formal and the didactic predominate.
Although the Narrator claims to recount his personal history, Ma-

---

[1] 4,814 lines; ed. Hoepffner, 2: 239-403 (cited hereafter as *DA*).

chaut in fact has written an *Ars amandi,* an unequivocally didactic treatise, which tells how love is born, matures, and declines, that is, an anatomy of the love affair. [2]

This anatomy of love is presented almost exclusively through the medium of allegory. In a sense, Machaut expands upon *DL,* but whereas in *DL* allegory coexisted with other elements (adventure, romance, comedy), in *DA* it is central to the plot, and the plot exists only to be interpreted allegorically. Unlike *DL, DA* is an Allegory in the generic sense (not just a poem containing allegorical elements), that is, a work of literature in which personified abstractions or allegorically interpreted beings and objects become the only participants in the action, and the only nonallegorical character is the author-narrator or his *persona.* [3]

The Narrator tells us that as a child he cherished little birds and, when he grew up, learned to enjoy bigger ones. Since throughout *DA* birds of prey represent women, we may assume that the Narrator always had an eye for the fair sex: that as a boy, even before puberty, he honored girls of his own age, and as he grew older, his affection for them developed accordingly. Machaut also reminds us of one of the central points elaborated in *DV*: that a man discovers *fin' amor* because the will to love is already present in his heart. Furthermore, it is appropriate that young boys should love, since, according to the troubadours, the qualities commonly associated with youth—generosity, enthusiasm, single-mindedness, a warm heart—are traits of the ideal lover and most likely to be found among the young. Not all young lads care for raptores, the Narrator tells us. The world contains men who do love hawking and men who do not, that is, categories of good and bad lovers, men who are faithful to the code of *fin' amor* and those who revile it (as we saw in *DL*).

On a literal level *DA* states that training in falconry, the noblest of sports, forms an essential part of a young man's education but, *allegorice,* that knowledge of love, the basis of life, is even more

---

[2] See Hoepffner, 2: lxvi-lxvii, and Gustav Gröber, *Geschichte der mittelfranzösischen Literatur,* 2d ed., revised by Stefan Hofer (Berlin-Leipzig, 1933), 1: 18.

[3] For this definition, see W. T. H. Jackson, "Allegory and Allegorization," *Research Studies* 32 (1964): 161-75.

important to his development. To find out about raptores the Narrator associates with other youths, specialists in hawking; he learns from observing them and from the answers they give to his questions. Four times he returns to these young falconers; the last time they show him courtesy because "Bien savoient que li mestiers / Des oiseaus moult m'abelissoit" (3836-37). Machaut tells us that a young man cannot discover *fin' amor* in isolation. He must frequent courtly society, for only by observing courtiers under "field conditions" can he learn the ways of love. Or, on another level, we may interpret the community of falconers and birds of prey as a representation of the psyche. As in *Le Roman de la Rose,* these young men symbolize traits *(Joinesce, Leësce, Cortoisie)* which contribute to the erotic experience. The Narrator then partakes of or acquires qualities without which he cannot fall in love.

Be that as it may, he wishes to own for himself consecutively a sparrow hawk, an allerion, an eagle, and a gerfalcon. Each represents a lady whom the Narrator has loved. Medieval man considered raptores to be the most noble of winged creatures; the Narrator's beloveds are presumed therefore to be the finest of all women. The allerion flies high in the air of good reputation ("bonne renommée," 2792). The eagle is praised for her beautiful tail-feathers, which represent Honor and Modesty. In addition, following an old tradition in the bestiaries, the Narrator informs us that the eagle can look directly at the sun. [4] He interprets this in the following way. The sun represents Good Love. Since only this one lady is sufficiently

---

[4] On points relating to falconry I have consulted, in addition to the items cited in chapter 4, note 8, the following: *The Art of Falconry, being the De Arte Venandi cum Avibus of Frederick II of Hohenstaufen,* tr. & ed. Casey A. Wood & F. Marjorie Fyfe (Stanford-London, 1943); Gustaf Holmér, ed., *Traduction en vieux français du De arte venandi cum avibus de l'empereur Frédéric II de Hohenstaufen* (Lund, 1960); Gunnar Tilander, ed., *Les Livres du roy Modus et de la royne Ratio,* 2 vols. (Paris, 1932), and *Dancus Rex. Guillelmus Falconarius. Gerardus Falconarius* (Lund, 1963); Håkan Tjerneld, ed., *Moamin et Ghatrif, Traités de fauconnerie et des chiens de chasse* (Lund, 1945); Alexander Herman Schutz, ed., *The Romance of Daude de Pradas called Dels Auzels Cassadors* (Columbus, Ohio, 1945); Gace de la Buigne, *Le roman des deduis,* ed. Åke Blomqvist (Karlshamn, 1951); Ernst Bormann, "Die Jagd in den altfranzösischen Artus- und Abenteuer-romanen," in *Ausgaben und Abhandlungen aus dem Gebiete der romanischen Philologie* 68 (Marburg, 1887); J. G. Mavrogordato, *A Hawk for the Bush* (Newton, Mass., 1961); Michael Woodford, *A Manual of Falconry* (Newton, Mass., 1960).

noble to perceive the nature of love directly, she is superior to other women.

We also discover how forbidding the lady appears to her suitors when the Narrator tells us that the sparrow hawk and allerion take great pleasure in the chase. The Narrator chooses a brancher hawk to be his first bird; we are told that these wild accipiters are the best. Here Machaut goes along with traditional falconry-lore but, on an allegorical level, indicates either that the Narrator's first love is a maiden, as new to Eros as himself, or a young woman who, whether married or not, has not yet indulged in a courtly relationship. It is better for a youth to love such a woman, says the Narrator, because she is less experienced in the ways of love, therefore harder to win.

Birds are free to fly where they will, but our falconer is tied to the ground. He finds it difficult to capture the wild sparrow hawk, for example, and must entice her to earth, waiting endless hours before she deigns to notice him. We are then told that it is good for the Narrator to spend a long time manning his bird. Although he must stay up nights caring for her, he will appreciate her all the more and become in the long run a better man for it. To possess an allerion also requires great expenditure of time, effort, and money. And she flies so high that the other birds cannot see her and dread her descent.

Machaut tells us that in *fin' amor* the lady remains free but her suitor is enslaved by passion and suffers in the cause of love. Even after she deigns to notice him, he continues to do *servitium amoris*, all the while suffering pangs of love day and night. The allerion flying so high represents the lady, and the lesser birds, traits belonging to her suitor (*souvenirs, pensées, plaisirs,* and *joies*), who recognize their inferiority and are terrified if by any chance she looks their way. But two of them dare to follow the allerion as best they can: *Volenté* and *Desir*.

While serving his lady, the Narrator acquires virtues pleasing to love. He keeps his own counsel while frequenting young falconers and in no way reveals that he is eager to learn about birds or to capture one. Once he catches sight of the sparrow hawk, he keeps silent and hides lest she take fright. Thus Machaut's ideal courtly lover discovers timidity, discretion, humility, and patience. The Narrator tells us that he seeks honor and avoids vice for the eagle's sake, to imitate her goodness and because she is worthy of the finest deeds on his part. He becomes a better man, "Pour l'aigle qui bien le valoit" (3681). (Treatises on hawking inform us that a good falconer devotes his entire lifetime to learning the craft; he expects to stay up day and night caring for his birds, and he must avoid laziness, gluttony, anger, negligence, and lust. He always studies, labors, and takes pride in his work. Gace de la Buigne says that a good falconer must be a virtuous man and uses the imagery of hawking to inveigh against the seven deadly sins.)

Despite his efforts, however, the Narrator encounters obstacles to winning a lady. First of all, she cannot make the advances herself. Although in *chansons de geste* passionate maidens throw themselves at the hero's feet, authors of romance condemn such uncourtly behavior (for example, in *Enéas, Cligès, Flamenca, Jaufré* and *Jehan et Blonde*). In *DA* the Narrator hangs about the aviary, insinuating in a thousand ways that he is taken with a gerfalcon. Her trainers take pity on him and would willingly have handed the bird over to him but for a wise man who insists that they refrain until the youth himself comes to ask for her. Machaut then interprets the allegory in the following terms. The keepers represent the girl's character traits. *Vouloir* and *Desir* agree to offer him her love, but *Cuer* insists they wait until they are assured of his good character, until he shows sufficient boldness to ask her himself, whereupon the lady will grant his request.

Nor can the Narrator triumph by physical constraint or money. He realizes he must neither try to capture the sparrow hawk the first time he sees her nor resort to brusque movements or the use of force. Like the gerfalcon, the allerion is not for sale. A raptor of the highest moral character, she belongs to a master too noble ever to dream of selling her. This lord, who gives but never trades, represents the God of Love. On the same subject Machaut tells the story of William Longsword and King Louis IX's stallion. William has an obsessive desire for King Louis's beautiful white horse but remains without hope since a king's mount is unobtainable. One day on the Crusades Louis needs someone to perform a delicate mission. William consents with alacrity even though the king had banished him from France, asking only that on this one occasion King Louis lend him his horse; and Louis, out of gratitude for William's presence in the army and willingness to serve, ends his vassal's banishment and gives him the steed. The king, with absolute sovereignty over his subject, stands for the lady, and the beautiful white horse for the gift of her love. Machaut says that love cannot be purchased nor is it subject to Fortune; only the God of Love himself will grant so noble a prize.

The allerion's guardians are willing to give her to the Narrator, except for one of them, who speaks against the transaction. His objections prove to be fruitless, however, when a lady favorable to the Narrator's suit knocks him down! This nay-sayer recalls the conventional *gilos*-figure in troubadour poetry, image of the husband or guardian, and the lady can be assimilated to a good servant (Brangien in the Tristan romances, Thessala in *Cligès,* Lunette in *Yvain, la Vieille* in *Le Roman de la Rose)* who seconds her mistress's amours. Certainly the episode can be interpreted in this way, although physical violence against the *gilos* belongs more to the fabliau tradition than to literature of the court. However, Machaut himself once again explains his allegory with reference to the lady's psyche. Certain figures symbolize personality traits—Reason, Grace, Honor, Measure, Humility—that accede to the lover's suit, while *Dongier,* "li despiteus, / Fel, desdaingneus et po piteus" (2435-36), intervenes against the lover. *Dongier* should no doubt be interpreted as the lady's natural pride, anger, and contempt,[5] which are then subdued by *Douce Plaisence,* the physically pleasurable side of an affair.

Machaut tells an anecdote about a king of France, who, having observed one of his own birds of prey kill an eagle, decapitates the victor. By attacking the king of birds, the falcon supposedly committed an act of treason. Despite the Narrator's claim to have been told the story orally (3398-400), we know that this *exemplum* is to be found in Alexander Neckam and Vincent of Beauvais (Hoepffner, 2: lxix, n. 1). Machaut says that the eagle represents the lady's honor, and the wicked bird of prey tale-bearers who kill a lady's reputation. More precisely, the falcon stands for the tongues of these *losengiers.* The king, who embodies honest speech, tears off the falcon's head (wicked, thoughtless speech), so that the lady's honor will never be sullied again.

---

[5] As in *Le Roman de la Rose.* See C. S. Lewis, *The Allegory of Love,* pp. 123-24 and Appendix 2.

Although false suitors and *losengiers* represent a permanent menace to the courtly lady, she is adept at confounding them. We are told that the eagle seizes other raptores' game; these others, who dread the eagle, not only abandon their quarry to her but cease hunting for the rest of the day. Machaut interprets this lore in the following way. The eagle stands for the lady's honor, the prey for her suitor. By taking him for herself, she confounds the tale-bearers who sought to defame her.

The lady often shows courtesy to her lover: witness a trait Machaut ascribes to the sparrow hawk. Sensitive to the cold of night, the hawk captures a small bird alive and clasps it in her claws to keep warm. The terrified victim expects to be torn apart at any moment. However, the accipiter releases her prey the following morning and takes care not to pursue him for the rest of that day. *Allegorice,* the lady, represented by the hawk, cannot herself make advances to her suitor nor, when he offers himself, can she accept his. At night he suffers from unrequited love. In the daytime, however, decorum permits the lady to bestow loving glances on him, which reveal that she cares for him and that his suit is not hopeless.

In Pierre de Beauvais's *Bestiaire* and Richard de Fournival's *Bestiaire d'Amours* Machaut finds that certain of the allerion's feathers are as sharp as razors. He refers undoubtedly to her emarginate flight feathers, three on each wing: on the right wing are located *Scens, Honnesté,* and *Courtoisie,* on the left wing their opposite. *Amour* explains that good and bad lovers are granted their just desserts. If a bad lover's suit is refused, he howls with rage; if he succeeds, he does not really enjoy his conquest, for he cannot appreciate true love. On the other hand, a good lover will know the joy of *fin' amor* when his suit is granted and, if refused, will continue to cherish his lady and hope for better things in the future.

Esperence will eventually bear fruit. When the Narrator asks for the gerfalcon, his suit is granted. Presumably he has fulfilled the necessary conditions to be recognized as a true lover, has demonstrated sufficient *hardement* for the lady to say yes. Yet his boldness does not imply *démesure* or ill-breeding; rather, he is daring in a humble way, and his humility inspires *debonnaireté* in the lady: "Car la cause d'umilité / Trait gens a debonnaireté" (3991-92). She then exhibits largess by giving her love freely. To capture the sparrow hawk, on the other hand, the Narrator uses a cage-trap: he ties down a small bird in the leaves of a tree and chases away all other game in the area that might distract the accipiter, who swoops down on the decoy and is caught when the Narrator springs shut the door. The tethered decoy stands for *Dous amoureus regart* or *Bel et courtoisement parler,* while the distracting birds represent vicious, uncourtly speech. Both allegories describe forms of *gradus amoris,* according to which a lover meets a lady, is received into her company, avows his love, and is accepted. It may not be entirely irrelevant that for both sparrow hawk and gerfalcon the Narrator's *words* bring off victory. The sincere speech of a lover (and perhaps the artful speech of a poet) are necessary for *fin' amor* to triumph.

Good things come to an end, however. All four birds eventually fly away, that is, all four liaisons are broken off. The sparrow hawk molts, upon which she becomes wilder. Her heart also molted, says the Narrator, and soon afterwards he lost her. The molting may indicate that the lady married (a likely interpretation if she was a maiden when the Narrator met her) or simply that her heart changed toward him, whereupon she fell in love with someone else. In the gerfalcon's case no doubt is possible. A mean, ungrateful bird, she changes humor without reason. One day she abandons her usual quarry to chase a screech owl. We may interpret the screech owl to represent either vices which have undermined the falcon's personality or, more likely, a vicious, unworthy lover. In a speech which recalls the Knight's lament in *JRB,* the Narrator bewails the loss of her but at the same time recognizes that since his lady has been corrupted by one seducer, she will surely yield to others, and her honor will be irrevocably tarnished. In fact, what disturbs the Narrator most is this threat to her honor, for he cherishes her still. If only she had chosen a noble bird for her paramour, he would have been consoled, but a screech owl is unworthy of her favors and of the Narrator's jealousy.

Despite his grief, a lover must remain loyal to his lady and to the God of Love. This is the doctrine expounded in the last, most elaborate scene in *DA* (4249-764). The Narrator wanders into a beautiful grove, a *locus amoenus* in the grand tradition, where he observes a variety of birds. One of them drops onto his lap and attracts an allerion, whom he also captures. The Narrator recognizes her to be his allerion from past days by a pearl which he had

attached to her foot. Machaut asks us to read this episode as
follows: the grove is the Garden of Love. Adventure, Love, and
Fortune bring the Narrator to this place, where he finds Nature
and Hope. The hedge surrounding the grove represents Good
Deeds and Speech; the grass, Sweet Thoughts; the trees, virtues; the
birds, resistance to love. The bird in the Narrator's lap stands for
Good Reputation: she attracts the lady who had been flying to
Honor in the clouds. He recognizes her by the pearl of Loyalty and
Truth. This rather cumbersome episode supposedly illustrates true
love. The poem closes with the Narrator in full possession of joy. He
will keep the allerion forever and, if by chance he loses her a second
time, never seek another hawk. Hence the title of the poem, which
Machaut himself called the *Dit des quatre oiseaus* (4814) but which
was known in his own day and to posterity as *Le Dit de l'Alerion*
(Hoepffner, 2: lxiii-lxiv).

In my opinion, of all Machaut's long narrative poems *DA* is the
least successful, and the reason for the tale's inadequacy lies in its
use of allegory. I do not presume to denigrate all allegory, whether
defined either as a specific late-medieval literary genre *(Le Roman
de la Rose, Le Pèlerinage de la Vie humaine, DL, Piers Plowman)*
or as a mode which appears throughout world literature. The best
twentieth-century critics refuse to exalt some genres or modes to the
detriment of others. [6] In fact, the last two centuries have witnessed
a revival of allegory in both dramatic and lyric verse (Hugo, Baudelaire, Claudel, George, and Hofmannsthal) and in fiction (Haw-
thorne, Melville, Orwell, Kafka, Gide, and Camus). Whether or not
allegory turns out well depends uniquely on how the individual writer
handles the medium in an individual work of art.

A modern reader finds it difficult to enjoy a love story narrated
in terms of the art of falconry; he simply does not have enough
knowledge of, interest in, or emotional attachment to "l'art de
chasse aux oiseaux" to react to the tale as poetry. It can be
maintained, of course, that twentieth-century allegory (e.g., Camus,

---

[6] Edwin Honig, *Dark Conceit: The Making of Allegory* (Evanston,
Ill., 1959); Angus Fletcher, *Allegory: The Theory of a Symbolic Mode*
(Ithaca, N. Y., 1964); Rosemond Tuve, *Allegorical Imagery*.

Orwell) appears meaningful to the contemporary reader only because the vehicle is familiar to him. An earlier generation of scholars condemned Guillaume de Lorris and Dante because their frames of reference were too far removed from our everyday concern; however, once students of literature took the trouble to familiarize themselves with the Garden or the Pilgrimage, *The Romance of the Rose* and *The Divine Comedy* were seen to radiate with life. It cannot be denied, hawking was an exciting pastime for the medievals; an allegory of love associated with falconry probably had the same effect on the fourteenth-century public as would a political satire today attached to the psychiatrist's office or the classroom. Nonetheless, whereas some medieval allegories, including *DL,* can appeal to the modern reader, such is not the case for *DA.* Unlike the themes found in successful allegory—quest, debate, siege, and garden—hawking is a pastime dependent on the historical moment, and, to some extent, it lacks universal significance. So too in six hundred years our hypothetical psychiatric or professorial satires will appear equally dated. To demand that today's reader become adept at falconry, watchmaking, and lady's fashions will not bring alive poems by Machaut, Froissart *(Li Orloge amoureus),* and Olivier de la Marche *(Le Parement et Triomphe des Dames d'honneur).* Only the greatest masters—a Dante, a Villon—succeed in combining topical relevance and appeal to posterity.

I find a certain incongruity approaching bad taste when a poet depicts a raptore's tail-feathers as virtues or a hawk's molting and a falcon's preference for a screech owl to her usual quarry as symbols for sexual infidelity. More to the point, whether we think of the Narrator's lady friends as people or birds, they never come alive, never display the warmth and charm we admire in *JRB, RF,* and *DL.* In fact, except for the faithless gerfalcon, all four raptores appear the same. No effort is made to differentiate them as literary characters nor as distinct manifestations of the female psyche. Although one protagonist alone dominates the action, we cannot identify with him or become emotionally involved in his problems. He remains too detached from his own love affairs to elicit our sympathy. The process of distancing—e.g., creating an objective, detached point of view—highly successful in Machaut's earlier tales, fails in *DA* because it lacks humor and because a single focus here leads only to thinness of characterization.

Both the lover and his ladies give the impression of being only personified abstractions. Of course, personification is a legitimate figure in medieval rhetoric. However, the act of reading implies that one is first made aware of a story, of characters doing and saying things, and only later of ulterior levels of meaning. If illustrative imagery cannot maintain the public's interest, it fails as literature and as allegory (vide Edwin Honig and Rosemond Tuve). In other words, successful allegory maintains a delicate balance between tenor and vehicle. Both should be consistent and believable, each in a state of congruity by itself and with rapport to the other. But here a rigid, inflexible scheme has been imposed upon the poem. Allegory undermines the literal narrative, and the narrative occasionally makes the interpretation appear silly. The result is a system of "imposed allegory" (to use Rosemond Tuve's phrase), which destroys both poetry and life.

Although Machaut employs parallelism and antithesis in the elaboration of his *dits,* never had he descended to the use of un-adorned, undifferentiated repetition. In *DA,* however, the same fundamental narrative increment recurs. Four times, in almost identical fashion, the Narrator tells us how he comes upon a lovely *raptore,* is taken with her, and wins her for his own; he then describes her salient traits and concludes by recounting how he loses her (with one exception: he loses the sparrow hawk before describing her). Since they are more or less identical, the four stories are strung out haphazardly, no inner form dictates their place in the narrative, nor is progression to a climax possible. A fifth increment (the al-lerion's return) then gives the impression of being an afterthought, introduced to bring about a happy ending. Ideally, a narrative whole will appear larger than the sum total of its parts, and the skeletal structure will have been filled out by the flesh of the narrative so that its outline can only be guessed at. In *DA,* however, the poem's structure is only too obtrusive, even to the casual reader.

Machaut several times pauses to narrate *exempla,* such as the sparrow hawk keeping her feet warm at night, William Longsword and the king's horse, and the execution of a hawk for *lèse-majesté.* Although these anecdotes probably generate at least as much interest as the central plot-line, they are never integrated into the narrative. Furthermore, after each digression the Narrator again pauses (a digression within a digression) to explain its significance.

Throughout *DA* as a whole the Narrator interrupts the story to present didactic material largely unrelated to the plot. Artistically, *DA* appears clumsy because the Narrator feels obliged to indulge in these interminable digressions, in contrast to *DL,* where allegory and symbolism are sufficiently transparent that the reader, with a little imagination, himself can divine what is going on.

In sum: the narrative and doctrinal lines are not sufficiently blended to form an aesthetically satisfying whole. Machaut's structure gives the impression of having been imposed from without instead of having developed naturally from the initial situation in which he placed the major characters. The story-line is rigid and static; the focus is blurred; the characters never come alive; discussions of courtly doctrine are not integrated into the plot. Human psychology, poetry, and symbolism are all sacrificed to a highly complex didactic allegory, yet a pretense to personal confession (pseudoautobiography) is maintained. The total effect is one of extreme tedium.

The *DA* is not a masterpiece; it is successful neither as a work of art nor as an *Ars amandi.* However, the poem does contain interesting patterns of imagery and some good individual scenes: the *exempla* of William Longsword's horse and a falcon's *lèse-majesté;* the Narrator's dream of a sparrow hawk (504-23); the gerfalcon's bizarre actions prior to infidelity; finally, the lengthy set-piece describing the grove where the Narrator will recapture his allerion.

This grove is of special interest. Containing green grass, birds, and trees, and surrounded by a hedge, it belongs to the *locus amoenus* tradition. In an instance of pathetic fallacy, as the hero's sorrow is transformed into joy, he penetrates into a joyful, springlike landscape which reflects the happy end to his trials. So too earlier in the story he lies under a tree in a garden, communing with birds and butterflies, whereupon his hawk comes into view. We are told that the garden of love exists in, and was founded by, Nature (4289-300), who, with Love, brings the young man to the grove just as they were originally responsible for his inclination to hawking (139-142). Love is part of nature, therefore essentially good; so is its only proper décor, the *locus amoenus.*

The Narrator recognizes the returning allerion by a bright shining pearl he himself had attached to her foot. The pearl stands for

Loyalty and Truth. Earlier in the story an opposition was created
between light and darkness, the bright light of day when the sparrow
hawk befriends her suitor and darkness of night when she imprisons
him in her talons. In *DA* the sun represents *Bonne Amour;* since
it is dangerous to gaze at the sun directly, only the eagle may do so
with impunity. For a lady to indicate by her gaze that she accepts a
suitor's love is compared to a bit of cloud ("un po de nuée," 1848)
passing in front of the sun. On another occasion, easing a lover's
pain is compared to a transformation from poverty to riches, from
shadow to light, and from winter to summer.

The most important image-pattern treats of birds. The nightingale,
lark, and blackbird appear often in the courtly lyric; perhaps the
most beautiful of these is Bernart de Ventadorn's "Can vei la lauzeta
mover." In the *conflictus* poems, from which Machaut took the idea
for *JRB,* birds play a major role in determining who is a better
lover, the knight or the cleric. In Marie de France's *Laüstic* a
nightingale symbolizes the joy of love, and the husband's killing
the bird is a sin against Nature and Joy; in *Yonec* a fairy-prince
takes the form of a giant bird; and the swan as a love-emissary
appears in *Milon.* A nightingale is sent to a lady as a love-token
in *Le Roman de la Poire.* Birds also have an important function in
Le Dit de la Panthère d'Amours, La Messe des Oisiaus, and the
Bestiaires d'Amours. In Canto V of the *Inferno* Dante assimilates
the great lovers of history to starlings, cranes, and doves. And
l'Ovide moralisé, a book we know Machaut read before 1349 but not
necessarily at the time he wrote *DA,* contains examples of the Greek
gods' assuming avian forms to seduce mortals, or of great lovers'
transformation into birds, the most famous example being the story
of Philomela. After Machaut the courtly bird tradition persists in
the works of Chaucer *(The Parliament of Fowls, The Legend of
Good Women)* and Jean Lemaire de Belges *(Les Epîtres de l'Amant
vert),* among others.

With more specific reference to birds of prey, in *chansons de
geste* raptores appear as costly gifts or booty. Old Provençal and
Old French lyrics compare the lady or love itself to a falcon chasing
the poet-lover or the lady to a raptore the lover hopes to train, that
is, win over to his suit. A sparrow hawk, the prize for a feat of
arms, sanctions Erec's right to marry Enide. In *Cligès,* as an
excuse for repairing to a secret tower, the hero pretends to train a

goshawk, which symbolizes Fénice. The lovers are discovered when a certain Bertrand climbs the garden walls to find a lost sparrow hawk. In *Guillaume au faucon* a falcon is sacrificed to *fin' amor;* in *L'Escoufle* a kite serves both to separate and to reunite the lovers; and in *Jehan et Blonde* Jehan tells Blonde's fiancé that he has set a trap to capture a sparrow hawk; the trap stands for his love, and the sparrow hawk for the girl.

Despite obvious anomalies, the medievals did not find it improper to assimilate a beautiful lady to a bird of prey. They considered such birds to merit first place in the avian hierarchy. Treatises on falconry, medieval and modern, proclaim that the best raptores are female, larger, nobler, braver, more intelligent, and easier to train than the male. And the eagle partakes of a political and religious aura: Jove's bird and a symbol of the Roman Empire, she also represents the Gospel according to Saint John, God's grace, the human soul baptized or strengthened by grance, Christ (for she renews her plumage, image of death and resurrection), and God the Father (for she dares to gaze directly at the sun, image of the Virgin Mary).

The psychoanalyst who declares that flight symbolizes sexual stimulation, and the flying bird a beautiful but unattainable object of sexual fantasy, only confirms medieval predicators who castigated hawking as a sinful pastime and depicted the sin of lust under the guise of falconry, [7] not to mention Chrétien, Dante, Du Bellay, Ronsard, Donne, Góngora, and so many others, who have assimilated the beloved to a flying bird. However, by assimilating *fin' amor* to hawking, Machaut undermines traditional courtly doctrine as he did in *JRB*. After all, man belongs to a higher species than birds; he is superior to his falcon or hawk, is the master, and the bird his pet or servant. The Narrator teaches the sparrow hawk, not she him. To man the bird, he presumably seals her eyes (completely or partially blinding her, albeit temporarily), underfeeds her, blunts the sharp points of her talons, and fits jesses and a bell to her feet. We are also told of the eagle's fidelity, that she is at the Narrator's beck and call and returns to him immediately after the chase. Their relationship differs strikingly from that of a timid lover who adores

---

[7] See D. W. Robertson, Jr., *A Preface to Chaucer* (Princeton, N. J., 1962), pp. 190-94.

his cruel, unattainable mistress *(DV, RF, DL)*. Machaut has created a pattern reminiscent of the *chansons de geste,* where man has the dominant role.

No matter how often the Narrator insists that these birds cannot be purchased or seized by force, that they will be handed over to him only as a free gift of love, winning a girl is nonetheless compared to acquiring a raptore. We cannot help seeing the loved one as an object, not a person, and, worse still, an object of exchange. Machaut employs the vocabulary of commerce, considers the bird a prize awarded or a treasure stolen. Since *Bonne Amour* says to the lover, "Se tu pers, je le paieray" (3013), we can hardly blame the Narrator for reifying the object of his affections, the courtly lady.

Machaut's protagonist is paid not only for good deeds and laudable character traits; he also triumphs through ruse. He praises the eagle for taking other raptores' quarry, an example of good trickery (3602-16). The king of France's councillor tells him that since sure knowledge, love, good conscience, subtlety, and boldness will gain him his ends, he should send one man (William Longsword) instead of an army on a particularly delicate mission. In fact, William manifests shrewdness not only on the king's mission but because he succeeds in acquiring the king's horse. And William serves as a model to the Narrator, who persuades falconers to hand over the allerion, eagle, and gerfalcon. He would like to seize the sparrow hawk but realizes that prudence obliges him to wait and set a trap — *Courtoise decevance:*

> 584   Et qu'il me couvenoit atendre
> Une autre fois, mieus pourveüs,
> Mieus avisés et mieus meüs
> Et dou prendre un po plus soutils
> Et garnis de soutis outis
> Pour haut lever ou pour estendre,
> Pour a ce gent esprivier tendre.

Lastly, *DA* tells of unhappiness in love, as a result of ladies' infidelity. All four birds desert the Narrator. He does not give precise details concerning the departure of the first three, except that the sparrow hawk molted, her character deteriorated, and she was taken away, but we can be sure that the Narrator did not abandon or sell any of his precious darlings. They left him, and theirs was the fault. As for the gerfalcon, her character deteriorates as did the sparrow hawk's, upon which she deserts the Narrator for a screech owl. She resembles the unfaithful beloved in *JRB:* both females prove to be disloyal, promiscuous, ungrateful, and of low character because they prefer a vile lover to a good one.

In theory, a lover must remain faithful to his lady, regardless of her behavior. But in practice the opposite of loyalty solves the Narrator's problems. The allerion, even though she wears the pearl of *loyauté* and *verité,* had left the Narrator, Lord knows why, yet returns to him with a clear conscience and is received like a prodigal son. The Narrator, too, consoles himself with four distinct mistresses, paying court to one after the other, and then takes up with one of his old flames. The falconers welcome the Narrator into their midst, recognizing him to be a seasoned bird-lover, an habitué of the court, a late Gothic and, perhaps, very chaste, Lothario but a Lothario for all that. Neither the four birds nor the Narrator have been faithful; all have followed King John's advice in *JRB,* in opposition to *fin' amor.* And none of them has been punished for his transgressions.

To the extent that *DA* contains a message, it is the following: Do not grieve over lost love, do not remain faithful to dead love. Live and love again. There is more than one fish in the sea, more than one bird in the sky. After each of the four raptores has abandoned the Narrator, allegorical personages—*Amour, Avis, Raison*—urge him to find a new lady. *Amour* says the following:

> 2995 Or use dont de ta science
> Et met en pais ta conscience,
> S'en oste hors erreurs et doubtes,
> Et saches une fois pour toutes,
> Se tu aucune chose pers,
> Soiez avisiez et apers
> Que tu puisses par bien ouvrer
> A point ta perte recouvrer
> Ou chose qui ta perte vaille.

Raison offers the Narrator justice not pity; she can do nothing for him unless he helps himself: "Aïde toy; je t'aideray. / Honnis toy; je te honniray" (4433-34). And when the Narrator follows her precepts, Reason leads him out from the Way of Sadness into the Grove of Nature and Joy where he is reunited with the allerion. As in *JRB,* Machaut tells us the Narrator will find joy after having given himself to Reason. Only by adopting a commonsense attitude toward his *vie sentimentale* can he expect to lead a normal, happy, fulfilled life.

The structure of *DA* is neither linear nor circular but repetitive. The same narrative increment—encounter, conquest, portrait, separation, regrets, consolation—is more or less repeated four times. For all its monotony and inelegance, this pattern does create a vision of life. One bird is like another, one woman like another, one adventure like another. They repeat each other in an extendible series. Love itself appears cynical, disabused, and a trifle world-weary. Like so many other sentiments, it too falls into a system.

Machaut does give us something new at the end of his poem, however. The old pattern is broken. After four successive tales of success and failure, the Narrator returns to one of his earlier mistresses (or rather the former mistress returns to him). They are reunited, and it is presumed that their story will be different from the others, that their love will endure. Although this denouement gives the impression of having been imposed from without, lacking evidence to the contrary, we must assume that it forms as integral a part of the tale as the preceding episodes. Machaut presumably believes that true love is attainable in the world and that the Narrator has learned the way to happiness.

He certainly has not conformed to the precepts of *fin' amor*. But he has been educated and indeed undergone transformation in the course of the narrative. Significantly, he more or less educates himself. No father or mother figure, such as the God of Love *(DV)* or Lady Hope *(RF)*, plays the role of teacher. The hero begins the story as a child, with the characteristics of a child. He then grows to manhood, frequents courtly society, enters into erotic relationships with several ladies, and uses his intelligence to win their love. At the same time he learns not to adhere foolishly to an outdated literary code but to live life as it comes, guided by Reason as well as Love. When an affair is ended, after a brief interlude of despair, he rises up, takes stock, and finds a new beloved.

In spite of this rather static pattern, the Narrator moves about more than any of Machaut's characters we have seen up to now. He frequents falcon-houses, traps raptores, mans them, loses them, begins again, and so forth. His seeking love and an object for his affections reflects an equally imperative quest for maturity. In the course of the poem he succeeds in growing up, discovering the true nature of love, and of establishing a *modus vivendi* with courtly society. At the end of the poem, one of his lost loves returns. Instead of chasing the lady, she comes to him, in a setting of calm, repose, and joy. Now that the Narrator has finally come to terms with himself and his world, his story draws to an end.

6. LE JUGEMENT DOU ROY DE NAVARRE

The Narrator spends the winter of 1349 locked in his room for fear of the Plague, meditating on the calamities of the age. With the advent of spring he goes out hunting, whereupon he is noticed by Lady *Bonneürté* (an allegorical figure representing Happiness or Good Fortune). *Bonneürté* reproaches the Narrator for the decision he made in *JRB:* that a knight suffers more from his beloved's infidelity than a lady from her lover's death. The two agree on a new trial, to be held before Charles the Bad, king of Navarre. As plaintiff, *Bonneürté* is assisted by allegorical attendants: *Franchise, Honnesté, Charité,* and others. The Narrator conducts his own defense. Both parties narrate *exempla* taken from *l'Ovide moralisé,* modern vernacular romance, or contemporary *faits divers.* Finally, King Charles and his councillors (*Avis, Raison, Mesure,* and *Congnoissance*) decide in favor of *Bonneürté:* their verdict is diametrically opposed to the one in *JRB.* The Narrator is condemned to write a *lay,* a *chanson,* and a *balade.*

As THE TITLE INDICATES, Guillaume de Machaut wrote *Le Jugement dou Roy de Navarre contre le Jugement dou Roy de Behaingne*[1] as a sequel to *JRB.* The generally accepted opinion on *JRN* is the following: "Le jugement attribué au roi Jean [in *JRB*], mais qui en réalité était de Machaut lui-même, a dû se heurter à des critiques violentes et nombreuses, surtout de la part des dames; le poète, dans sa pièce même, nous l'a bien fait entrevoir. C'est pour leur plaire et se concilier de nouveau leurs bonnes grâces qu'il a composé

---

[1] 4,212 lines, followed by *Le Lay de Plour,* 210 lines; ed. Hoepffner, 1: 137-291 (cited hereafter as *JRN*).

ce nouveau poème, où, tout en ayant l'air de défendre son premier jugement, il finit par se prononcer dans le sens exactement contraire" (Hoepffner, 1: lxix).

However, an analysis of the trial will show that the issues and Machaut's viewpoint as author are more complex than Hoepffner would have us believe. The reasons for a decision favoring *Bonneürté* are given by *Mesure and Raison* (3577-3724, 3767-3832, 3971-4006). From their speeches we discover that the Narrator has been condemned essentially on four points:

1. He pleaded his case badly, that is, some of the anecdotes he submitted as evidence were inappropriate and the reasoning based on them false. Three such examples are cited.

In the story of the clerk of Orléans, who goes insane when informed that his mistress is unfaithful, the clerk suspects her without foundation, since he never inquires whether the allegations against her are to be believed. The Narrator has neglected to inform the court of all the details in the case; therefore, his *exemplum* fails to hold water.

The story of the knight who, when his lady requests him to return her ring, cuts off his ring finger and sends it to her, is an example of sheer madness. We must condemn, not praise, the knight's action.

The Narrator should not have brought up *La Châtelaine de Vergi,* praising the lover, since the Châtelaine proves to be more noble than he, whose unpardonable indiscretion is responsible for her death and his own. From *Bonneürté*'s first speech it is apparent that the trial has been transformed into a debate on the respective virtues of men and women, that is, whether man or woman loves more deeply. Consequently, all three of the Narrator's arguments turn against him, for in all three the quality of the man as lover is held up to question.

2. *Raison* and *Mesure* adjudge the Narrator guilty of having defamed the honor of the fair sex, of having spoken against ladies and against the God of Love. Certainly, Machaut did write *JRB,* and in the course of the *JRN* trial he has the Narrator declare that men suffer from Eros more than ladies, that men are loyal and worthy of respect, whereas women prove to be fickle. He cites case after case of cruel ladies and the pain they bring upon their lovers.

Faithful women exist, of course, he says; but you'll find only one good one in 500,000, so finely is the grain scattered! According to *Raison,* the God of Love does not tolerate such accusations: if any one speaks ill of ladies and then does not repent, he must pay for his crime.

3. The Narrator has shown inexcusable discourtesy to his adversaries. While hunting in the field he neither greets nor even notices *Bonneürté,* an insult to ladies in general ("Trop po les dames prisiez," 768) and to the courtly world, for he was not as dazzled by her as he should have been. Then he dares to plead against one so "high" as *Bonneürté,* to defend the false judgment pronounced in *JRB* instead of admitting at once that he was in the wrong. And in the course of the trial he accuses *Franchise* of lying and hypocrisy.

4. Finally, it is wrong to estimate jealousy a greater ill than bereavement, for death is the cruelest of all misfortunes and the pain of death worse than all others:

> 3620 Je di que Guillaumes a tort;
>   Car de tous les crueus meschiez
>   La mort en est li propres chiez;
>   A dire est que tous meschiez passe,
>   Et pour ce que nuls n'en respasse;
>   Car on se puet trop mieus passer
>   De ce dont on puet respasser.

What is the effect of this judgment? Does *Mesure*'s and *Raison*'s verdict in fact undermine the doctrine of love propounded so vigorously in earlier *dits,* especially *JRB* and *DA*?

That the Narrator as a literary character proves to be a bad lawyer does not in and of itself repudiate his cause nor does it prove an about-face from the author, Guillaume de Machaut. A perfectly valid thesis may be defended ineptly without its being discredited on its own terms. As the Narrator himself points out, whether or not the clerk of Orléans's mistress was unfaithful has no relevance whatsoever to the Narrator's main point: that a man suffers unbelievable pain when he believes, truly or falsely, that he has been deceived. Similarly, whether or not the knight acted according to the most elegant precepts of *fin' amor* in cutting off his finger does not affect the Narrator's argument that the knight had been driven to despair by his lady's betrayal. Machaut the Author has chosen to have Machaut the Narrator lose his suit in this way, committing minor errors in procedure, while his main argument remains intact. After all, it is he, Guillaume de Machaut, who "composes" the *dit* and prepares the speeches on both sides, for the ladies and for "himself." He could have awarded flawless pleading to the Narrator and have the ladies make mistakes. Machaut was indeed a poet of the court, ladies may well have put pressure on him to decide in their favor, and the public was perhaps woman-oriented and the feminine element predominant: all this no doubt placed the author in a dilemma. But he then found a way to resolve it. Because his side must lose, because the ladies must win, Machaut undermines the Narrator's skill as a lawyer in order to conserve his doctrine intact. He is condemned for being inept but not for being wrong.

No one can deny that the Narrator has treated the fair sex with discourtesy. The evidence he submits and the conclusions he draws are clearly anathema to the courtly tradition represented by *Bonneürté*. To honor ladies is one of the cardinal precepts of *fin' amor*. Andreas Capellanus says: "Dominarum praeceptis in omnibus obediens semper studeas amoris aggregari militiae" (Commandment VII) and "Maledicus esse non debes" (Commandment IX). Because he loves one lady, the courtly lover must honor all ladies. However, although speaking against ladies is obviously a heresy within the confines of *fin' amor,* neither Guillaume de Machaut nor his public are necessarily orthodox devotees of the faith. For a noncommitted outsider, the Narrator's opinions may be either true or false, valid or invalid; presumably his trial has been convened to determine their validity. But the judges refuse to go into such matters. Their condemnation of the Narrator is based on a simple tautology: to defame ladies indeed consists in the defaming of ladies and is surely a crime within a system which proclaims from the beginning that the defaming of ladies is a crime. Unfortunately, Machaut and many of his readers may adhere to a different system with different rules.

The Narrator's rudeness to *Bonneürté* and *Franchise* falls under the first two points we have discussed. A good advocate does not insult his adversaries, especially if they are of higher social standing than he and if the trial takes place on their home ground. In addition, all of the allegorical figures assisting *Bonneürté* and *Bonneürté* herself are members of the fair sex. By insulting them as adversaries the Narrator also insults them as ladies. The Narrator's greatest sin of all is to plead against these ladies (and ladies in general), daring to tell the truth as he sees it, in opposition to courtly love.

Of the four points, only the last — that death is worst of all — bears directly on the subject at issue. Unfortunately, *Mesure*'s brief and rather elliptic pronouncement lends itself to ambiguities in interpretation. Does she mean that the Lady of *JRB* suffers more than the Knight because death is the *summum malum* that can befall a mortal and, therefore, the Lady suffers because her Lover has endured so much? Or does *Mesure* say that, since death is irrevocable, due to hopelessness the Lady suffers more than the Knight? Or that because legendary heroines (Dido, Hero, Thisbe, etc.) died for love, death being the greatest of ills, ladies love more deeply than men? In any case, so peremptory a decision, delivered in only seven lines, gives the impression of being an afterthought on *Mesure*'s part, a pretext for disposing the case expeditiously. But on doctrinal grounds it neither converts the Narrator nor wins over his public.

To the nonprejudiced observer it is apparent that, aside from these perhaps intentionally unsatisfactory judgments, Guillaume de Machaut, in the person of his Narrator, defends with vigor the ideas he espoused previously in *JRB* and *DA*. The Narrator never recants what he has said, and if he must yield to the court, does so because he opposed a "dame de si haut pris" (4196), not because he was wrong. Woman's inconstancy, pride, and cruelty are alluded to more often and with greater vigor here than in any of Machaut's other *dits*. Above all, the Narrator repeatedly proclaims his right to tell the truth as he sees it. If *Raison* decides against him in the end, it was she who originally urged the Narrator to defend himself, and he declares he will remain with her (not Love, not Happiness) for the rest of his life. Although Hoepffner said that Machaut "a composé ce nouveau poème, où, tout en ayant l'air de défendre son premier jugement, il finit par se prononcer dans le sens exactement contraire," one can equally well maintain the contrary: that the poet, while he gives the impression of refuting *JRB,* in fact defends it with wit and pluck.

If anything, once more Machaut proposes for emulation the ideals of prudence, measure, lucidity, and common sense—*sagesse,* as the French say. Several lovers are criticized for having acted fanatically:

the swallow who murders his unfaithful mate; the clerk of Orléans who goes insane perhaps for no reason; the knight who, in a gallant gesture, cuts off his ring finger. Machaut's Narrator declares that betrayal is a common portion of love, that evil is committed by both men and women, and that both sexes suffer from it. *Charité* points out that even if the clerk's mistress did marry, he should forgive her and honor her in her new state. Lovers ought to separate without bitterness, she says. And finally, *Raison* and *Mesure* condemn the Narrator not for being in the wrong but for being inept, because he fails to practice those social virtues so highly prized by the House of Valois and Charles of Navarre, by courtiers who no doubt approved Machaut's restatement of *aurea mediocritas:*

> 2915 Mais on dit—et c'est veritez—
> Qu'adès les deus extermitez,
> C'est trop et po. Einsi l'enten ge:
> Ne doivent recevoir loange;
> Mais qui en l'amoureus loien
> Est loiez, s'il tient le moien,
> Il ouevre bien et sagement.
> Et li sages dist qui ne ment
> Qu'adès li bonneüreus tiennent
> Le moien partout ou il viennent.

What I have said up to now is based on the assumption that, like Machaut's first four tales, *JRN* is fiction not autobiography, and that a trial scene with allegorical adversaries must be viewed as spectacle not personal experience. It is true that by obtrusively identifying the Narrator as Guillaume, author of *JRB,* by having him named as such by the other characters (573, 601, 651, 686, 695, 726, 746, 760, 779, 802, 862, 915, 974, and so forth) and himself (4199-4200), Machaut individualizes this traditional *persona* more than in *JRB, RF,* or *DL.* For all that, however, the semiautobiographical I-narrator in fiction is not and cannot be strictly identified with the author. (Rubrics in the text distinguish what "Guillaume" says at trial from narration by "L'Acteur.") The *JRN* Narrator still manifests quite a few conventional traits, and whether or not the real Guillaume de Machaut was a saucy but inept pleader at court is as difficult for us to ascertain as whether the same Machaut was a pure, timid, virtuous, but immature wooer when he wrote *RF.* No doubt, some of the comedy, in *JRN* as in *RF,* derives from both similarity and dissimilarity between the Author as Narrator and the Author as Poet, the irony generated when Machaut tells a fictional tale in his own voice, quite probably reciting it himself before Charles of Navarre, a tale in which both men play roles.

As we saw in Chapter 1, the dominant tradition in medieval narrative was that of a "poetic" or universal I, an Everyman representative of mankind. As a reliable Narrator with a valid claim to authenticity, he would generally be objective, unobtrusive, and unselfconscious. Guillaume de Machaut's "I" is still the center of consciousness and single focus for the narrative. What he says is to be given credence; he participates actively in the story as hero. Yet he is also obtuse and naive, not aware himself of all the comic overtones inherent in what he says. Machaut, even though he may identify with the Narrator, erects a barrier between himself and his all-too-human literary creation. He is more sophisticated than his Narrator, and his attitude toward the events recounted in *JRN* may be quite different.

Machaut the Author appears inside and outside the story: as a literary character, a defendant at court; as the same character, telling the story later on; and as himself, the master pulling the strings. From this situation emerges distance and control — the unself-conscious, unobtrusive Narrator separated from the only too self-conscious, obtrusive litigant and from the author hiding behind the scenes. Machaut the Author provides both support and correction, sympathy for and criticism of, the Narrator as hero.

Two aspects of the Narrator's *persona* generate humor: his cowardice and antifeminism. We discover that this eminent poet and defender of noncourtly love is terrified both at being late for *Bonneürté*'s summons and later at pleading against her. Along with melancholia, doubts enter his heart, for he believes he must be under a spell to have dreamed of such recklessness. Cowardice and timidity, traits ascribed to the Narrator as lover in *RF* and to the Narrator as witness in *JRB,* are incongruous in a lover, but even more so in a great specialist on love who defies courtly conventions, a nonknight who denies the prerogatives of the knightly world and unconsciously parodies so well the timid courtly lover he disdains.

Partly from cowardice, partly from good breeding, the Narrator treats his trial adversaries with exemplary deference. Yet in his heart he is an antifeminist. Once the debate is engaged, the Narrator's polish wears thin. He first accuses *Franchise* of bad faith, then urges an end to digressions on the respective merits of men and women. But in the midst of this plea he himself delivers a powerful but wholly gratuitous diatribe against the fair sex and, despite the remonstrances of *Largesse* and *Doubtance,* concludes that only one good lady can be found in 500,000. Although, except for *Avis* and King Charles, the entire assembly is made up of ladies, the Narrator insults them.

The defendant would like to appear the fine, gracious poet, at ease in any situation, especially among courtiers. He may even think of himself as a great lover and have expected an erotic adventure when summoned by *Bonneürté*'s squire.[2] Unfortunately, he suffers from timidity, rudeness, cowardice before great ladies, and ferocious misogyny. Both cowardice and misogyny are traits traditionally ascribed to the clergy. It is appropriate that a canon at Reims should be afflicted with them, but incongruous that a master in the doctrine of love and potential lover should fear or dislike the object of love. Furthermore, his reactions are obsessive. Repeatedly coming to light at inappropriate moments, they undermine the resilience of his character and give the impression that he is unable to cope with everyday happenings which a well-balanced personality will take in stride.

We laugh at the Narrator but do not reproach him. First of all, his faults are not serious enough to darken the comic mood. Second, Machaut depicts him as a predominantly decent character, with whom we can sympathize. *Bonneürté* herself commends the Narrator for an exemplary private life: for adhering to *jolieté* and *honnesté,* for working hard during the day and studying hard at night (600-612). Her praise is ironic because 1) it is written by Guillaume de Machaut the Author, told by Guillaume de Machaut the Narrator, and directed at Guillaume de Machaut the Litigant, and 2) immediately thereafter *Bonneürté* declares she will destroy his happiness. Nonetheless, the passage places the Narrator in a good light, as a poet-scholar of some importance and a good man. Our laughter is directed as much at *Bonneürté* as at her prospective victim, and we laugh with the Narrator, not at him.

In spite of being a coward, the Narrator demonstrates a fair amount of pluck in his dealings with the allegorical world. Before

---

2 Wimsatt, *Chaucer and the French Love Poets,* pp. 99-100.

the trial he demands to know exactly what crime he is accused
of and when and where he committed it. A vague accusation will
carry no weight; if *Bonneürté* cannot be precise, he must be
exonerated at once (840-61). The Narrator declares he will defend
his writings himself. He can be beaten but will do his best. The
account of the trial enhances our opinion of him. Although he
argues alone against ten noble ladies, who attack him each in turn,
it is a moot point as to who presents the more convincing arguments.
Furthermore, if the Narrator loses his temper and the thread of
his discourse, the ladies are far more guilty of courtroom indecorum,
as we shall see later on.

The Narrator appears to be an outsider at this court of love, one
who does not belong to the official hierarchy. The court stands
against the poet and will not take him seriously. What chance does
he have crossing swords with abstract virtues personified as the cream
of aristocratic society? In a very real sense, despite the vigor of his
defense, he cannot win. Consequently, we the readers feel sympathy
for him as an underdog, a man who suffered from the Plague and
now must suffer anew, ripped away from his innocent pastime by
an all-too-human and vengeful Grande Dame. A closed, artificial
society condemns the Narrator; in return, to ever so slight a degree,
we condemn it.

Finally, the Narrator stands in the limelight. He is the center of
consciousness, the author's *persona;* the world of *JRN* is his world,
filtered through him. To the extent that he maintains a certain
objectivity and remains detached as narrator from his predicament
as litigant, we respect him. To the extent that he surreptitiously
deforms the courtly world, rendering it through his own ironic
perspective, we accept his point of view, since it is the only one we
know. In this poem the Narrator adopts some traits often ascribed
in comedy to the Fool. He is the butt of society yet also its critic,
a wise observer and uncouth scapegoat, *eiron* and *agroikos*. [3] We do
not necessarily judge him nor are we forced to agree or disagree with
his views. We see him as a person as well as an ideological spokesman. We may even enjoy his duel with the courtly world, admire
him, and identify with him.

---

[3] See Northrop Frye, *Anatomy of Criticism*, pp. 172-76.

Although the humor of *JRN* derives first of all from the Narrator's *persona*, its full potential is realized in a group relationship, when he interacts with his adversaries. These allegorical ladies at first comport themselves with dignity but, before the poem's end, prove to be a cackle of gabby, gossipy females, every bit as comic as he is. We come to doubt their reliability as impartial arbiters in a court of law. *Bonneürté* and her friends continually insult the Narrator instead of reasoning logically with him. *Foy* and *Charité* interrupt the deliberations to confer together in whispers (2381-2406). Later, in a less flattering moment, *Honnesté* interrupts *Charité*, who had opened her mouth to speak, because she herself wishes to take the floor (2561-74). Then, after the Narrator has delivered an unusually sharp misogynistic remark, the ladies lose their collective tempers and begin to murmur; upon which, the misogynist requests that his adversaries be permitted to continue their pleading in unison, to have done more quickly. And they do speak all at once, whereupon King Charles smiles and the Narrator rejoices:

> 3157 Si firent elles, ce me samble;
>   Qu'elles parloient tout ensamble,
>   Dont li juges prist a sousrire
>   Qui vit que chascune s'aïre.
>   Et certes, j'en eus moult grant joie,
>   Quant en tel estat les vëoie.

Humor is generated when so many distinguished ladies feel obliged to accuse one man, when they attack him one after the other or all together but are sufficiently inept that he, for all his foibles, ends up reasonably well, and when they become so infuriated at his occasional lapses from decorum that they insult him themselves. They are as prone as the Narrator to rigid, mechanical behavior and Bergsonian fixations, such as the sanctity of womankind and the courtly code. They appear perhaps even more laughable than he because of repetition (the ladies all act alike, each one more or less repeats what the others have said) and snowballing (an accumulation of speeches which builds up to that magnificent temper tantrum when they all speak at once). For the first time Guillaume de Machaut has developed a continuous comic situation from the interactions of a small group of people. Each person gives full expression to his comic potential when he is placed in contact with the others, when they contribute together to the elaboration of a comic world.

This world is based upon the fiction of the trial. Machaut follows the workings of the law closely, whether it be the Narrator's insistence upon hearing the particulars of his indictment, *Bonneürté*'s formal accusation, the rapid play of argument and careful scrutiny of evidence by plaintiff and defendant, the judges' retiring to reach a verdict *in camera,* and the Narrator's explanation of how he found out what was said in their secret deliberations.

His seemingly realistic parody of judicial proceedings contributes a sense of authenticity to *JRN* but also generates humor because we can never forget that the trial is so preposterously and obviously a figment of the author's imagination. The subject at issue concerns whether a lover suffers more from his beloved's death or his beloved's infidelity, but from *Bonneürté*'s first speech the trial degenerates into a war of the sexes, a debate on the respective virtues of men and women. At no time do the judges correct this flagrant travesty of justice; nor do they reprimand the litigants for indulging in irrelevant casuistry: arguments over who suffered more, Pyramus or Thisbe, Hero or Leander; over who loves more deeply, a person dying from a broken heart or one who has gone insane for the same reason; over whether the insane lover remains permanently in ex-cruciating torture or suffers only the instant he went mad. The ladies attack the Narrator one after the other; the arguments they use and the stories they tell are roughly the same. For all the importance of tradition and authority in medieval law, and reverence for *auctores* throughout medieval culture, the fourteenth-century public could not help but recognize the absurdity of attempting to prove universal psychological and moral judgments based upon a few contemporary or historical anecdotes. It is no accident that *Raison* rambles on about meteorological phenomena and the rules of scholastic debate and that *Mesure* praises herself in so unrestrained a manner. Nor is it an accident that the proceedings as a whole cannot be fair: King Charles's four supposedly impartial councillors are of *Bon-neürté*'s retinue and as much her servants as the ten ladies who fulminate directly against the Narrator.

We cannot take seriously a trial where a fear-stricken defendant proclaims it will be fun to hear the fine arguments on both sides, at which *Bonneürté* laughs. We cannot take seriously a trial where the verdict and sentencing provoke peals of laughter. An absurdly minor point of love casuistry, discussed in a poem at least ten years old, unleashes a full-fledged legal confrontation before the king of Navarre; and the result of this massive trial machinery is to condemn the defendant, a poet, to write more poetry.

In passing, we note that it is the ladies, not the cleric-narrator, who cite *exempla* from Greco-Roman antiquity: the stories of Dido, Ariadne, Medea, Thisbe, and Hero. They, not the Narrator, prove their case with arguments taken from *escripture* (3657). In a debate between the cleric and the court, between Reason and Love, between rational man and irrational woman, the courtly, love-oriented, un-learned ladies triumph in the world of books, beating the Narrator at his own game. On the other hand, the Narrator, who should have relied on classical authority, cites three contemporary anecdotes and three medieval French tales of love. In this strange amatory debate his adversaries are the ancients and he the modern. He may lack courtly etiquette, but common sense is on his side. To the extent that book-learning and authority are called into question, the ladies' position suffers, not the Narrator's.

Unlike *DL,* the plot of *JRN* is not based on the *roman d'aven-tures* pattern. But the themes of adventure and the chase do con-tribute to the narrative and in a comic register. Once the plague has lifted, the Narrator goes hunting. He is so engrossed that he fails to notice *Bonneürté* ride by. Hurt by the Narrator's discourtesy, *Bonneürté* summons him into her presence. From this interview the trial follows directly. The hunt brings the Narrator and *Bonneürté* into contact but, because of the Narrator's distraction, it keeps them apart. *Bonneürté* accuses the Narrator of having failed to show due respect to her as a lady and thus having insulted ladies in general. His action parallels in humorous fashion the more serious affronts he made as a poet in *JRB* and will make in the trial scene to come.

How should we interpret the hunt? Medieval man often con-sidered the chase a symbol of idolatry and riding on horseback a symbol of vanity. To ride down a little furry animal, a rabbit or hare (*JRN,* 505), is an obvious erotic situation which evokes the sin of lust and was condemned in moral and satirical treatises. [4] Influenced in part by the example of "bad" hunters in scripture

---

[4] Robertson, *A Preface to Chaucer,* pp. 113, 263-64.

(Nimrod, Esau), the church protested against clerics' participating in the chase: because of disturbance to the contemplative life, the risk of arousing passions, and the expense. On the other hand, imagery of the chase, as of falconry, was assimilated to the noblest impulses of *fin' amor*. I am thinking of troubadour and trouvère poetry and *Enéas, Erec et Enide, Aucassin et Nicolette,* and *Le Roman de la Rose*. Machaut undoubtedly knew either from Jean de Meun or *l'Ovide moralisé* that Venus advised Adonis to hunt rabbits and hares *(Amor)*, not fierce beasts *(Militia)*. The "hunt of love" then became a familiar theme in late medieval allegory, in *La Prise amoreuse* by Jehan Acart de Hesdin, *Li Dis dou cerf amoreus,* and *Die Jagd* by Hadamar von Laber.

It is possible to interpret the Narrator's pastime as lustful, non-courtly amorous pleasure, insulting to *Bonneürté,* or an effort on the Narrator's part to be a courtly lover in the grand style. I wish to suggest still another hypothesis. In courtly literature the hunt also stood for an alternative way of life, in opposition to, or in competition with, the erotic. Such is the case in *Guigemar, Parto-nopeus de Blois, Guillaume de Dole, Durmart le Galois,* and so many episodes of *l'Ovide moralisé,* where a youth or maiden in the service of Diana will not submit to erotic advances, even from a god. The examples of Daphne, Actaeon, Narcissus, and Arethusa point to a fundamental opposition between love and the chase, representing totally irreconcilable attitudes toward life. When a mythological personage (Meleager or Adonis) seeks to combine the two or to pursue them at the same time, he is doomed. In *JRN* then the Narrator's participation in the chase is anathema to *Bonneürté,* for by so doing he partakes of a pleasure different from love. He remains ignorant of love and of *Bonneürté's* presence, enjoying himself fully in a parody of the only true joy a priestess of *fin' amor* will admit. And finally, he dares partake of a court pastime; he, a non-noble, a coward, and a poet, presumes to act like a knight, even to defend rabbit-hunting as a noble sport in which he can attain honor. Instead of bagging the rabbit for a good stew, he will discover that he is the hunted not the hunter in a quite different sport.

The Narrator excuses his discourtesy by claiming to have been seized or ravished *(ravis,* 795) out of his senses, hence his failure to recognize the ladies. He refers to his rabbit hunt as a *queste* (553) for *honneur* (502, 508, 510, 516), and to an encounter with *Bon-*

neürté's messenger as an *aventure* (536). If talebearers had spoken against him, that would have been an *aventure* too (835). Later, he is accused of being *forfais* (811, 860) to ladies. His fear of the trial is compared to enchantment (1340), his *honneur* (1064) again at stake, and *Bonneürté* refers to the whole affair as a *merveille*, unique in its kind (1477-78). Without reproducing the mold of *DL*, Machaut places his Narrator in a situation which recalls the cadre of Arthurian romance. He encounters *Bonneürté* and her messenger as by accident or in some miraculous way and is observed by her, unaware of her presence. For a much longer time *Bonneürté*'s identity remains hidden from the Narrator and the reader; like so many figures in Chrétien de Troyes, her name is revealed toward the end of the story, at her great moment of triumph (3851). She resembles the fairy-queen of the Other World, potentially a dangerous enemy. After having endured threats and insults, the hero metaphorically undergoes an ordeal, a parody of sacred combat, expiates his sins, and is delivered from enchantment. The court is free to revel in joy.

These romance motifs have been introduced into *JRN* entirely for the sake of comedy. In fact, the Narrator takes no risks, fights no battles, has engaged upon no covenant. A mighty hunter of rabbits, his only prowess is verbal. He defends the wrong side (from the courtly point of view) and loses in the end. Fair ladies harm rather than help him, and his ordeal turns out to be a joke. With the adventure motif, as with the trial and love casuistry, we see the hand of a master of comedy. Machaut demonstrates that men are foolish because they cannot live up to the courtly ideal, and that they are foolish to try to live up to an ideal which itself is untrue to life. The Narrator is a foil to the ladies, just as they serve as foils to him.

Up to now I have not discussed at all the first part of *JRN*, those five hundred or so lines which describe the Narrator's experiences during the plague winter of 1349. This section of the poem has received a great deal of attention from the critics and has been praised for its extraordinary realism. [5] However, scholars have wor-

---

[5] Alfred Coville, "Poèmes historiques de l'avènement de Philippe VI de Valois au traité de Calais (1328-1360)," in *Histoire littéraire de la France* 38 (1949): 259-333, esp. p. 330: "la peste, décrite avec des traits vigoureux et réalistes qui font de cette peinture une des plus remarquables pages de notre littérature du moyen âge." Also Hoepffner, 1: lxvi-lxvii; and Machabey, *Guillaume de Machault: La Vie et l'Œuvre musical*, 1: 43-45. For

ried about an apparent disharmony between the poem's two seg-
ments: the Narrator's experiences during the Plague (locked in his
house all winter), and those of the following spring (forced to defend
himself before a "court of love"). The "realism" of Part 1 forms a
striking contrast to the more romantic, allegorical, seemingly friv-
olous artificiality of Part 2. Boccaccio provides a frame for his
Decameron which also treats the Black Death. But, according to
these scholars, Boccaccio fuses courtly and naturalistic elements
into a synthesis of universal validity, whereas Machaut is left with
two unconnected, incongruous fragments. [6]

In my opinion, it is quite legitimate to provide an apparently
realistic frame for a romantic or allegorical tale. Part 1, the frame,
then acts as an authenticating device for events told in Part 2.
Machaut may also be telling us that, though the real world exudes
plague, religious fanaticism, civil war, and death, within it may yet
be found the joy of King Charles's court. Beauty exists, and it is
our duty to seek it out. Court poetry and the way of life it exalts
provide resistance to decadence, to the monstrosities perpetrated in
contemporary reality. [7] Or the plague scene may rank as an ironic
commentary on the artificially effete courtly society depicted in
Part 2. Although Machaut does not flail out at courtly orthodoxy
in the manner of Jean de Meun, he undermines it from within, an
attitude not all that different from Boccaccio's. With both writers
a contrast in tone between frame and narrative kernel (Jürgen
Grimm, p. 146, calls it the "einleitende Kontrastfunktion") has an
important role: creating irony. Both masters tell us of the beauty
and fragility of existence, that we must view the world with humane,
civilized detachment.

In any event, I submit that Part 1 constitutes not only a semi-
realistic frame set in contrast to the central episode but also an

---

Machaut's place in a tradition of plague literature dating back to Homer
and the Bible, see Jürgen Grimm, *Die literarische Darstellung der Pest in der
Antike und in der Romania* (Munich, 1965), esp. pp. 143-54. Grimm
emphasizes the medieval, nonrealistic, purely aesthetic side of *JRN*.

[6] For example, Grace Frank, "French Literature in the Fourteenth Cen-
tury," in *The Forward Movement of the Fourteenth Century*, ed. Francis Lee
Utley (Columbus, Ohio, 1961), pp. 61-77, esp. p. 65; Charles Muscatine,
Chaucer and the French Tradition (Berkeley-Los Angeles, 1957), pp. 100-101.

[7] Poirion, *Le Poète et le Prince*, chapt. 1, raises this idea concerning
lyric production in the later Middle Ages.

integral section of the total narrative. The calamities striking France in the winter of 1349—flame, tempest, earthquake, war, plague— are manifestations of contemporary reality but also conform to a traditional medieval motif, the universe upside-down. The world is rife with corruption and decay; man has wasted God-given bounty. The Narrator flails at the abuses of his time, then demonstrates how God punishes man for his sins. All four elements that man has corrupted are now used by God to scourge him: earthquake, the flame of war, poisoning of water by Jews and of the air by the plague. If the universe has now decayed *(mundus senescit)*, in an earlier, happier age men lived at peace with God and themselves; when I was young, says the Narrator, the world was good and no such calamities befell *(Laudatio temporis acti)*.

The *Mundus senescens* reflects a comparable state within the Narrator. Examples of "pathetic fallacy" were by no means rare in the Middle Ages. The outer world and inner man were united by a bond; the microcosm of man's individual destiny and the macrocosm of world history were one in God's eyes. We hear repeatedly that the Narrator suffers from melancholia (37, 106, 109, 115, 142, 454, 543, 591, 715, 1336, 1429), a condition that was linked to an excess of black bile in the body, under the influence of the Greater Infortune, the planet Saturn, and matching autumn or winter in the life of the year and old age in man's life. [8] It is no coincidence, then, that the Narrator becomes melancholic in autumn; meditates on the calamities of an old, decaying world set against the happy times of his youth; evokes the historical personage Guillaume de Machaut, who was about forty-nine years old when the action of the poem supposedly took place; and later in the story opposes the doctrine of young love espoused by *Bonneürté*. Let us not forget that Guillaume de Lorris banished both *Tristesce* and *Vielleice* from the Garden of Mirth. A melancholic man is presumed antisocial and prone to cowardice and the sin of *acedia* (especially rampant in those who practice the contemplative life), as much a state of sadness as of sloth. Hence, the Narrator spends all winter alone, hiding in his cold, gloomy room, dreading the plague and, later on, the prospect of defending himself in court. A melancholic man is also

---

[8] See the excellent monograph by Henrik Heger, *Die Melancholie bei den französischen Lyrikern des Spätmittelalters* (Bonn, 1967).

subject to brusque changes in temper, hence the Narrator's oscillation between optimism and despair in Part 1 and between deference and insult during the trial.

Another theme common to both parts of *JRN* is that of madness. In Part 1 the world has gone insane. The Flagellants are the most notorious example of unreason, though no doubt Machaut ranged makers of war and the miscreant Jews under the same heading. Earthquake, tempest, and landslide signify that the rational order of the universe has been undermined. We know that the medievals considered a tendency to madness proper to the melancholic man and unhappy lover. The Narrator's actions during that winter, his sudden changes in temper and enforced self-isolation, hardly reinforce our confidence in his mental equilibrium. Although in Part 2 he shows no symptoms of *folie* other than having contradicted *Bonneürté,* insanity (generally related to Eros) crops up during the trial. The Narrator tells of a clerk of Orléans who went mad for twenty years, a dog whose rabies was cured by removing a worm in his tongue, and a knight who cut off his finger out of gallantry. Although they do not wish to denigrate *fin' amor,* the ladies too cite examples of famous people who, in *l'Ovide moralisé,* are driven mad by love: Dido, Ariadne, and Medea, among others.

Melancholy and insanity are linked to death. According to the Narrator, God has unleashed Death upon the world. Nine of every ten people perish from the plague, and still others from wars, natural disaster, or because Jews poisoned the water. Fear of dying impels the Narrator to remain in seclusion all winter. Later, during the trial, we are told one story after another in which a lover dies of a broken heart or commits suicide over the presumed death of a loved one (the maiden of Paris, Pyramus, Thisbe, Hero, Tristan, Iseut, and the Châtelaine de Vergi's lover), because his passion has been betrayed (Dido, Ariadne, the Châtelaine de Vergi), or who perishes for some other reason related to love (the swallow's mate, Leander, Dido's unborn child, Jason's children). Then, at the end of the poem, for a bereaved lady the Narrator composes *Le Lay de Plour,* which contains the traditional imagery associated with this theme: rivers of tears, a great tree pulled out by its roots, and the lady sobbing over her lover's coffin.

The fundamental question of *JRB*—whether infidelity or death is a greater obstacle to love—is pushed to one side, but the death theme contributes to *JRN* nonetheless. On the one hand, the historical calamities in Part 1 anticipate ironically the rather artificial *Liebestöde* of Part 2, derived from romance and *l'Ovide moralisé*. On the other hand, death remains a terrifying, agonizing force in the universe. The Narrator is wrong to denigrate its power. Love and death are bound together, in the literary tradition (Virgil, Ovid, *Tristan*) or in everyday life. Not only, as the Freudians have demonstrated, is the sexual act itself both a refusal to die and an anticipation of dying, but Western man has converted Eros itself into a death-wish. [9] For all the humor in *JRN,* Machaut never lets us forget that love is accompanied by pain and death, and can never escape from either of them.

The Narrator's answer to his predicament lies in an attempt to avoid love and death. He seeks refuge from the plague and contests the rules of courtly orthodoxy. In fact, however, he has spent the winter in a sort of prison (485). With the coming of spring, season of love and sunshine, he breaks out of his cell. From the immobility of containment within four walls, he proceeds to ride to the chase. But he succeeds no better in the world of life than he had in the world of death. Lady *Bonneürté* summons the Narrator to court where, terrified, he again is overcome by melancholia and must defend himself in hostile surroundings. This second "imprisonment" is, to be sure, presented ironically, in the comic vein. Because the Narrator remained alone in winter, then in springtime went hunting alone with no concern for others, he is now forced to share human company. From the author's viewpoint, the court is a good prison, beneficial to the social order. A contrast is drawn between savage, dreary, cold, wintry solitude and the elegant, sunny, warm, spring-like court of love. Machaut evokes the world of the court in laudatory if ironic terms, as a possible refuge in a *mundus senescens.*

The Narrator's opposition to *fin' amor* is presented as both valid and invalid. Love is a powerful force; we may eschew the excesses of love-madness and the irrelevant, artificial clichés of an exaggerated code, but we should not reject love altogether. Common sense and wisdom *(sagesse)* require some form of accommodation to so vital

---

[9] Despite carelessness in his use of sources and an unfortunate infatuation with the Catharist heresy, Denis de Rougemont's *L'amour et l'Occident* (Paris, 1939) contains much of value for the specialist as well as the general reader. It remains one of the seminal books of our time.

a force in nature and polite society. The poet, more than other men, must avoid hubris and learn to accept the best the world has to offer, since his place ultimately lies, as Poirion has shown, in the world and at the court.

From Parts 1 to 2 winter gives way to spring, isolation to the court, Saturn to Venus, and death to rebirth. With an end to the plague the Narrator hears a fanfare of musical instruments, for men are no longer dying. People celebrate the return of spring with games and pastimes, the hunt, and a mock trial. The trial reflects the archetypal struggle between the old and the new, dying winter and the birth of spring. In this combat the mature, antisocial, melancholic Narrator represents, against his will perhaps, the old. His aristocratic patrons permit him to enter their society. He serves as a scapegoat, whose presence contributes to the festivities, since he must lose and his views be defeated. Death and the calamities of a *mundus senescens* are overcome at King Charles's court. Spring wins out; the rebel is converted or, at any rate, subdued; and his sentence delivered with laughter and joy.

The Narrator has been tried for statements made in *JRB,* that is, for poetry written in the past. He is then sentenced to create a new work of art, *Le Lay de Plour,* in the future. In the present he takes pride in the quantity and variety of books he has written (881-900) and is cured of melancholia, a trait ascribed to poets. *Bonneürté* always thinks of the Narrator as an artist, whether she praises him for studying hard at night or castigates him for what he wrote years ago. The *JRN* as a whole is a palinode, a recantation in the medieval tradition. But, unlike Andreas Capellanus, Petrarch, Juan Ruiz, and the author of the *Canterbury Tales,* Machaut does not renounce love poetry in favor of a higher truth, the only Truth and Love for a canon at Reims. Instead, following Nicole Bozon and anticipating Jean le Fèvre and the Chaucer of the *Legend of Good Women,* he recants misogyny for *fin' amor,* the inspiration of poets, and he continues to write. In crime, punishment, and all that falls between, two hundred years before Du Bellay and Ronsard, five hundred years before Vigny and Hugo, in French letters we find the poet as hero.

Although Guillaume de Machaut pretends to recount a trial scene in all seriousness, in fact he regards the proceedings with more than a little skepticism. Evidence can be twisted by either side; both plaintiff and defendant lose their tempers. But what difference does it make, once we realize that the author is not primarily interested in an ideological war of the sexes but in the experiences of men and women as human beings and their comic interrelations in society? The *JRN* radiates wit, charm, good humor, and the smile of a man of the world. Behind *Le Lay de Plour,* behind the trial of *JRN,* behind the Narrator's *persona* stands a master of irony, who pulls the strings and creates a dynamic, believable, richly comic world.

7. LE CONFORT D'AMI

The Narrator comforts his Friend, a prisoner. He
tells stories of famous people who suffered from
injustice but later triumphed, and he offers counsel
on how to live.

ON APRIL 5, 1356, John II, king of France, seized his enemy,
Charles II, king of Navarre, who remained John's prisoner until
November 8, 1357. Within this period of a year and a half, Guillaume
de Machaut wrote *Le Confort d'Ami*.[1] Like *JRN,* Machaut's new
dit was composed for Charles of Navarre. Unlike Machaut's earlier
tales, however, *CA* is devoted entirely to a moral exhortation directed
to Friend (King Charles); we do not find a narrative frame which
encloses or sets off the didactic. It is as if *DV, RF,* and *DA* had
been reduced to explanatory lectures on love and fortune by the
God of Love, Lady Hope, and the *DA* Narrator respectively. Furthermore, and this is perhaps an even more significant departure, for
the first time in his career Machaut devotes a long poem to a subject
other than love. Although Friend is said to be in love and his
amatory problems are touched upon from time to time, the Narrator's primary concern lies elsewhere.

The *CA* contains two main elements: a *consolatio,* designed to
solace King Charles in particular and, more generally, all who have
suffered from political injustice; and a *regimen principum,* an educa-
tional treatise on morals, ethics, free will, love, politics, war, and
affairs of state. As a *consolatio,* Machaut's tale participates in a

---

[1] 3,978 lines, followed by a twenty-six-line passage, a reply from *Ami,*
which should not be attributed to Machaut; ed. Hoepffner, 3: 1-142 (cited
hereafter as *CA*).

tradition which goes back to Boethius (for a list of medieval *remedia Fortunae,* see Chapter 3, p. 57). As a mirror for princes, *CA* follows in the wake of treatises by Jonas of Orléans, Godfrey of Viterbo, John of Salisbury, Giraldus Cambrensis, Helinand de Froidmont, Gilbert of Tornai, Vincent of Beauvais, William Perrault, Thomas Aquinas, Aegidius Romanus, Robert de Blois, and Watriquet de Couvin. [2] The *dit's* originality derives largely from the fact that the two elements—*consolatio* and *speculum*—are combined in one work and because, written for a particular prince, it treats his immediate problems.

Machaut adheres to tradition by placing his *dit* in a Christian Context. It is in fact his first long poem which contains any overt religious inspiration. The *RF* was strictly secular in nature and, although it used *De Consolatione Philosophiae* as a source, avoided metaphysical problems raised by Boethius. But in *CA* secular philosophy and a specifically Christian ethos are combined. The result, a *consolatio* both secular and religious, recaptures some of the original Boethian spirit, if not its extraordinary aesthetic power, and paves the way for later vernacular treatises by Christine de Pisan, Alain Chartier, and Michault Taillevent, among others.

As he had done in *DA* and *JRN,* Machaut livens up *CA* by telling stories of famous people. From *l'Ovide moralisé* he relates the legends of Orpheus and Eurydice and the Abduction of Proserpina; he also alludes to Paris and Helen, Hercules and Deianira, and the Revolt of the Titans. More striking, no doubt, is the poet's use of sacred history. In keeping with the religious orientation of *CA,* he retells the stories of Susanna and the Elders, Nebuchadnezzar's dream, Daniel in the burning fiery furnace, Belshazzar's Vision, Daniel in the lion's den, and the conversion of Manasseh; briefer mention is made of Mattathias, Joseph, Job, and Christ. Machaut's prime source is the Book of Daniel, although he also translates or adapts passages from 2 Chronicles, 1 Maccabees, Proverbs, Job, and the Wisdom of Solomon (Hoepffner, 3:ii-vi). These *exempla,* whether of Greco-Roman or Hebraic provenance, help substantiate the

---

[2] See Josef Röder, *Das Fürstenbild in der mittelalterlichen Fürstenspiegeln auf französischem Boden* (Emsdetten, 1933); and Lester Kruger Born, "The Perfect Prince: A Study in Thirteenth- and Fourteenth-Century Ideals," *Speculum* 3 (1928): 470-504.

doctrine he propounds, contribute an aura of dignity, and, last but not least, provide variety and a change of pace in what otherwise would be a tedious poem.

Ernest Hoepffner, while granting *CA* some qualities as literature —elegant versification, precise expression, appropriateness of imagery, lively narration, and judicious commonsense remarks of an intellectual nature—nonetheless proclaims that "Trop souvent, malheureusement, ces qualités sont noyées dans un flot d'idées impersonnelles, de lieux communs et de banalités qui ne rendent pas toujours des plus attrayantes la lecture de ce long ouvrage" (3:xviii). To some extent I agree with Hoepffner. Of course, an ideological poem cannot be judged by the same criteria as for a work of fiction. It will not suffice to condemn nonimaginative literature for being nonimaginative. I admit that Machaut's forte lies in the realm of sophisticated narrative, such as *DL* and *JRN*. He does not possess the energy, slashing wit, mastery of abstract concepts, and simple talent for vulgarization we find in Cicero, Jean de Meun, Montaigne, Bossuet, and Diderot. However, despite certain obvious deficiencies, the medieval public appreciated the *dit*; it ranks second only to *JRB* in the number of manuscript copies which have survived (Hoepffner, 3:xviii-xix). No doubt the medievals appreciated its *sapience* in a way foreign to our modern perspective.

It has been suggested that *CA* can be divided into three parts: 1) a religious *consolatio* (1-1660); 2) moral counsel applying specifically to Friend's imprisonment (1661-2872); 3) practical advice to princes in general (2873-3944).[3] I am not sure how valid such distinctions are. Parts 2 and 3 contain religious exhortation, although the Christian theme is not as preponderant as in Part 1. Part 2 also contains much general advice to princes (do not overeat, lose your temper, or display melancholy) we should expect to find in Part 3. In my opinion, in all three sections narrative *exempla* present comparable themes which are then developed or commented on in the more strictly didactic passages.

The theme of justice and injustice is central to the first two sections of *CA*. The Elders accuse Susanna of adultery Daniel,

---

[3] Hoepffner, 3: ii; also Georges Becker, "Guillaume de Machaut," in *Dictionnaire des Lettres françaises: Le Moyen Age* (Paris, 1964), pp. 353-58, esp. p. 356.

even though he interprets Nebuchadnezzar's dream satisfactorily, later is placed in a burning fiery furnace and in the lions' den. Their sufferings take place during the period termed the Babylonian Captivity, when the Children of Israel suffered at the hands of foreign oppressors. Manasseh the renegade is incarcerated by his enemies and taken to Babylon. And Pluto holds captive Eurydice, Proserpina, and the Titans. Machaut points out that King Charles of Navarre endures a similar fate: "Tu es pris de tes annemis, / Mais trop as estroite prison" (1652-53), and that his captor, King John of France, and so many others are prisoners of the English. Sometimes the victim deserves punishment, but more often (Susanna, Daniel, Eurydice, Proserpina, John, and probably Charles) they are innocent. Each case is a striking instance of the disproportion between man's actions and his rewards in the secular world.

A prime cause for injustice appears to be evil, wicked judges. Because in the monarchical system so much power is concentrated into the hands of one person, whenever an evil man is made king, the whole machinery of justice grinds to a halt. However, in *CA* the judge and king have jurisdiction over sacred as well as lay affairs; God's vicars on earth, they play the role of priest as well as potentate. An evil judge will defy God's law, and any miscarriage of justice is an affront to the proper functioning of religion as well as the state. Susanna's judges are false priests (195). These lecherous old men not only commit the capital sin of *luxuria* but also seek to corrupt others and to betray them by means of calumny. Nebuchadnezzar casts Daniel's companions into the furnace only after they refuse to bow down before a graven image. Nebuchadnezzar's son Belshazzar also builds idols. King Darius of the Persians has himself declared God and demands that the people worship him. Darius's hubris is then surpassed by Manasseh, a Hebrew who leads his own people into apostasy. Guillaume de Machaut himself, in the Narrator's voice, holds idolatry to be *cornardie* (1288); he intervenes in the narrative to deliver an eloquent diatribe against the practice (1283-1344). His emotional stance does not appear out of place since, in *CA,* a king or judge commits evil only after he himself has in some way placed himself above the Divinity, and good people are mistreated because they, unlike these kings, refuse to betray God.

Belshazzar profanes the gold vessels taken from the Temple of Solomon. His father, Nebuchadnezzar, the man who originally seized the temple treasure, builds idols of pure gold, as will Darius. Apparently obsessed by riches, Nebuchadnezzar and Belshazzar form a striking contrast to Daniel, who is content to starve in the lions' den and remains indifferent to Belshazzar's offers of money: "Rois, de tes dons ne de ta terre / N'ay cure" (781-82). Friend too once had all the material things a man can desire (gold, precious stones, money, horses, fine raiment), but, the Narrator tells us, in spite of, or rather on account of, these things, he forgot God.

A king commits evil either because he himself is evil or because, meaning well, he has been corrupted by wicked councillors. After princes and satraps, jealous of Daniel's titles, persuade Darius to enact a decree they know he cannot obey, people denounce Hananiah, Mishael, and Azariah to Nebuchadnezzar. The evil courtier, the sower of discord, the envious, jealous troublemaker is blamed for much iniquity in the world. A political *losengier,* who corresponds to the *vilain* of *fin' amor,* he plays a comparably negative role in the governmental sphere.

To underscore his vision of a disjointed, upside-down world, Machaut creates a pattern of demonic imagery (I use Northrop Frye's sense of the term). The false king or judge is portrayed as a tyrant—authoritarian, greedy, irrational. He is associated with Babylon, with wild beasts (wolves, lions, black horses), or with storm and tempest; he razes the countryside and slaughters his servitors like a butcher on the farm. The innocent victim trembles with downcast eyes and drinks bitter tears as he bows under the winds of Fortune. He is persecuted by fire, image of choler, an attribute of the planet Mars and of Satan in Hell, or he is condemned to be devoured by lions, who also represent pride, anger, and lust. In any case, he is rendered immobile in a prison, separated from the community by hard, impenetrable walls, and sacrificed to bright metallic idols. [4] Even Susanna's lovely garden, a *locus amoenus* appropriate to love, cannot preserve her from the Elders, who enter the grove, spy her out, and seek to defile her in a cruel travesty on *fin' amor.* Proserpina too was gathering flowers in a *locus amoenus* when Pluto

---

[4] This is the kind of imagery analyzed by Bachelard in *La Terre et les Rêveries de la Volonté* (Paris, 1948).

carried her off. Even though he conquered Hell, Orpheus fails to bring back Eurydice and is later slain; Deianira involuntarily kills Hercules; Paris and Helen's love ends in disaster. From a world of light and joy Susanna, Proserpina, Eurydice, Daniel, Daniel's companions, and Manasseh are plunged into darkness, "En une chartre moult obscure, / Pleinne de pueur et d'ordure" (1413-14). Pluto himself is said to be blacker than Hell. And do not a dark prison, a dark jailer, and Babylon symbolize death and the terrors of the Inferno?

Machaut writes of tragedy as the medievals conceived it: the fall from high to low estate of a man who had the folly to commit himself to Fortune. In this poem, in which Boethius is cited twice (1904, 3752), the author returns to the theme of *RF*. Although he cannot release Friend from prison, he will console him and all men at grips with Fortune. First of all, says the Narrator, Friend's sufferings are his own fault; he used to be rich and powerful, but then he forgot God. God is punishing him for sins Friend committed in youth, just as he did to Manasseh. Friend's tribulations, like Manasseh's and Nebuchadnezzar's, form part of God's divine plan and, in the best Boethian tradition, will dissuade him from ever again committing evil. Since Friend had too much material happiness in youth, says the Narrator, he now pays for former extravagance. Friend has the right to consider his former prosperity a blessing, for surely its memory will console him in present misery. He can also take comfort in the fact that all men are borne up, then down, on Fortune's wheel. Indeed, a prince has no business grieving the loss of worldly honors, since he never possessed them in the first place. He may hoard riches but will be separated from them when he dies, if not before. As Boethius and Jean de Meun proclaimed, true nobility is to be found in the heart, an attribute of a man's virtue, not wealth or birth. Unlike riches, virtue is not subject to Fortune. Man has freedom of choice: he can choose the way of virtue or of wealth and honors. And when Fortune lays him low, he can show resignation in the face of adversity. Job, Mattathias, Christ, Socrates, Orpheus, Ceres, Proserpina, Paris, Helen, and Hercules are cited for their loyalty to Hope. Since Fortune is an extension of divine providence, man should appreciate that her actions serve his own best interests. Offered a choice between damnable despair, a sin against the Holy Spirit, and Hope, the sweetest of the theological virtues, the Christian prince's choice is clear.

As in *RF*, however, Machaut's final argument is based upon the belief that things are not as bad as they appear, and that it is possible for a prince to be virtuous and to regain happiness in the world. We discover that Nebuchadnezzar and Darius are not as wicked as the other tyrants; convinced of the error of their ways, they restore Daniel to his former glory. In fact, Darius wanted to help him all along but could not. Daniel tells Belshazzar how God humbled Nebuchadnezzar until the latter repented, then restored him to glory. After having abandoned his faith, Manasseh also returns to the way of the Lord. In Machaut's own day, John of Bohemia, the arbiter in *JRB*, is cited as an exemplar of the good king, a man whose greatest conquest is of honor. The Narrator saw him on his campaigns; he can testify that John suffered terribly in the field but persevered without ever losing hope. We are even informed that Friend's judge is not evil. This anonymous personage (King John the Good of France) is proclaimed loyal, wise, truth-seeking, and compassionate. Friend should have confidence in him, for he will pardon Friend's wrongdoings, if indeed any have been committed (1830-35). Later, King John is referred to by name and compared favorably to seven of the Nine Worthies (Judas Maccabeus, Hector, Caesar, Alexander, Charlemagne, Godfrey of Bouillon, and Arthur) as well as to Ajax, Achilles, Troilus, Gawain, Tristan, Lancelot, Roland, Ogier, Guillaume, Oliver, and Pompey (2795-807). Surely such a master is more reliable than Belshazzar or Susanna's lecherous Elders.

Fortune is discomfited because God himself ensures the ultimate triumph of right over wrong. As in Racine's *Athalie*, although the deity never steps directly into the narrative, he may be nonetheless considered the protagonist. In the first 1,000 lines of *CA* he is alluded to by name forty-three times. [5] The first piece of advice the Narrator gives Friend is to love God. The idolater is a fool because one God only created the four elements and governs the universe, has counted the grains of sand on the shore and the drops of water in the sea,

---

[5] Lines 3, 10, 19, 41, 49, 54, 82, 162, 167, 173, 216, 257, 273, 293, 318, 326, 334, 345, 353, 363, 382, 387, 397, 422, 464, 590, 596, 600, 602, 614, 626, 691, 760, 785, 823, 843, 855, 858, 873, 883, 904, 913, 975.

and has named the stars. God is the Good Judge, omniscient and omnipotent, who will confound false judges who speak in his name but corrupt his law. At critical moments Susanna and Manasseh pray and are saved. The infant Daniel's intervention on Susanna's behalf is indeed a miracle. Daniel and his friends are preserved from certain death, and Habakkuk transported miraculously to Daniel's side. The Narrator urges Friend to be comforted by these stories of innocent prisoners whom God saved. God loves you, says the Narrator, and never will abandon you. All his children will find comfort, greater than mortal man can give.

Friend is also consoled in his love life. The captive prince, separated from his lady, suffers pangs of desire. Machaut dramatizes this old courtly theme by delivering in Friend's voice a moving *complainte* (2057-102). But the Narrator replies that where desire does not exist, love is absent too. It is better to love and be separated from one's beloved than not to love at all or to have been forgotten. Obstacles are considered beneficial to a relationship; they should be accepted, even honored, for the good they bring. Of course, while in prison Friend must adore his lady and keep her image present in his heart. *Souvenir*'s daughter, *Douce Pensee*, seconded by *Bon Espoir*, will help him. The Narrator also refers to the *compaingnie amoureuse* (2260) in Friend's heart, a Trinity comprising hope, the lady's image, and the lover's own self. But for *Esperence*, Orpheus would never have conquered hell, Hercules given battle for Deianira, Paris kidnapped Helen. At least in the short run, all three classical figures succeed in their endeavors. So too Friend is granted an immediate consolation—the expectation of victory. Hope and the reward of love's mercy are not separate in the lover's mind. He has the right to seek both; if one is granted, he can expect the other to follow.

In love and politics the greatest of virtues is *mesure*. As a wooer and as a political prisoner, Friend should avoid both despair and facile optimism; as a practicing ruler, he should avoid excessive desire for power, money, and conquest. King John of Bohemia is praised for *souffissance* (moderation), especially in money matters. Daniel too is left cold by offers which entail sacrificing principle. The ideal ruler ought not to give vent to his emotions upon receipt of good or bad news:

> 1754 Pour nouvelle qu'on li aporte,
> Pour povreté ne pour richesse,
> Pour grant joie ne pour tristesse
> Ne doit muer qu'il ne soit fermes
> Com Socratès.

A prince ought never to fear excess of honor, however. He should hold the mirror of honor before his eyes, seeking its reflection and perfecting himself in its image. Honor, the best of flowers, smells as sweet as a rose, while dishonor is worse than the loss of one's eyes or teeth. God tests Friend in the same way as he did Susanna, Daniel, Manasseh, and Orpheus. Only after Friend has proved his worth as a prince of men and servitor to God can he claim that title to nobility found in the heart.

Friend is taught the practical side of kingship. Sections 2 and 3 of *CA* contain advice on politics, ethics, finance, war, personal hygiene, and etiquette. According to Hoepffner, of these precepts, "quelques-unes sont d'une naïveté amusante." He also comments, referring to Part 3: "Sauf dans la partie consacrée à l'art de la guerre, qui forme un ensemble compact (vv. 3097-492), il est impossible de découvrir ici quelque disposition logique ou quelque idée dominante. Tous ces préceptes sont amenés au petit bonheur, sans la moindre vélléité de composition" (Hoepffner, 3: vi, x).

In my opinion, Hoepffner, although not entirely mistaken, has exaggerated the absence of structural coherence in *CA*. In sections 2 and 3 these practical counsels may be organized into thematic bundles which reinforce themes illustrated by the *exempla* and developed in the more philosophical portions of the *dit*.

Women. Friend is urged to prevent his soldiers from rape and to punish rapists severely. The Narrator advises him, in accordance with the laws of chivalry, to honor all women, married or single, of high or low degree, especially widows and nuns. He also advises him against lechery and divorce. Machaut thus proposes a line of conduct in stark contrast to the practices of Susanna's judges and Pluto. If Friend follows the Narrator's advice, he can expect a just reward from his own beloved.

Gluttony. The prince is advised not to eat too much, to lead regular hours, to speak in honest and measured tones, and to refrain from malicious gossip. By so doing he will avoid committing sins of the tongue. Belshazzar's orgies with the vessels of the Temple brought him to ruin. Daniel, on the other hand, instead of becoming food to the lions, relies on spiritual sustenance and, by a miracle, is supplied with natural food as well.

Sloth. A good prince takes the trouble to keep well groomed. He does not hide behind his castle walls nor does he cringe in fear when beaten or outnumbered. And if no war is to be found nearby, he will help his friends or seek adventure abroad. By avoiding sloth and its accompanying traits, melancholy and cowardice, he practices the most important virtue in a *miles dominans:* prowess.

Honor. Friend is advised to act in accordance with the code of chivalry, especially in time of war. A good prince never breaks a truce; he always gives way if his adversary is morally in the right; he never tortures or executes an adversary who has fallen into his hands. The Narrator reminds Friend that a vengeful man can neither eat nor sleep in peace and that there is no excuse for unnecessary violence. By following these precepts, Friend will establish himself as a good ruler, in contrast to Nebuchadnezzar, Belshazzar, Darius, and Pluto, who betrayed their public trust.

Sovereignty. The good ruler maintains a proper relationship with his subjects, that is, a fitting exercise of sovereignty. He does not exploit them as a tyrant nor is he remiss in the proper exercise of his rights. In wartime he refuses counsel of clerics or callow youths but sends for wise, experienced veterans, from foreign parts if necessary. He wins the love and respect of his men by being available to them, not hidden away like a sacred relic. And he never exploits the poor. Once again, Daniel and John of Bohemia are the models to be followed, the Old Testament tyrants to be avoided.

Riches. Friend is urged to earn his men's loyalty by tangible manifestations of largess, not to exploit his subjects nor debase the state's currency. He should banish from court ambitious spendthrifts, who adopt the latest modes in masculine attire. Although, because of his royal state, Friend must own beautiful clothes, he should flaunt them only on ceremonial occasions. Since one's financial status changes like the face of the moon and, like the moon, is subject to Dame Fortune, a good king renders equal justice to rich and poor alike. In fact, if a poor man criticizes the king, he should not be punished, for he cannot be held responsible. The Old Testament kings were guilty of miserliness, a form of *cupiditas* which places love for things above man and God. A miser will never win battles nor the love and respect of his men. Machaut depicts the way of life these evil rulers lead in terms of reification and commerce (cf. pp. 134, 137-38). Potentates are concerned only with amassing wealth and immobilizing it for their own selfish purposes, never with distributing it to help the community. A medium of exchange, transformed into an object precious in its own right, loses its natural function. Sovereignty is now based on structures of monetary exchange, not loyalty or the social hierarchy. Human beings become subservient to an inanimate object, whether it be gold coin, courtiers' fancy clothes, or a graven image. They are rewarded to the extent that they second the tyrant's obsession and thus dehumanize their own lives. In the end, this thing, which has been endowed with a simulacrum of life, is worshiped as a god, and the men who worship it deny their immortality by denying God and parodying in so blasphemous a way his cult. *Cupiditas,* in all its connotations, is the negation of *Caritas.* The ruler who constructs an idol of gold or exploits people for miserly ends will harm good servitors, be they Daniel or Charles of Navarre, as he harms his Creator. On the other hand, by using his wealth to fortify the state and reward his subjects, and by moderating his own desires, the good prince proves his capacity to love God and man *(Caritas).*

Religion. Most important of all, the Narrator advises Friend never to go to sleep or make war in a state of mortal sin, divorce or repudiate his wife, gamble, or fornicate. He must defend widows, orphans, and the church, pray to God, and seek his guidance in all things. A magnanimous man to his subjects, he remains ever humble in the sight of God. Although a commonplace in medieval literature, such advice has a special function in a poem which speaks of Daniel, Susanna, Belshazzar, and Darius. The *CA* is a mirror for Christian princes; Machaut focuses on the ruler in Christian society, who serves God, remains subservient to his wishes, and is supported by him in his infinite wisdom.

We ought not to be surprised at the variety of precepts in *CA,* of divergent scope and importance. When a course of study is prescribed for a hero of romance, formal book-learning and ethical indoctrination are mentioned in the same breath with the chase, falconry, field sports, war, languages, music, and court graces. [6] The *corpus sanum* which coexists with a *mens sana* was considered no less important in the Middle Ages than in the time of Rabelais and Montaigne. Machaut also follows the *De Regimine Principum* tradition in which personal hygiene, etiquette, warnings against bribery and corruption, preparedness for war, taxation, and the choice of good councillors, a wife, and a doctor are treated with the same gravity as the philosophy of kingship.

It should never be forgotten that these treatises (and by extension *CA*) are manuals in the art of politics. Friend is advised to keep well groomed and neither overindulge in food and drink nor lead irregular hours because only thus can he retain his subjects' respect. Honor and largess are political instruments which help preserve the state. Friend should treat his enemies fairly, never break a truce or despise a seemingly weak adversary, always maintain good relations with at least one of his neighbors, listen to his advisers, and be willing to change his mind—because such actions are morally commendable and because they pay off in the domain of *Realpolitik*.

Seemingly trivial matters assume importance because the king is a mirror for his people in much the same sense that the treatise is a mirror for the king. A model to be imitated, his own person, public and private, has to be without fault. And since he is the soul of the Body Politic, the proper functioning of the kingship is presumed to depend on his conduct. To be a good king he must first of all live virtuously. In other words, the ideal king is an ideal man; only an ideal man will make a good king; and only with such a king can the state function at its best.

All these questions—administrative, financial, military, ethical, domestic, and the various biblical and classical *exempla*—deal with the prince as a man. His personal conduct is the dominant criterion which will determine his success or failure as a ruler, the future of his state, the welfare of his subjects, and his salvation or damnation in the eyes of God. From beginning to end Machaut urges the prince to virtue and dissuades him from vice.

---

[6] See Madeleine Pelner Cosman, *The Education of the Hero in Arthurian Romance* (Chapel Hill, N. C., 1966).

In terms of character development, *CA* is more static than any of Machaut's other tales. Although certain minor figures (Nebuchadnezzar, Manasseh) are transformed in the course of the poem, Friend himself is not. He lies in prison in the beginning and at the end. Although perhaps the public has reason to assume that the Narrator's counsel will spur Friend into action, that he will find consolation now and rule wisely in the future, we do not see this evolution take place. However, we do see the process that will lead to Friend's eventual though problematic transformation: the instruction he receives from the Narrator. As so often in Machaut the hero's education is a dominant theme. For the medievals, as for the men of classical antiquity and the Renaissance, an ideal ruler possesses strength and courage, on the one hand, and prudence, experience, and wisdom, on the other—*fortitudo et sapientia.* As Fulkes II the Good is supposed to have said to King Louis IV (quoted by Giraldus Cambrensis and Vincent of Beauvais, among others): "Noveritis, domine, quia rex illiteratus est asinus coronatus." Already by the twelfth century, he who wishes to rule must first learn to know himself and others, to become a *miles clericus.* In vernacular fiction, too, we find the brave, wise hero, expert in arms, letters, and love (a good lover because he is both *chevalier* and *clerc*), a *topos* which received its finest literary statement in *Flamenca.* By the late Middle Ages learning was accepted as both a knightly and clerical ideal, appropriate to men of either estate called upon to occupy a place of leadership in society. [7]

In the three parts of *CA, exempla* are taken from scripture, *l'Ovide moralisé,* and contemporary history (John of Bohemia) respectively. They evolve according to a pattern: from ancient to modern, from sacred to secular, from theoretical to practical. Although while in captivity Friend is compelled to adopt the *vita contemplativa,* his normal state in life is the *vita activa,* to which he will presumably return. Hence he is given practical advice in addition to theory, and his training includes subjects placed by

---

[7] Curtius, *Europäische Literatur und lateinisches Mittelalter,* chapt. 9; Vittorio Russo, " 'Cavalliers' e 'clercs,' " *Filologia Romanza* 6 (1959): 305-32; Alberto Vàrvaro, "Scuola e cultura in Francia nel XII secolo," *Studi Mediolatini e Volgari* 10 (1962): 299-330; also in *La narrativa francese alla metà del XII secolo* (Naples, 1964), pp. 5-41; Poirion, *Le Poète et le Prince,* pp. 585-91.

medieval encyclopedists under the heading of *practica* not *theoretica*. Machaut follows the example of Brunetto Latini, who said that the final goal of learning is to rule cities and who placed his treatise on politics in a place of honor at the end of *Li Livres dou Tresor*. Susanna, Daniel, Manasseh, and, to a lesser extent, Proserpina succeeded in freeing themselves from imprisonment. They progressed from darkness to light, from symbolic death to spiritual rebirth; they were delivered from an archetypal Inferno and restored to honor. So too, Friend has a chance to regain joy, honor, freedom, and love. Like Orpheus, he can attain knowledge of the world and of himself. If he follows the path of reason, he will become an ideal man, then an ideal king.

Friend is enabled to change because of the Narrator's instruction. The Narrator cannot be considered an active, participating character in the plot, since there is no plot, but he does intervene occasionally in somewhat obtrusive fashion. From the outset he tells Friend he can be of no material help but will provide consolation; in any case, he goes on, Friend is wise enough to take care of himself. Offering advice to so great a prince, impertinent though it may be, is an effect of gratitude and love. The Narrator intervenes again after the biblical *exempla* to remind Friend he seeks to comfort him but can offer no concrete benefit: for that, Friend must turn to God. The Narrator delivers highly emotional tirades against idolatry and effete court dress. He also claims to have been an eyewitness to King John of Bohemia's feats in the East. In the *conclusio*, he tells Friend to accept whatever good he finds in *CA* and to reject the bad. Even though I am not worth anything myself, says the Narrator, my teaching is: "Mais uns cornars a teste fole / Dit bien une bonne parole" (3955-56). Then he reveals his name and King Charles's in an anagram. Machaut supposedly permits the reader to discover his identity so that he may be criticized, for his work merits blame as well as praise.

As in Machaut's other tales, the Narrator's *persona* is complex and ambiguous. Partaking of the universal poetic "I," the Narrator serves partly as an authority figure, a sage, and an eyewitness of John of Bohemia's doings. His mere presence is an authenticating device. Second, his exhortations to Friend or diatribes against the evils of the day contribute to *CA* a sense of drama and personal involvement. But the Narrator also decries his own importance. His pretended humility is no doubt appropriate given the narrative situation—a cleric proffering advice to a king—and serves to attenuate what might otherwise appear untoward presumption (Hoepffner, 3: xvii). It can also be interpreted within the larger canvas of medieval rhetoric, in particular the topic of affected modesty. [8] Throughout the Middle Ages *captatio benevolentiae* was considered an excellent way of winning the public's sympathy. Favorite variations included fear of boring the public, inability to tell the story with sufficient skill, Christian humility before God, and secular humility before king or emperor. Machaut works the old topic into the fabric of his *dit*, where he (as Narrator) presumes to speak directly to the king of Navarre (as Friend).

Although, unlike Rutebeuf or Dante, he does not exhort the reader directly, the Narrator seeks our indulgence for what he is doing. He serves as a bridge between Friend and the public. Since the poem is filtered through a single consciousness, his, and since his point of view and the public's coincide, he alone can create sympathy for Friend. We relate to his norms and accept his beliefs. He is responsible for the serious, partially detached, yet sympathetic and humane manner in which Friend's predicament is related.

Nebuchadnezzar, Belshazzar, and Darius had a good councillor, Daniel, but preferred to heed evil councillors. The Narrator warns Friend to choose his advisers well. He should reject rash young courtiers in favor of experienced, older ones. It is perhaps not coincidental that, at the writing of *CA,* Guillaume de Machaut himself was in his mid-fifties. At any rate, within the context of *CA,* as Daniel admonished pagan kings and the Children of Israel, the Narrator gives Friend the advice he seeks. The protagonists of *DV, RF,* and *DL* learned the ways of love from authority figures; so too the *CA* hero stands in need of a teacher. The Narrator, who so often in Machaut's tales plays the role of lover or bystander, in *CA* himself becomes the master. He is an outsider, a wise man who gives Friend the benefit of his moral vision.

Perhaps the most important of the Narrator's topics is the problem of friends and enemies. Enemies exist throughout the world. A prophet of the Bible suffers from them as do fourteenth-century kings.

---

[8] Curtius, *Europäische Literatur und lateinisches Mittelalter,* chapt. 5 and Excursus 2.

In the *speculum* as in the *consolatio* the Narrator teaches Friend how to deal with such people: how to fight them in war, deceive or outmaneuver them in time of peace, and bear up under their persecutions when in their power. Of course, as Boethius and Jean de Meun pointed out, ill fortune provides one major compensation: you learn to distinguish true friends from the false, since only the former will remain. The good prince also is taught how to make friends with his neighbors, earn the good will of his subordinates, and ally himself to God, thus benefiting from the protection of that greatest of Friends. He also benefits very much from the friendship of a mortal relatively low in status—the Narrator. The Narrator apologizes for daring to refer to King Charles as one of his friends. Yet he, the Narrator, plays the same role of adviser, confidant, elder brother, and man of the world as does *Ami* in *Le Roman de la Rose*. In spite of the ostentatious deference with which he treats his royal charge, the Narrator does act as a friend to him. Just as Charles enters into friendship with God, so high above him, the Narrator may in turn befriend the hero-king. Since the hero is named *Ami*, whose friend can he be but God's and the Narrator's? A series of patterned relationships between beings unequal in status but united by bonds of affection and mutual trust defines the inner structure of *CA*. In purely human terms, the poem is successful to the extent that Guillaume de Machaut renders credible the bond between Friend and the Narrator—a complex relationship of man to man, master to servant, king to subject, patron to poet, student to teacher, young to old, and friend to friend.

8. LA FONTEINNE AMOUREUSE

> Although he tries to fall asleep at night, the
> Narrator is kept awake by love-plaints from a man
> in a room nearby. This man (the Lover) bewails that
> he must go into exile and that, separated from his
> Lady, he cannot communicate with her. The next
> morning the Narrator and the Lover stroll together
> into a garden where, near a Fountain of Love, they
> fall asleep and dream that Venus has brought the
> Lady to comfort her suitor, thus assuring him of
> her devotion. After they have awakened, the two
> men return to the castle. The poem ends when the
> Lover crosses the sea into exile, but with joy in
> his heart.

AFTER AN ESSAY in political *consolatio* Guillaume de Machaut returns
to his old manner. *La Fonteinne amoureuse* [1] is a tale of love which
contains such traditional courtly motifs as springtime, a lovely
garden, the fountain, a dream-vision, and a descent of the Goddess
of love. As in *CA,* the Narrator offers advice to a noble patron,
in this case John, Duke of Berry and Auvergne, third son of King
John II of France, Friend's judge in the previous work. [2] And, as

---

[1] 2,848 lines; ed. Hoepffner, 3: 143-244 (cited hereafter as *FA*).

[2] The Duke of Berry, John of Bohemia's grandson, was one of Machaut's
most generous patrons during the last twenty years of the poet's life. A
document proves that Machaut was one of the Duke's clients in 1371; Duke
John possessed in his library two Machaut manuscripts, one of which is the
present Bibliothèque Nationale, fond français 9221, and the other was
probably made up for the Duke by Machaut himself. We also have some
reason to believe that at least two of Machaut's lyrics — the *balade* "Amis,
je t'aporte nouvelle," *La Louange des Dames* 212, and the *rondel* "Cinc,
un, treze, Wit, nuef d'amour fine," *Rondeaux notés* 6 — may have been composed by Machaut for John's wedding to Jeanne of Armagnac, the Lady in

in *CA,* the protagonist endures a kind of imprisonment, since the events narrated in *FA* refer to Duke John's forthcoming voyage to England (October 30, 1360) as a hostage, as stipulated by the Treaty of Brétigny. However, Duke John is depicted almost exclusively as a lover; his amours are the subject of *FA,* a work of extraordinary beauty only paralleled by *DL.*

Love, the dominant force in the hero's life, demands absolute submission. Wise and powerful men—Solomon, David, Aristotle, Virgil—have accepted love's primacy. The Lover admits that his Lady is of higher social status and should grant her favors to one nobler than he, but he argues, as do several of Andreas Capellanus's characters, that by deigning to love him she will raise him to her level. Her eyes grant him *scens, maniere,* and *vigour* (245), create joy from tears, and assuage his sadness. They are the source of all goodness and, like the host in the Grail poems, provide sustenance. All the treasure buried in the earth and the crowns of France and England are worthless compared to love of "la bele et la blonde / Qui a chief sor" (945-46). Even though they shall be separated, she will retain his heart, he will guard her honor, and after he dies his spirit will pray to God to keep her from harm. Although she is not yet his mistress and he has no certainty that she will ever love him, he is content to adore her from afar, since she is the best of all ladies. We are told that chastity is essential to *fin' amor;* only evil, hypocritical suitors yearn for love's final stage. Nonetheless, the Lover does beg her *grace* and *merci* (352), declaring that to obtain one quarter of her love will draw him out of hell into paradise. On the other hand, if the Lady refuses, he will fall into despair and be damned. He wants very much to win her but, given his forthcoming exile, has little hope, for he could more easily climb the clouds and capture the moon than succeed in his suit. Therefore, he manifests traditional symptoms of lovesickness: his heart and body burn, his skin-color is pale, he cannot sleep, and he is so distracted when people address him that they believe him to be mad.

The Lover's misery can be attributed primarily to separation from the Lady. He is forced into exile and at the end of the poem

---

FA. (Hoepffner, 3: xxvi-xxx, 261.) However, Williams, "An Author's Role in Fourteenth Century Book Production," p. 452, believes *Rondeau* 6 was written over a decade before John's wedding.

will leave France, not knowing for how long. Machaut gives expression to this obstacle in traditional courtly prison imagery. We are told the Lover's heart is imprisoned in the Fortress of Sadness, that he is a hostage in a cage, and that he leaves his heart in the Lady's prison (her body) without hope of ransom. A young knight, he sought to undertake knightly campaigns, to seek renown and thus merit her love; instead, because of the prison, his honor will diminish, and he may lose her.

Although he and the Narrator sleep in contiguous or near-contiguous rooms, they are separated by a wall and are unaware each of the other's existence. Both men are rendered immobile in the darkness of night, enclosed as in a prison. A warm bed within four walls at night often creates a mood of security, of the womb,[3] but in *FA* the Lover is disconsolate and the Narrator terrified by illusory enemies or phantoms. For all his greatness in the secular world, the Lover sleeps alone, without his lady and, except for one knight, without retainers. His only real companions are *Dous Penser* and *Bon Espoir*. He has no one to confide in. Although by pure chance the Narrator overhears him, this occurs without the Lover's knowing it and affords him no consolation at the time.

The Lover is so alienated that he can no longer communicate. Obstacles prevent him from speaking to the Lady or gazing at her. He recognizes that, even if she loves him, her honor forbids making advances by correspondence. Nor can he write to her, for he is too timid to make a declaration and, in any case, cannot risk public discovery of his suit. Presuming that the Lady does love him or will do so at some future time, the Lover fears she will forget him while he pines away in exile. Torn by jealousy, he begs Morpheus to discover and report back to him whether she loves another. The Lover also claims repeatedly he will perish if she does not reciprocate his love. We have seen the death instinct in *JRB, RF, DL,* and *JRN*. Death is the final obstacle, Thanatos the ultimate jailer; in his prison the Lover will remain forever alone, immobile, and separated from the Lady. To some extent Machaut duplicates the baleful, demonic, prison atmosphere of *CA*. Not only does the Lover refer incessantly to his misery, the Narrator too suffers from

---

[3] Gaston Bachelard, *La Terre et les Rêveries du Repos* (Paris, 1948), and *La poétique de l'espace* (Paris, 1957).

melancholia and insomnia. A tone of pathos is appropriate for an adventure which was "diverse et obscure / Au commencier et päoureuse" (58-59).

However, the Narrator goes on to say that his fearful, impenetrable adventure turned out to be joyful in the end (60). The Lover will eventually win his Lady's love—in large measure due to the intervention of other people, including the Narrator himself. The "I" helps young lovers in two of Machaut's earlier tales: *JRB* and *DL*. But never has he been so close to the protagonist of a *dit amoreus;* never have the two been involved together in the love quest. The Lover and the Narrator converse in the grove before falling asleep; while the former bares his sorrow, the latter confesses he overheard the Lover's *Complainte* the night before. After the dream they continue to talk late into the night. Although the Lover feels depressed, he is again comforted by the Narrator. The Lover confides in his companion, releases tension by speaking of his troubles. The "I" helps the Lover by being there, literally providing a shoulder to lean on. Furthermore, himself a lover and a poet, a man whom the Lover has cherished for many a year, he more than others is capable of understanding his princely patron. As a *doctor amoris,* he must know the disease to cure it. The Narrator loves him as much as a "povre homme" (1262, 1263) can; though his affection is worth little, he offers it anyway. They become friends. Indeed, unlike the silent protagonist of *CA,* the Lover is more than eager to accept the Narrator's offer of friendship. Man to man, and master to man, a warm, human relationship between the two is established. At the fountain they lean on each other's shoulders, fall asleep, and the Narrator has a dream in which the Lover's problems work out successfully. Although the Lover dreams the same dream—and it is possible he could have been comforted without the Narrator's intervention—we see the Lover's consolation in the Narrator's dream, filtered through his consciousness. Without him the Lover might never have gone into the grove, stopped by the fountain, and fallen asleep. As in *DL,* the Narrator serves as a helpful catalyst-character, who provides concrete material aid to the hero in quest of his beloved.

The Narrator contributes another important element to *FA:* comedy. Hearing strange noises in his room at night, he hides in bed under the sheets, more afraid than a rabbit: "Que j'en os horreur et frëour, / Doubtance, frisson et päour" (75-76). His dread is then turned to ridicule when we discover that the strange noises are a courtly knight's plaint and when the Narrator seeks to justify himself in an excessively lengthy, pendantic digression on the nature of cowardice. He claims that knights too show fear after dusk: that, unlike them, he is unarmed; that it is better to run away than to fall in combat; and that cowardice is as proper to a cleric like himself as courage to a knight—in fact, for him to manifest bravery would be an offense against Nature. He also says that he was often afraid during King John of Bohemia's campaigns in the East but nevertheless stuck close to John's side: because he had no real choice, was safest in the monarch's train, ate better food there, was dispensed from open combat, and in case of flight could justify himself by the need to follow his master. Although the Narrator excoriates in his own voice cruel, rapacious barons, he disclaims criticism of any individual:

> 181   Je parle tout en general
>   Sans riens dire d'especial,
>   Si est fols qui a li le tire
>   Et qui a mal faire s'atire.

And then he is terrified when Venus appears in his dream.

A man of letters, the Narrator suffers from *déformation professionnelle*. At night he transcribes with glee the Lover's heart-rending plaint. The next morning, he is overjoyed at having written it all down without mistakes and amazed at the Lover's tour de force (*La Complainte de l'Amant* (235-1034): 800 lines divided into fifty stanzas of sixteen lines each, each stanza based on a two-rhyme pattern, the plaint as a whole containing 100 dissimilar rhymes). Later, when the Lover asks the Narrator to compose a *lai* or *complainte* alluding to his plight, the latter comes up with a transcription of the Lover's own words. These episodes generate humor because of this incongruous relationship between the Lover and his new friend and because we know the plot-situation to be false. The Lover could not possibly have bewailed away the entire night in rhyme, and the Narrator could not possibly have reproduced his neighbor's bewailing (800 lines) without a mistake, even in shorthand. We know that Machaut the poet wrote the *Complainte,* that he attributes it to the Lover as a compliment to the Duke of Berry which, however, neither the Lover nor the Narrator takes very seriously.

The Narrator manifests distinctly human virtues and failings. He is a professional writer, a cleric, a coward, a busybody, and a bit of a snob, who enjoys hobnobbing with the gentry. He is tactful and charming, possesses a sense of humor, and above all cherishes his own personality. These are not the traits of a real person, however, but a particularly successful rendering of a character-type found often in Machaut's *dits:* the cowardly, inept Narrator. The protagonist is a *miles,* a lover, a master; his friend is a *clericus,* a witness to love, a servant. Because both the Lover and Trojan Paris (told about in the Narrator's dream) are princes of the blood, they belong to the realm of Venus; she has chosen them because of their nobility. A disciple of Pallas, the Narrator serves as a foil to the more serious, dignified Lover. Machaut tells us that knights break their word, exploit their people, and even display cowardice, whereas the Narrator learns the meaning of courage from King John of Bohemia. Even wise men yield to *Amor* (the Narrator is said to love, although his *vie sentimentale* has no role in the story), and the Lover-prince is transformed into a poet. However, although Love and Reason, the knight and the cleric, the active and contemplative lives are not mutually exclusive, they do represent distinct elements in the human condition. To the extent that the Narrator belongs, *grosso modo,* to a different estate than the Lover, his character-type will differ also. A semicomic figure, to be taken less seriously than the hero, somewhat closer to the average man because of his failings and his plebeian origins, he serves as a bridge from the Lover to the public. Yet, to the extent that the Lover and Narrator become friends and share (or exchange) traits, the two estates are brought into synthesis.

The Lover's problems are solved when he and the Narrator together dream of a visit by Venus and the Lady. The Narrator cannot look Venus in the face. She projects the aura of a Greek goddess and an astrological House. She represents an elemental power of nature, the love that moves men's souls, and, in the tradition of Arthurian romance, is a good fay who aids the hero to win his bride. Indeed, she leads by the hand the prize the Lover has yearned for so pitifully—his Lady. The two appear, in Jungian terms, as anima-figures, images of beauty, harmony and transcendence. They partake of the great mother and virgin bride archetypes, divine goddess and fairy princess, respectively (1594-95).

These anima-figures function as teachers. Venus tells of the Wedding of Peleus and Thetis and the Judgment of Paris to the Narrator before delivering a lecture on *fin' amor* to his friend. Then, in a lyrical passage called *Le Confort de l'Amant et de la Dame* (2207-526), the Lady refutes arguments the Lover proffered in his *Complainte,* thus delivering her own *Ars amandi.* Good lessons are to be obtained from these *puellae senes,* who possess not only the beauty of young girls but the wisdom and compassion of older women. Nor are they depicted as rigid stereotypes. Venus, in particular, comes to life as a sprightly, coquettish creature with a sense of humor. She recounts her obsession with Priapus's anatomy and joshes the Lover by asking him if he has noticed his Lady's beauty and whether he failed to seek Venus's help out of ignorance. She is on the whole very sympathetic, unlike the more common medieval Venus, the embodiment of *concupiscentia,* or the figure of unbridled passion we find in Jean de Meun.

First Venus, then the Lady, console the Lover. These two ladies are closely tied to the Lover and the Narrator, who dream of them in the same dream. Inside the net of *Amor* are the Lover and the Lady. Although involved, Venus and the Narrator stand outside; they are mentors, advisers, and confidants, aiding the Lady and Lover respectively. However, the Narrator is of lower social status than his friend, whereas Venus ranks high above the Lady; the Narrator is a kind of servant to the Lover, but the Lady serves Venus in turn. As in *CA,* Machaut establishes a hierarchical pattern. A poet-cleric on the fringe of society, the Narrator stands at the bottom of the scale, but can nevertheless participate in courtly doings. The Lover dominates the secular world but is a slave to his Lady, while both are in thrall to Love: in the domain of Eros the conqueror is conquered, and the amorous life (Venus) triumphs over the active (Juno) and the contemplative (Pallas).

As in Machaut's other tales, the Lover is taught hope and joy. All-powerful Venus promises him happiness. The Pagans of Antiquity readily sacrificed to her, for she is the most powerful of goddesses. The Lover should trust in her and in his Lady. If he had appealed directly to Venus, his problem would have been solved long ago. However, since his failure to do so was undoubtedly the result of ignorance not malice, Venus will take pity on him.

In her *Confort,* which parallels the Lover's *Complainte,* the Lady informs him that she shares his love. True, they must remain separated for a time, but in exchange for his heart lodged prisoner in her breast, he may keep her heart and image within himself. All her joy comes from him, and her desire for him is as great as his for her. She swears she will neither forget him nor listen to the advances of another suitor. Their passion, however, cannot be consummated, for the seeking of concrete sensual fulfillment is unworthy of a good lover. Venus will help him only if he remains chaste in thought and deed. The Lover should not complain to Dame Fortune of his predicament. Fortune treats all men in similar fashion indiscriminately. Nor should he worry about losing his reputation for prowess. The Lady prefers him alive and healthy to his dying in battle, being wounded, taken prisoner, or insulted by the rabble.

The Lady's desire for her sleeping prince is spelled out in no uncertain terms (2255-90), and she embraces him in a scene both graceful and very sensuous (cf. also vv. 2621-24):

> 2495 Adonq la dame s'abaissa,
> Qu'onques pour moy ne le laissa,
> Et plus de cent fois le baisa
> En son dormant;
> Et puis elle le resgarda
> Et de son droit braz l'embrassa
> Et li dist: "Amis, trai te sa!"
> En sousriant.

Venus too is blind neither to Priapus's anatomy nor to the pleasures of the table at Thetis's wedding feast. Although intercourse itself does not take place, both Lover and Lady are warm, sensual human beings, equals in love, each in love with the other. As in his other *dits,* Machaut takes a commonsense approach to life's problems. The Lady prefers a live, healthy lover to a renowned captain fallen in battle. The Narrator sees nothing wrong in hiding between the sheets at night nor in flight, provided one's honor is preserved. Finally, Paris awards the Apple of Discord to Venus, rather than to Juno or Pallas, for the most practical considerations: having been informed that he is of noble birth, Paris declares that he will readily acquire wealth and wise councillors. Only in the realm of love can he benefit from divine intervention. He chooses Venus and like the Lover will receive his reward.

From their dark, solitary rooms Lover and Narrator step out into a fresh spring morning. In sunshine they perceive a grove, containing a wide variety of flowers, trees, and birds, and in the center a Fountain of Love. This fountain, taken directly from *Le Roman de la Rose,* is the central image of the poem, from which its title is derived. Both Lover and Narrator bathe their hands and face, an act of purification, but they fear to drink. Its water, like Brangien's filter in the Tristan romances, possesses magic qualities. This tabu fountain, associated with the story of Troy, evokes love's power as well as the fecundity of Mother Nature. Machaut does not mean us to feel dread or awe at the fountain, however. The worst that can happen to his characters is to fall in love, and they both already have. The fountain and the garden as a whole are images of goodness, hope, and joy. No place in the world, not even the terrestrial paradise, is more beautiful, we are told. Although like the earthly paradise Machaut's garden contains a serpent, it by no means gives an impression of the demonic. The serpent has been built into the fountain, *is* the fountain, and from its twelve heads spouts water onto a marble basin. Pygmalion created it under Venus's orders and at Jupiter's instigation. Indeed, Cupid, Venus, Jupiter, and assorted nymphs and fays use the garden for their festivities. Albeit with a touch of irony, this *locus amoenus* recasts both the terrestrial paradise and the classical Golden Age: it is a place of repose, where man exults in serene, idyllic nature, where his only dread is love's *dolce-amar.* It serves as a catalyst for the dream and permits Venus's initiated disciples to find consolation.

A man who, in his plaint, begged to receive a green hat from Love (green is the color of hope, of renewal, of May Day), finds contentment in a green world with a golden serpent, where he loves a Lady with golden hair, is consoled by a goddess wearing a golden crown, dreams of a golden apple and is told about Jupiter appearing to Danae in a golden shower and about a banquet served on tables of gold. The Lover no longer stands alone, isolated from others: he communicates first with the Narrator, then with Venus, finally with his Lady. To pledge their love, the Lady takes his diamond ring and leaves her ruby in its place. According to the Lapidaries and other medieval texts, the diamond, an image of fidelity, cures madness, takes away lust, and ensures against hurt from enemies; the ruby, "la gemme des gemmes," superior to all others in splendor, symbolizes nobility and power, prevents defeat in battle or before a tribunal, cures despair, and grants love. [4] As in *RF,* the exchange of rings is an authenticating device which links the dream to waking reality; for after he awakens, the Lover discovers the ruby on his finger. It also indicates equality in Love and consecrates a symbolic marriage.

The key word is *joy,* in this tale of an adventure which began *diverse, obscure,* and *päoureuse* but turned out to be *joieuse* (see above, p. 149), of a love which, conducted according to the precepts of *fin' amor,* ends in happiness. The Narrator enjoyed merely writing down the Lover's plaint; now he takes joy in his friend's happiness and in the marvelous events which become part of his own experience and eventually the subject of a *dit amoreus.* The Lover, for all his suffering, was happy merely to adore so perfect a Lady; now his joy is complete, knowing that she loves him and that he already possesses all he may rightfully seek. The dream over, attended by "maint chevalier cointe et gent, / Cointe, apert, faitis et gentil" (2758-59), the two friends repair to the most beautiful castle in France or the Empire, where they hear Mass and dine together. A stranger in the land, the Narrator is accepted into the court, a community of gracious, handsome, well-born people; and the Lover, master of all he surveys, also joins in the group. In an atmosphere of gracious living, pomp, and decorum, both men find the fitting resolution to their problems.

On the following day, the court moves to the seacoast (Calais) where, three days later, the Lover takes a boat into exile. Although he was first separated from Venus and the Lady, now from the Narrator, he takes with him into exile Venus, the Lady's image in his heart, her ruby on his finger, his servants, and the Narrator's offer of his heart, body, and power. With these he is properly armed against desire, sighs, and tears. For the Lover is not the same man he was at the beginning. He had been spiritually incarcerated, was

---

[4] See Léopold Pannier, *Les lapidaires français du moyen âge, des XIIe, XIIIe et XIVe siècles* (Paris, 1882), and Paul Studer and Joan Evans, *Anglo-Norman Lapidaries* (Paris, 1924).

then released, and now will return to a physical prison but with his heart and soul free. He will no longer be subject to despair. Joy triumphs over sadness, even though the protagonist goes into exile. Indeed, it is appropriate that he develop a fully integrated personality on his own. The *FA* recounts that decisive moment in his life when a man learns to cope with his problems; once he comes to terms with himself, the poem can legitimately be brought to a close.

Transformation occurs while the Lover is asleep. The themes of sleep, insomnia, and dreaming are fundamental to *FA*. As we have seen, the Lover suffers from conventional lovesickness, one of whose symptoms is insomnia: "Il est certain qu'en mon lit ne repos / Ne n'i sommeil / Et que je n'ay bien, joie ne repos" (701-3). Since he cannot rest, he complains against love, his Lady, and the God of Sleep. The Lover declares grandiloquently that he has taken the 100 rhymes of *La Complainte de l'Amant* from his Lady's beauty, which kept him awake from dusk to dawn (1021-24). So long a poem, containing repetitions and some dull passages, is properly ascribed to a man who had nothing else to do all night but compose it. Equally appropriate is his pallor the following day, attributed by the Narrator to the *nuit blanche* rather than to conventional lovesickness.

The Narrator too suffers from insomnia. When he is finally on the point of falling asleep ("quant repos en moy nature / Voloit prendre," 69-70), he hears noises through the window, takes fright, and eventually copies down the Lover's *Complainte,* with a result that he too stays up all night. The Narrator's sleeplessness forms a humorous parallel to the Lover's. The next day, after dozing off at the fountain, both men experience an unusual dream because they endured so long a period of sleeplessness beforehand. We find similar phenomena in Ovid, the *Enéas,* Guillaume de Lorris, Chaucer, and Christine de Pisan.

As always, Machaut's dream-visions correspond to the reality of the dream-experience in everyday life. For example, Venus will tell the story of Troy, holding the Apple of Discord and accompanied by the Lady. This manifest dream content reflects episodes from the dreamers' day residue: 1) the previous night the Lover thought exclusively of the Lady, 2) he and the Narrator lie down near a fountain, on which are carved images of the Abduction of Helen and Fall of Troy, 3) they talk of love, the Lady, and the

Pagan gods who built the fountain, and 4) just before falling asleep the Narrator thinks of his own beloved. It is also significant that the Narrator and the Lover are spiritual twins. They both suffer from insomnia and melancholia. They are both unhappy lovers. They both write poetry. They fall asleep together and dream the same dream, each a character in the other's dream, and are both instructed by Venus. As in *DL,* the Lover is, to some extent, the Narrator's double, an alter ego on whom he has projected his own frustrations. By rendering the Lover even more miserable than himself and by placing him in a situation more hopeless than his own, the Narrator renders his own burdens lighter. And by having the Lover ultimately succeed, he creates hope for himself. From both points of view, the Narrator indulges in wish-fulfillment and releases tension in a fantasy-world where an anima-figure brings happiness to his surrogate. Time, distance, and social status are abolished. In the dream he and the Lover are granted a revelation which transcends normal self-knowledge. They discover the secrets of nature and are made better because of it. Sleep and the accompanying dream have therapeutic value for both men. They were unhappy before falling asleep; whether or not they are aware of a change, their unhappiness has evaporated upon awakening.

According to Machaut, this metamorphosis is brought about through the direct personal intervention of two mythological characters: the God of Sleep and his son, Morpheus. In his *Complainte* the Lover tells the myth of Ceyx and Alcyone, describing how Iris, Juno's messenger, goes to the God of Sleep to ask that Alcyone be informed of her husband's fate. Like Venus, the God of Sleep wields supernatural power; even Iris almost dozes off in his palace, dreads him, and vows never to return. After agreeing to Iris's request, the god sends Morpheus to appear before Alcyone in Ceyx's guise and recount his death at sea. The Lover then prays to Morpheus to grant him sleep, to inform the Lady of his love, and to return with the information whether or not she loves him in return. She cannot tell him so of her own volition (the discretion motif), but Morpheus can. With his help, the two will communicate as did Ceyx and Alcyone. The Lover counts on Morpheus's *franchise,* declares Morpheus to be his only hope, and prays to him and to the God of Love that his request be granted. And in a humorous passage he swears to make an offering "Au dieu qui dort" (876), gifts of a nightcap and a feather bed, "Pour mieus dormir" (808).

The Lover does not pray to Morpheus in vain. Venus and the Lady appear to him in a dream with the news he wishes to hear. Whether the two feminine figures come in their own person or are an illusion created by Morpheus is not made clear. But, after he has awakened, the Lover thanks Venus and Morpheus and promises to make an image of Morpheus in gold on a marble pillar and build a temple to Morpheus and the God of Sleep. Morpheus's intervention is equally decisive in the three classical *exempla* Machaut has inserted into his text: The stories of Ceyx and Alcyone, the Judgment of Paris (Hecuba's vision of the Fall of Troy), and 100 Roman senators whose collective dream was interpreted by the Sybil. The *FA* is thus rendered more coherent as a work of art by the three *exempla* and the theme they illustrate: the power of Morpheus, God of Dreams. Machaut himself, in *Le Voir-Dit,* refers to *FA* as the book of Morpheus, its title in two surviving *FA* manuscripts (Hoepffner, 3:xxi). Perhaps, as in the case of *DA,* Machaut called his poem *Morpheüs,* but, for one reason or another, the title *Fonteinne amoureuse* won favor with the public. In any case, Machaut's having introduced the God of Dreams into a *dit amoreus* set a pattern for later writers: Froissart, *Le Paradys d'Amours, L'Espinette amoreuse, La Prison amoreuse, Le Bleu Chevalier,* and Chaucer, *The Book of the Duchess,* among others.

The dream motif contributes to an interesting tension between illusion and reality. The Narrator claims his dream to be true, not a lie (1565-68). When they wake up, both Narrator and Lover perceive on the latter's finger the Lady's ruby, which he supposedly received in exchange for his own diamond. Thus, as in *RF,* we are expected to believe that dream-events or a vision are reality not fiction. So too in his *Complainte* the Lover insists that, because "Songier souvent ne doit mie estre fable" (783), if Morpheus appears to the Lady in a dream, she will remember it and respect its contents the following morning. The story of the hundred senators supposedly proves that identical dreams had by more than one person will come true, "Car c'estoit grant signefiance / Des choses qui sont a venir" (2650-51). We are told that Morpheus appeared physically to Alcyone and told her the truth about Ceyx, and we may assume Hecuba's dream of giving birth to a torch that will burn her city is an accurate prediction of the birth of Paris and his later activities—his passion for Helen (the flame of lust), which will bring about the destruction of Troy by fire. Machaut makes an effort to give these dreams an aura of the *somnium coeleste*. For the medieval public, they are, to some extent, authenticating devices which guarantee the truth of his narrative.

On the other hand, the God of Sleep is surrounded by a thousand sons and daughters, "vanitez et songes" (628). Mention of these *vanitez* will remind us (if we had forgotten) that Morpheus, Venus, and the Lady are not the Christian God and his angels, and that the dreams of Alcyone and the Narrator not *visiones* in the accepted theological sense. Machaut recognizes that the stories in *l'Ovide moralisé* need not be taken literally, that they are myths. He is aware that Morpheus creates illusion when he appears to mortals, and that Morpheus, his father, and their palace are themselves creations of an author's imagination. This is undoubtedly one of the reasons why, in Ovid as well as Machaut, Iris's visit to the cave of sleep is portrayed in comic terms. Even the "realism" we noticed earlier, the way Machaut creates believable dream psychology, undermines the dream's authority since, for the medievals, a dream derived from the subject's personal anxieties and reflecting his day residue is an *insomnium* or *somnium animale,* of subjective and, therefore, limited value. In Machaut's century the dream-vision had become a literary convention. It could be interpreted objectively or in psychological, subjective, specifically human terms (as we moderns do with our dreams). Machaut chooses to maintain both levels, to treat the old convention seriously and poke fun at it at the same time. He proves the dream's authenticity while reminding us that the entire poem is a fiction. Although the Narrator and the Lover, as literary characters, believe in the reality of what they experience, Guillaume de Machaut the poet knows better. He shows us that the Narrator himself is an illusion and his dream-world an artificial, literary transformation of the real one.

Machaut concludes his tale with the following line: "Dites moy, fu ce bien songié?" (2848) Perhaps he is reminding us that the Narrator's dream-experience "turned out well," that, in terms of the plot, the Lover benefited from it; or he may be taking pride in his craft as a writer, content that the dream-section of *FA* was rendered successfully in artistic terms. It is also possible (cf. Hoepffner,

3:xxxii) that the Narrator here reveals that the whole poem, or at least all of it but for the introductory scene which depicts the Narrator alone in bed at night, was dreamed by the Narrator, that all the action—including the Lover's *Complainte,* his encounter with the Narrator, and their falling asleep together—makes up the Narrator's own original dream. If this interpretation be valid, then the Narrator dreams that he and the Lover are dreaming and that in their dream Venus tells the story of Hecuba's dream. In other words, *FA* contains a dream within a dream within a dream. Machaut has created a complex, ambiguous poem, quite unlike other medieval dream-visions, where illusion and reality fuse, and the reader can never be certain whether his characters are dreaming or awake. Ambiguity extends to the point that we are not told when the "I" fell asleep or that he fell asleep at all. Dreams are treated as seriously as reality, and reality portrayed in terms of a dream. In his own way Machaut creates a poetic world which anticipates, *mutatis mutandis,* one aspect of the Spanish baroque and German romanticism. For, without wishing to press too hard the analogy, I must allow that the construction in or near the Garden of Love of a Temple to the God of Sleep underscores the theme that truly life is a dream and dreams are life.

In *FA* structure is determined by a series of contrasts or antitheses: night and day, insomnia and sleep, imprisonment and freedom, immobility and movement, exile and home, solitude and community, ignorance and knowledge, lover and witness, man and woman, human beings and Gods, dream-reality and waking-reality. Even the Fountain of Love functions both as good and evil, for it renders some poeple happy, others miserable. The plot is interrupted by two splendid lyrical monologues: the Lover's *Complainte,* and the Lady's *Confort* in answer to his *Complainte.* And their understanding is symbolized by a symmetrical exchange of rings.

These oppositions are not articulated statically, in a one-to-one relationship, however. In the course of the plot, the characters step out from their dark, enclosed, silent, lonely rooms into the bright light of day. They rejoice in freedom, open air, and movement, and come together with others to form a community. Images of the garden, the fountain, the golden apple, the torch, and the feast symbolize their transformation. Yet the Lover is then separated first from his Lady, then from the Narrator. He returns to the state of loneliness, imprisonment, and exile in which we found him in the beginning. This circular structure is reinforced by the dream within a dream within a dream. The real world serves as a frame for a dream-world which in turn frames other dreams. The poem revolves around the encounter between the Lover and the Narrator and their subsequent dream (within a dream) at the fountain, a miraculous initiation. This dream contains a *Confort* which answers the earlier *Complainte,* just as the dream itself "answers" the *nuit blanche* of the previous evening. The dream indeed is framed by architectural references—a description of the Fountain of Love, and the Lover's promise to build a Temple of Sleep—and by two court scenes, a relatively unintegrated social situation where the Lover is miserable and the lone Narrator, unrecognized, looks on from outside, and one where Lover and Narrator are integrated into the community. These court scenes are in turn encircled by "realistic" descriptions of everyday life. Thus *FA* may be envisaged as a circular or ring pattern which contains within itself the parallelisms and antitheses it eventually resolves.

Two other increments contribute to the structure of *FA:* myths from classical antiquity, and the two lyric *complaintes.* Machaut has his characters tell of Ceyx and Alcyone, the Wedding of Peleus and Thetis, and the Judgment of Paris. (Since the *exemplum* of the 100 Senators is of little importance to the narrative, I will not discuss it here, and in any case technically it does not belong to the corpus of Greco-Roman mythology.)

The myth of Ceyx and Alcyone treats the same themes of isolation, loss, unhappy love, and insomnia that the Lover faces in his own life. Like the Lover, Alcyone cannot sleep because she has been separated from the person she adores. Ceyx perished apart from his wife, just as the Lover fears death due to separation from his Lady (who is also his wife, if we assimilate him to Duke John of Berry). Alcyone's grief as a woman corresponds to the Lover's grief as a man. Her predicament gives Machaut an excuse to tell of Morpheus and to discuss the nature of sleep and dreams. Like Venus, the God of Sleep has tremendous power; Iris dreads him as greatly as the Narrator does Venus. And Iris's trip to the Palace of Sleep is as much a death-rebirth experience as the Lover's dreaming at the fountain. Finally, by appearing to Alcyone in her sleep, Morpheus enables her to communicate with Ceyx. Morpheus (as

Ceyx) appears to Alcyone at Juno's behest, thus paralleling a later episode when the Lady (or Morpheus as the Lady) appears to the Lover at Venus's command. Juno's protégée learns the truth, a tale of death (and she too will die), symbolized by a turbulent sea, Nature as enemy, whereas the Lover is revealed a truth of joy, whose symbol is the contained, controlled water of the Fountain of Love. (In the end the Lover must go into exile over the sea, but it is presumably a calm voyage, and he expects to return.) The two stories resemble each other, however, in their emphasis on the authenticity of dream revelations, human sorrow, divine pity, and the loving fidelity of the dreamer. Although Alcyone suffers, in the end she and Ceyx are reunited after they have been metamorphosed into birds. So too the Lover hopes that his problems will be resolved when he and the Lady see each other again.

Venus gives the Narrator an eyewitness account of the Wedding of Peleus and Thetis, the Apple of Discord, and the Judgment of Paris. Paris's decision to award the apple to Venus rather than to Pallas or Juno underscores the invincible power of love. The Lady cites the myth of Danae to show that Amor destroys all obstacles, even prison walls, for, if young lovers remain steadfast, Venus will find a way to unite them. Although Paris suffered from loneliness and was exiled from his heritage in Troy, like the Lover, he is initiated to the ways of love and becomes Venus's servant. By anticipation, just as Paris won Helen's love and regained his rightful place in Troy, so too the Lover will one day return from exile to his Lady.

Paris had originally been cast out because Hecuba dreamed of giving birth to a torch which burned Troy. The fruit of Hecuba's love for Priam burns; on the Fountain we see Venus set Helen aflame with her torch; Paris and Helen love each other with traditional flame-imagery; and their passion will unleash a war resulting in the burning of the city. Troy will fall due to the feats of Achilles, and later his son Pyrrhus, yet even Achilles succumbs to Polyxena's charms (another triumph for Venus), thus bringing about his own destruction. How appropriate then for Venus to begin her story with a wedding of two happy lovers (another analogy to John of Berry and his bride), from whom descend those warriors who will fulfill Hecuba's dream and burn Troy. The story carved on Machaut's Fountain of Love is more complex than the corresponding myth of Narcissus in *Le Roman de la Rose*. Machaut has expanded a secondary motif in Guillaume de Lorris's poem to form an episode of central importance in his own.

One hallmark of the European Renaissance is a changed attitude toward the ancient world. Frenchmen of the sixteenth century took pagan myths seriously, treated both mythological and historical personages of Antiquity with respect, as models for their own lives. Such is, however, already the attitude of Jean de Meun and Guillaume de Machaut. Mythology lives again in the latter's evanescent dream-world. We are made aware of the power which emanates from the Fountain and from the Apple of Discord, from Venus and Morpheus—supernatural forces beyond man's comprehension. At the same time, we must not forget that true myth comes into being only after people have ceased to believe in the gods, have learned to cherish the marvelous as fiction stored up in the imagination. [5] In *FA*, even more than in *JRN*, Machaut handles classical material with a light touch. He smiles at Iris's fear, Paris's shrewdness, Venus's pride, quick temper, and sensuality. Venus is almost as rich a comic character as the Narrator himself. As with the poets of the Renaissance, reverence for Antiquity does not preclude parody and banter, the tribute of loving intimacy. The *Livre de Morpheüs* projects an aura of sophistication worthy of Ronsard and La Fontaine. Drawing from his own medieval heritage, Machaut writes a court poem for the Duke of Berry in which *sapientia* precedes *fortitudo* and the Lover, whatever his opinions on *imperium,* benefits from a *translatio studii* brought about directly by the gods.

More than any other of Machaut's *dits amoreus, FA* is a Poem of Complaint and Comfort, given expression in lyrical passages of great beauty. Although the two lyrics slow down the narrative, they provide *détente* and a change of pace. The separation of styles was, as Erich Auerbach points out, less pronounced in Froissart's century than in Voltaire's. Machaut's public saw no incongruity in a juxtaposition of lyrical and narrative elements in the same work. In fact, a finely written *complainte* inside a *dit* was considered an artistic tour de force. Unlike some other poets of the time, however, Machaut carefully integrates his *complaintes* into the narrative. Given

---

[5] C. S. Lewis, *The Allegory of Love,* chapt. 2.

the Lover's melancholic insomnia, it is fitting that he delivers a plaint and that it is a long one. *La Complainte de l'Amant* embodies his emotions more dramatically than if they were recounted in conversation or in the Narrator's own voice. With the *Complainte* Machaut succeeds in establishing a rapport between his protagonist and the public. We sympathize with him in part because we momentarily forget the Narrator.

The Lady's *Confort* parallels the *Complainte*, refutes it even, and thus depicts in lyrical terms that joy which corresponds to the earlier mood of unhappiness. Her *Confort* is a much shorter poem than the *Complainte*, however (twenty stanzas against fifty). Not only is the Lady free from insomnia, but to tell of happiness perhaps offers fewer opportunities for artistic embellishment than to tell of misery. The Lover's repetitive, accumulated plaints would have been out of place in the *Confort*, where *fin' amor* gives way to common sense and a natural, shared passion. The tone is lighter. In the *Confort*, Machaut parodies his own *Complainte*, treating the genre itself with gaiety and irreverence. Even the woeful genre of the *complainte* [6] must yield to laughter, joy, and a community spirit.

At first the Lover exists only as a dispossessed poetic voice in the night. His *Complainte* informs the Narrator of his presence, keeps both men awake all night, and provides an excuse for the Narrator to seek closer relations with the Lover and for the Lover to bare his heart to the Narrator. But for the *Complainte*, even if the two were to make contact later (the Narrator came to the Lover's castle for that purpose), they would probably never have spoken of love. Without the *Complainte*, the plot of *FA*, as we know it, would have been impossible. The Lady's *Confort* is less essential: we can imagine her speaking to the Lover in octosyllabic couplets or her message presented indirectly by Venus. However, by placing the *Confort* in her voice and in lyrical form, Machaut emphasizes its message of communication and joy. In fact, it forms the Lover's final initiation, a moment of exultation.

The Lover delivers a plaint containing 100 dissimilar rhymes, a tour de force of craftsmanship. Later in the narrative, on the ride from his castle to Calais, he sings a variety of songs:

---

[6] Poirion, *Le Poète et le Prince*, chapt. 10.

2800 Il disoit des dis et des chans
      De lais, de dances et de notes,
      Faites a cornes et a rotes,
      Tant que tous nous esbaudissoit;
      Et tout ce qui de li issoit
      Estoit si plaisant a oïr
      Que tous nous faisoit resjoïr.

Then, upon boarding ship, the Lover turns to the Narrator and in a lovely voice, "Pleinne de tres grant melodie" (2822), sings the following *Rondel:*

2825 "Eu païs ou ma dame maint
      Pri Dieu qu'a joie mi remaint.
      Se j'ay heü peinne et mal maint,
      Eu païs ou ma dame maint,
      Espoir ay qu'en aucun temps m'aint,
      S'en dit mes cuers qui siens remaint:
      Eu païs ou ma dame maint
      Pri Dieu qu'a joie mi remaint."

The Lover is shown to be an artist. Love has made a poet of him (and of the Lady too, for that matter), so that, in the course of the narrative, he also becomes a master of *sapientia,* a devotee of Pallas as well as of Venus.

For all the Narrator's modesty, Machaut is proud of his *dit* as a work of art and his own role as its creator. The Narrator's astonishment at the technical perfection of the Lover's plaint serves as a subtle, witty compliment to Machaut the author. Machaut compliments himself less obliquely by having the Lover praise the Narrator as an artist and treat him as a friend. Significantly, Orpheus, the subject of an *exemplum* in *CA,* attends Peleus's wedding feast where he performs along with Venus's half-brothers Apollo and Pan. The Fountain of Love itself (*cum* serpent) is a beautiful artifact, created by Pygmalion, as are the sculpture and temples promised to Morpheus, Venus, and the God of Sleep, and the gold table at Peleus and Thetis's nuptial banquet. The theme of art and the artist is central to a tale, where the two protagonists are poets, which describes highly prized works of art in its plot, and itself ranks as a most elegantly finished aesthetic whole.

This triumph of the aesthetic does not resemble Art for Art's Sake in the least. Rather, it contributes to a style of courtly living.

Machaut's characters lead an elegant, refined, sophisticated existence. Gracious manners, delicate speeches abound. Machaut's people attain a sense of community in highly formalized but nonetheless organic social relationships, such as friendship between the Narrator and his social superior, the Lover, one link in a chain which includes the Lady and Venus herself. They succeed in creating the ultimate in civilization.

9. LE LIVRE DU VOIR-DIT

> *Toute-belle* sends a *rondeau* to the Narrator, in
> which she says that she offers him her heart. The
> Narrator replies in kind. Soon the aging poet and his
> youthful admirer are involved in an amorous corres-
> pondence. He visits her several times, and they
> indulge in physical intimacies. After the Narrator
> returns home, he dreams that *Toute-belle*'s sentiments
> toward him have changed. The lovers continue to
> write to each other. However, a harsh winter, the
> plague, fear of highwaymen, and *losengiers'* reports
> against *Toute-belle* cause the Narrator to postpone
> further meetings. Finally *Toute-belle* convinces him of
> her good will, and the book ends as they swear eternal
> love and plan once more a reunion.

Le Livre du Voir-Dit[1] has received more attention than any of
Guillaume de Machaut's other tales. It is perhaps the only one
which has caught scholars' fancy. However, most studies devoted
to *VD* are concerned largely with whether or not the poem is "real,"
that is, recounts an autobiographical episode in the poet's life.

---

[1] Ed. Paulin Paris (Paris, 1875) (cited hereafter as *VD*). The Paris edition
contains 8,437 lines, plus forty-five interspersed epistles in prose. Due to an
error of 600 lines in numeration, pp. 272-73, Paris's version appears to claim
9,037 lines. In reality, however, the original text of *VD* is longer than 8,437
lines, for, as I pointed out in the Introduction, Paris leaves out bunches
of lines, of a descriptive or allegorical nature, without warning the reader, as
well as a more important 265-line sequence, Polyphemus's song to Galatea,
published subsequently by Antoine Thomas: "Guillaume de Machaut et
l'Ovide moralisé," *Romania* 41 (1912): 382-400. I have consulted Ms 1584,
fond français, of the Bibliothèque Nationale, and will quote from it when
appropriate.

In the title of *VD* (The True Story), Machaut makes an unusual claim for authenticity; he invites comparison with other romances of the day and with his own previous *dits,* presumed less "true" than the new one. Machaut justifies his choice of title, which may have appeared pretentious, in the following words:

> p. 17   *Le Voir-dit* vueil-je qu'on appelle
> Ce traictié que je fais pour elle,
> Pour ce que jà n'i mentiray.

(Cf. also Letter **XXXV**, p. 263: "Et aussi, vostre livre avera nom le *Livre dou Voir dit;* si, ne vueil ne ne doy mentir.") He declares that the *VD* narrative occurred in real life, that he has told of his amours with *Toute-belle* at her command. She wants everyone to know their story, even if her reputation suffers because of it.

Machaut's first modern editor, Prosper Tarbé, accepted the Comte de Caylus's suggestion that *Toute-belle* stands for Agnès d'Evreux, sister to King Charles II of Navarre (who played so important a role in *JRN* and *CA*) and wife of Gaston Phoebus, Count of Foix.[2] Tarbé, like Caylus, assumed Agnès wrote the poems ascribed to *Toute-belle* in *VD,* as well as other lyrics in the Machaut canon where the speaker is feminine, and attributed them to her in a separate edition.[3] In 1875 Paulin Paris demonstrated that Agnès de Navarre cannot have been the prototype for *Toute-belle,* characterized in the story as an unmarried young girl, by proving that Machaut wrote *VD* in the early 1360's, a good fifteen years after Agnès had wed Count Gaston Phoebus. Instead, he identified *Toute-belle* with Peronne or Peronnelle d'Unchair, Dame of Armentières, a wealthy heiress, whose stepfather was Jean de Conflans, Vidame of Châlons and Lord of Vielmaisons in Brie (P. Paris, pp. i-ii, xviii-xxxi). However, Paris joined Caylus and Tarbé in proclaiming

---

[2] M. le Comte de Caylus, "Premier Mémoire sur Guillaume de Machaut, poëte et musicien dans le XIVe siècle: Contenant des recherches sur sa vie, avec une notice de ses principaux ouvrages," in *Mémoires de littérature, tirés des registres de l'Académie royale des Inscriptions et Belles-lettres* 20 (1753): 399-414, esp. 413-14; Prosper Tarbé, ed., *Œuvres de Guillaume de Machault* (Reims-Paris, 1849), his introduction entitled "Recherches sur la Vie et les Ouvrages de Guillaume de Machault."

[3] Prosper Tarbé, ed., *Poésies d'Agnès de Navarre-Champagne, dame de Foix* (Paris-Reims, 1856).

that *VD* is fundamentally autobiographical and that in this quality of truth resides one of the poem's chief merits: "On ne lira pas sans plaisir cette espèce de Journal amoureux du quatorzième siècle: il présente au moins un mérite assez rare dans les Journaux, celui d'être sincère et parfaitement véridique" (P. Paris, p. xxxi). Tarbé and Paris set the tone for subsequent scholars, some of whom proclaim that Machaut invented the *roman vécu* or *mémoires intimes* and that, a Romantic *avant la lettre,* he anticipates Rousseau, Goethe, Chateaubriand, and Stendhal.

In my opinion, the finest piece of scholarship devoted to *VD* is an 1898 doctoral thesis by Georg Hanf. [4] Hanf's work, which has not received the recognition it deserves, sets out to prove that *VD* in its entirety is a work of the imagination—fiction, not reality. His arguments are sufficiently important to be summarized in some detail.

1. Machaut's narrative contains internal contradictions, plausible enough if *VD* is a work of fiction jotted down hastily by an author in his sixties but not if it is an autobiographical memoir transcribed only months after the events took place. For example, in Letter XVII (p. 134) the Narrator refers to *Toute-belle*'s book, that is, *VD* itself, although supposedly he has not yet begun to write down their True Story. In a *complainte Toute-belle* shows she is aware that the Narrator compared her to Semiramis (p. 243), but, if we accept Machaut's text at face value, there is no way she could have discovered this fact.

2. The *VD* is full of gross chronological errors. In Letter VI, purportedly answering one of *Toute-belle*'s epistles received in April 1363, the Narrator promises he will make an effort to visit her by Easter time. Yet in 1363 Easter Sunday had already fallen on the second day of that month. Letters XXXIX, XL, and XLI are all dated November 13 [1364]; however, a long time passes between the writing of XXXIX and XL alone. Then Letter XLIII, which answers XLII (June 16) immediately, is dated October 10, to be followed only fifteen days later by Letter XLIV, dated March 8.

---

[4] Georg Hanf, "Ueber Guillaume de Machauts Voir Dit," *Zeitschrift für romanische Philologie* 22 (1898): 145-96.

3. Several times letters are alluded to which are not transcribed in the text. Rather than that Machaut should have lost them or forgot where they are situated in the narrative, Hanf believes that these allusions were invented for the occasion, for needs of the plot.

4. The Narrator's correspondence and *Toute-belle*'s are indistinguishable. Their letters are constructed identically and written in the same style. They both contain motifs such as: I have received your letter; I am in good health; I am glad you are in good health; I will not forget you; I hope you will not forget me; I desire so much to see you. So too, the lyrics ascribed to *Toute-belle* employ identical rhyme, meter, imagery, and diction as the Narrator's. Her poems are of the same high quality as his. So extraordinary a talent as *Toute-belle*'s, bursting forth at the age of twenty, making her the equal of the leading French poet of the age, would have been noticed by her contemporaries. But they say nothing of Agnès de Navarre, Peronne d'Armentières, or any other lady poet until Christine de Pisan. According to Hanf, the brilliant young poetess existed only in Guillaume de Machaut's imagination. A fictional character, she is not to be identified with Peronne d'Armentières or anyone else who actually lived in the fourteenth century.

Almost forty years after the publication of Hanf's thesis, Walther Eichelberg arrived at a totally different conclusion. [5] He does not deny inconsistencies and contradictions within the narrative but proposes that they be ascribed to the failing memory of an old poet. Machaut would have had in his possession almost his entire correspondence with Peronne. In the process of arranging the letters chronologically and pinpointing the exact circumstances of their redaction, he presumably committed the errors observed by Hanf. Although Eichelberg agrees that much of *VD* is fiction, a residue of courtly convention, he maintains that the central plot line and all the poems and letters are authentic.

I readily grant Eichelberg's point that internal contradictions do not necessarily prove the narrative to be fictional. It is possible that Machaut first composed the letters, both the Narrator's and *Toute-belle*'s, and later fitted them into a frame. His process of creation

---

[5] Walther Eichelberg, *Dichtung und Wahrheit in Machauts "Voir Dit"* (Frankfurt am Main, 1935).

would then indeed have anticipated, *mutatis mutandis,* Rousseau's in *La Nouvelle Héloïse.* But, in my opinion, Hanf's most important argument stands unrefuted: the lyric poems and the letters, whether ascribed to the Narrator or to *Toute-belle,* must have been written by Machaut himself. Astonished at *Toute-belle's* facility as a poet, some scholars, including Eichelberg, suggest that the Narrator may have "touched up" her contributions prior to publication, noting that in the story *Toute-belle* asks him specifically to do it. However, no amount of correcting can account for the extraordinary genius she demonstrates. To any objective reader, her poems can only be the work of Machaut himself. Furthermore, it has been demonstrated that two lyrics purportedly composed months apart (according to *VD*) in fact were written at the same time, and that lyrics *VD* claims to have been composed during the period of the Narrator's amours with *Toute-belle* were written long before 1362-1365.[6]

The letters and poems are central to the plot of *VD,* the skeleton on which the story itself hangs. In a sense, the story exists to set them off, to explain why they were composed. Once they are admitted to be fictional, not much is left to the domain of reality. It is quite possible that the prototype for *Toute-belle* was a certain Peronne; perhaps this Peronne can be identified with Machaut's young contemporary, Jean de Conflans's stepdaughter. But we will never know the exact relationship between this Peronne and the author of *VD,* whether or not they exchanged a poetic correspondence, whether or not they were in love. The "I," whether he be the lover in *Le Roman de la Rose,* the pilgrim in the *Divine Comedy,* or Marcel in *A la recherche du temps perdu,* must never be assimilated in absolute terms to the historical Guillaume de Lorris, Dante, and Proust. The narrators in these three masterworks are the presumed or mock authors. They resemble to a greater or lesser extent their creators but also partake of convention and artifice, are literary characters, no less vital to the structure of their respective narratives than are Reason, Virgil, and Swann. At the very most,

---

[6] Paris, *Le Livre du Voir-Dit,* p. 25, n. 2; Reaney, "A Chronology of the Ballades, Rondeaux and Virelais set to Music by Guillaume de Machaut," and "Towards a Chronology of Machaut's Musical Works"; Günther, "Chronologie und Stil der Kompositionen Guillaume de Machauts"; Poirion, *Le Poète et le Prince,* p. 200; Williams, "An Author's Role in Fourteenth Century Book Production," p. 453.

the details of Machaut's private life gave him inspiration. Just as Proust drew upon his experience to create *A la recherche du temps perdu,* so too Machaut's creative imagination has transformed auto-biographical elements into a work of art, the world of his novel.

The majority of scholars have failed to distinguish between reality and realism. Although realism encourages the reader to believe in a narrative's authenticity, to bring about Coleridge's temporary suspension of disbelief, it is a literary technique, subject to the laws of literature and capable of depicting only literary reality. Tendencies toward a form of realism existed in the Old French period, even in highly idealized genres such as epic and romance. The later Middle Ages then produced an aesthetic combining the most outlandish stylization with concrete detail and an intimate, *creaturlich* representation of the domestic scene. [7] Of course, realism is a relative term at best. We can only use it to reflect measurable contrasts within a work of art or between closely allied works. It must never be presumed aesthetically desirable in and of itself. But as long as authors seek to represent life as it really is (as distinguished from how it might be), to depict characters and events existing in the realm of the probable instead of the merely possible, or simply to obtain an aura of credibility in readers' eyes, the study of reality in art will never be entirely fruitless.

Realia. Perhaps the most obvious trait of realism, especially in the modern novel, is the concrete representation of objects, décor, property—the external world of surfaces. In courtly romance and late epic, extended descriptions of dress, habitation, arms, food, and entertainment serve as ornament or to provide local color but rarely enter into the narrative fabric of the work in question. The same

---

[7] Pierre Jonin, *Les personnages féminins dans les romans français de Tristan au XIIe siècle* (Aix-en-Provence, 1958), and "Aspects de la vie sociale au XIIe siècle, dans *Yvain,*" *L'Information Littéraire* 16 (1964): 47-54; Anthime Fourrier, *Le courant réaliste dans le roman courtois en France au moyen-âge* (Paris, 1960), I; Jeanne Lods, "Quelques aspects de la vie quotidienne chez les conteurs du XIIe siècle," *Cahiers de Civilisation Médiévale* 4 (1961): 23-45; William Calin, *The Old French Epic of Revolt* (Geneva-Paris, 1962), chapt. 5, and *The Epic Quest,* chapts. 1 and 2; Faith Lyons, *Les éléments descriptifs dans le roman d'aventure au XIIIe siècle* (Geneva, 1965); Huizinga, *The Waning of the Middle Ages,* chapts. 16, 21, and 22; Erich Auerbach, *Mimesis: dargestellte Wirklichkeit in der abendländischen Literatur* (Berne, 1946), chapt. 10.

can be said for Machaut's own depiction of an ideal court in *JRB*, *RF*, and *FA*. The pilgrimage to Saint-Denis in *VD*, however, has a different function. After having dined, *Toute-belle* wishes to sleep; a sergeant of arms, so drunk that tears flow from his eyes and he weaves back and forth on his feet, sends them to a peasant's house on the other side of town, where, sharing two beds, *Toute-belle*, her sister, her confidante, and the Narrator doze off. This episode evokes the reality of life at a fair and also treats an interior scene, the intimacy of the bed, in a manner foreign to the early Middle Ages.

Space and Time. The action of *VD* takes place neither in the mythical world of King Arthur nor in the idealized, allegorical dream-locus of *Le Roman de la Rose*. On the contrary, its locale is shown to be the France of Machaut's own time, known perfectly to him and his public. The Narrator lives in Reims, *Toute-belle* in Paris and the South; she travels to her lands in Brie; he visits her in Paris and Duke Charles in Normandy and Brie; they both travel to Saint-Denis.

By dating the letters and through other devices, Machaut pinpoints chronology. In spite of the occasional contradictions noted above, scholars have determined when the major events in the story took place. [8] *Toute-belle* first contacts the Narrator in August or September 1362. He sets out to visit her on April 27, 1363. The lovers go to the Lendit Fair on June 12, and *Toute-belle* gives the Narrator the "key to her treasure" on June 20 of that same year. The story is not compressed into one highly charged day or day and a half, as in some of Machaut's early tales. It develops over a span of years; the characters also are transformed in time. We notice weather and the change of season: a rainy day when *Toute-belle* visits the Narrator in church or winter storms that prevent him from rejoining her. Anticipating one aspect of the novel, *VD* creates a sense of duration quite modern in tone.

Contemporary allusions. These storms, characterized by wind, rain, snow, freezing cold, the uprooting of trees, and collapse of houses, correspond to unusually harsh winters in 1362-1363 and

---

[8] Hanf, "Ueber Guillaume de Machauts Voir Dit," pp. 158-60, 170-92; Chichmaref, *Guillaume de Machaut*, I: liii-lxiv; Armand Machabey, *Guillaume de Machault: La Vie et l'Œuvre musical*, I: 56-62.

1363-1364. Further obstacles separating the lovers are a resurgence of the Plague in the second half of 1363 and the presence of the "Grandes Compagnies," bands of mercenary soldiers that roam the countryside and pillage at will. The leader of one of the most ferocious bands in Champagne, Arnaud de Cervoles, Archpriest of Vélines, is mentioned by name, and *Toute-belle* continually warns the Narrator of the risks he takes when visiting her. Aside from the Narrator himself (assimilated to the poet Guillaume de Machaut), other verifiable personages of the 1360s are alluded to in passing: Machaut's brother Jean; the Duke of Normandy; and the Duke of Bar. The Duke of Normandy, John of Bohemia's grandson and brother to John of Berry, is known to have had warm relations with the poet. Machaut praises him in *La Prise d'Alexandrie* and, according to reports, entertained him in his own home during one of Charles's visits to Reims (December 1361). In *VD* the Narrator is summoned to the Duke's court on several occasions and, in a dream-sequence, has a long conversation with a "King," who probably also may be assimilated to the man who, in 1364, became Charles V, king of France. These seemingly irrelevant episodes illustrate the poet's snobbery, a pride in high connections, but also help create an aura of verisimilitude for the tale as a whole.

Class and moral problems. It has been claimed that modern realism coincides with the rise of the bourgeoisie and reflects an author's willingness to depict social classes other than the aristocracy and to treat the most deep-seated issues of his day. From this perspective, *VD* remains firmly imbedded in the Middle Ages. Although she does not dwell in a fairy castle, *Toute-belle* is a Lady, a member of the nobility. True, she participates in the daily life of her age— goes on pilgrimages, visits fairs, has a family and a secretary, is never free to choose her husband. But those issues which ripped apart French society in the fourteenth and fifteenth centuries— poverty, famine, civil war, plague, rebellion—have no real impact on her life. When they are mentioned at all, they serve only as a backdrop to her amours.

The Narrator is identified as a poet and cleric, of unmistakably plebeian origins, and whose professional commitments—a novena, a trip to the court—play a role in the action. He is also a writer, and passages in *VD* shed light on physical circumstances of book production in the fourteenth century.[9] However, the theme of the poet who adores a lady of vastly superior status entered romance literature with the troubadours. In *VD* the Narrator exists only to love and write poems. How he earns a living, whether or not he keeps warm in winter, what he does when not meditating on *Toute-belle* are of no concern to the author or his public.

On one occasion Machaut does satirize contemporary manners. When, in a dream, the Narrator visits the King Who Never Lies to seek counsel, he first lectures the king on how to rule (cf. *CA*) and later complains of the ills that beset his age: taxes, war, brigands, and the plague. However, this one dream-episode is structurally not indispensable to *VD*. The profound concern for moral issues which characterizes works such as *Raoul de Cambrai* and *La Mort le roi Artu* was foreign to Machaut, as to most other writers of his century.

Psychology. Unlike many protagonists of allegory and romance, the two main characters of *VD* give the impression of being individual, clearly delineated, believable human beings. *Toute-belle* is a coquettish, egotistical *vravelette* (p. 111), attracted by the fame of an older poet, then perhaps caught up in her own game. She permits him to kiss her and enter her bed, knowing she runs little risk, and can then reproach him both for timidity and aggressiveness. Whether the critics attack or defend *Toute-belle,* they never have been indifferent to her peculiar charm. The same is true for the poet who is torn by jealousy, uncertainty, an inferiority complex, and the purely physical incapacity of old age. His scruples over paying court to *Toute-belle* and over writing down their story for the world to see partake of centuries-old literary conventions but are indeed appropriate to a sexagenarian who dreads ridicule. Certain episodes sparkle with life: the Narrator in bed with *Toute-belle,* content yet afraid to touch her and rationalizing his cowardice with a tirade against "bad" lovers; the Narrator, riding home from a visit to his lady, terrified at assault by brigands, and then joyfully at ease, relaxing in his room, contemptuous of the brigands, who cannot hurt him now, God curse them! or the Narrator's fits of estrangement, alternating with equally violent manifestations of tenderness, which portray the reality of Eros in a way not generally to be seen in French literature prior to the Classical theater.

---

[9] Williams, "An Author's Role in Fourteenth Century Book Production."

Plot. With the exception of the Narrator's dreams and a few episodes where allegorical figures appear, the plot of *VD* is remarkably credible. For all intents and purposes, the supernatural makes no appearance, nor is the action complicated by a piling-up of adventures, secondary characters, or the intrusion of melodrama. In general, it is more amorphous, less consciously literary, than in Machaut's other *dits.* Whatever the loss in purely aesthetic terms, however, it gives the impression that normal, believable events happen to normal, believable people. And sexual matters are treated with a greater freedom than is usually the case in fourteenth-century poetry or, to judge from the scathing moral denunciation the Narrator or *Toute-belle* has received from certain scholars, the habitual reading matter of nineteenth- and early twentieth-century academics.

The letters and the poems serve to guarantee the narrative's authenticity. Machaut creates the illusion that they existed first as historical fact and that he wrote the frame-story later to explain how they came into being. In reality, we do not know whether the letters or the frame were composed first, or both approximately at the same time. Structurally, the frame-tale exists independently, the letters do not. The latter serve primarily to document the frame, perpetuating the illusion of historical truth. That Machaut succeeded in this endeavor is proved by the fact that so many scholars believe the tale to be autobiographical and that, although for his edition Paulin Paris often deleted material from the narrative frame and on one occasion (perhaps by inadvertence) from the lyrics, [10] to the best of my knowledge he cut not one line from the epistles.

---

[10] Page 243, vv. 5556-57 read:

> En dueil, en tristesse et en plour,
>   Sans nul meffait,
> Resgarde, amis, comment je plour,
> Oy mes souspirs, oy ma clamour ...

Cf. also p. 255, vv. 5870-75, read:

> Aussi Pallas, vostre sage baisselle,
> Li Dieu feront feste de la nouvelle,
> Et quant tous biens avez soubz vostre aisselle
> (Qu'il vous servent bonnement sans cautelle),
> Serez-vous donc a mon depri rebelle? ...

And lines 5907-34, pp. 256-57, part of the narrative frame and separated from the *complainte* by a miniature, should not have been printed in smaller type, as if they were a continuation of the lyric.

Style. According to Auerbach, the use of low style (*sermo humilis*) or a mixture of low, middle, and sublime styles is central to the development of realism in Western literature. In this respect, *VD*, like Machaut's other tales, partakes of an older, nonrealistic tradition. Machaut's elegant, charming couplets adhere to roughly the same register as in Chrétien de Troyes and Guillaume de Lorris: a worldly, sophisticated, aristocratic *sermo mediocris*. With the exception of a few minor lyrics (Chichmaref, 2, *Appendice*), nowhere do we find in Machaut's canon the scurrilous vulgarity of some *chansons de geste* and *fabliaux,* nowhere the extraordinary variety of styles in Adam de la Halle, Jean de Meun, and Dante. On the other hand, Machaut's style corresponds perfectly to the milieu he portrays, especially in his handling of dialogue. *Toute-belle*'s short, charming speeches are eminently appropriate to her status and character. Furthermore, on at least one occasion, Machaut employs *sermo humilis* to add verisimilitude to what is obviously a nonrealistic scene: when *Honte* and *Espoirs* visit the Narrator in his hostel (pp. 85-91). *Honte* leaps at the Narrator like a bear or wild pig, crying, "Qui t'éust tantost mené pendre, / Il n'éust perdu que la corde" (p. 86); upon which, *Espoirs* berates *Honte,* calling her "garce ... chetive, nice et fole" (p. 89), a spoilsport and killjoy, who, if she drowned in the ice floes of Prussia, would not be mourned for long.

Stylistic variety is provided by the lyrics, written in *sermo gravis,* and the prose letters, which may have given the impression of a more humble register. The sublime, passionate amatory epistle *à la* Ovid, Abelard, and the Provençal *Salut d'amour,* is here reduced to a repetitive, long-winded, frankly dull correspondence. Machaut consciously emphasizes the prosaic character of the epistles to give the impression that these letters are authentic historical documentation. The medievals, like our twentieth-century public, considered prose the appropriate medium for history. Although the *VD* epistles, which correspond to forms elaborated in the *Artes scribendi,* are as stylized as a *ballade* or *rondeau,* they do reflect the epistolary style of their century; letters like theirs were written. Therefore, this artificial, fictional correspondence is indeed "realistic," though not quite in Auerbach's terms.

Compared to most other romances and allegories of his day, Machaut's *VD* portrays reality in a relatively honest, forthright manner. We must not exaggerate his success in this domain, however. The *VD* remains a medieval poem adhering to the conventions of medieval narrative. Eichelberg has convincingly demonstrated that traditional courtly motifs appear throughout. We are told of love's power, how, tormented, the Narrator nonetheless praises to the sky *Amour* and *Toute-belle*. He and *Toute-belle* become enamored from afar on the basis of good reputation, before ever having laid eyes on each other. They exchange hearts and other, more tangible love-tokens. *Toute-belle*'s friend Colombelle, her cousin Guillemette, her sister, her secretary, her confessor, the Narrator's secretary, his brother, and other friends serve as confidants and intermediaries. Machaut compares the good *amant couart* with the bad *fol hardi* and emphasizes the role of trust in a relationship. Finally, whole episodes are devoted to allegory: a debate between *Honte* and *Espoirs, Esperance*'s career as a bandit, and lengthy portraits of *Amour* and *Fortune*. The total fabric of *VD* gives an impression different from that of a modern novel or even the *Decameron* and the *Canterbury Tales*.

Traits which appear to reflect contemporary life and succeed in convincing the modern reader of the story's authenticity may have originated as literary convention or opposition to convention. It seems likely that many of the early troubadours and trouvères adopted a distinct literary personality: Bernart de Ventadorn the timid lover, Peire Vidal the boaster, Arnaut Daniel the lunatic, [11] Colin Muset the glutton, Rutebeuf the pauper, Adam de la Halle the frustrated would-be scholar. Machaut too adopted a *persona:* the timid, inept, bumbling narrator-witness or narrator-lover. Frequent changes of season in *VD* may be pathetic fallacy, the joy of the Lendit Fair a symbolic marriage. Machaut describes *Toute-belle*'s attire in detail (pp. 82-84); however, this lush, concrete evocation of external reality serves in part to elicit an allegorical interpretation of the colors she is wearing.

In *VD,* as in Rabelais, Cervantes, Fielding, Diderot, and Stendhal, realism is a manifestation of antiromance. The author exposes traditional courtly artifice, indulges in a parody of *fin' amor*. The

---

[11] See D. R. Sutherland, "L'élément théâtral dans 'la canso' chez les troubadours de l'époque classique," in *Actes et Mémoires du IIIe Congrès international de Langue et Littérature d'Oc* (Bordeaux, 1965), 2: 95-101.

courtly and the noncourtly, the romantic and the down-to-earth, are juxtaposed, one convention played off against another for literary purposes, to create a mood of laughter and sophisticated, ironic detachment. For example, the Narrator burns without evidence of heat and light and shivers without being cold. When *Toute-belle* has not written for a time, he falls into melancholia ("Si pris à merencolier ... Si devins merencolieus," p. 24), turns pale, changes color, loses sleep, and cannot eat. In a *ballade* (pp. 25-26) the Narrator swears he will die unless God and ladies help him; later in the story he is about to perish at the hands of *Desir*. Needless to say, he does not pass away. Someone or something always turns up to cure him: *Toute-belle,* her poem, her letter, her portrait, the God of Love, *Esperance,* or a messenger. Yet no matter how often the Narrator recovers, he shortly reverts to melancholia and, as often as not, is put to bed within an inch of his life. This oscillation between joy and sadness is a hallmark both of courtly lovers and poets born under the sign of Saturn. [12]

The Narrator has not been felled by lovesickness alone. He was ill in bed before ever having heard of *Toute-belle,* even though at that time he had not been in love for a good ten or twelve years. He suffers from the gout, several times is physically incapacitated, and bewails that he is neither handsome nor worthy enough to appear before his beloved, a reference perhaps to the fact that he has lost the sight of an eye, for he refers to himself as "vostre borgne vallet" (Letter XIII, p. 118). These plaints represent not the conventional humility of a well-read courtly lover but an inferiority complex deriving from concrete, physical infirmity. The truth of the matter lies in the fact that to some extent the Narrator evokes Guillaume de Machaut, who was in his sixties when he wrote *VD*. Machaut's poem narrates a love story between a young girl and an old man. *Toute-belle* declares, and the Narrator agrees, that their love has come too late. The Narrator also compares his lady to Hebe, who, in *l'Ovide moralisé,* rejuvenated Iolaus; in similar fashion, says the Narrator, *Toute-belle* restores my youth and cures my ills (pp. 210-11). Thus are to be explained allusions to the Narrator's feeble health and his having been immune to love for so many years.

---

[12] See above my analysis of *JRN*, pp. 123-29, and Heger, *Die Melancholie bei den französischen Lyrikern des Spätmittelalters,* pp. 217-19.

Andreas Capellanus denies love to men over sixty and women over fifty years of age (p. 14). Whereas Andreas's strictures are based on purely physical criteria (that love is grounded in physical desire, which must at least bear the potentiality of consummation), we know that the troubadours exalted youth or *jovens* as one of the qualities most important in a lover.[13] True, Moshé Lazar has striven to minimize the term's concreteness. He writes: "*Jovens* ne signifie guère (sauf dans quelques rares passages...) jeunesse d'âge, jeune homme, esprit particulier à la jeunesse. Il semple plutôt représenter un ensemble de vertus et de devoirs exigé par le code de la *cortezia,* une somme de qualités morales qui font qu'un homme est courtois."[14] Nonetheless, however general or abstract the virtues associated with *jovens* may have been, youth still means youth. The medieval public, when confronted with the word and/or the traits it evokes, could not remain oblivious to its more concrete, direct meaning. Furthermore, are not many of the virtues associated with *jovens* and *cortezia* — enthusiasm, good nature, a warm heart, exaltation of love and the love discipline — often ascribed, even if mistakenly, to youth? In the courtly realm, as throughout world literature, love is a game for the young. Sons triumph over fathers, young girls over their guardians, young women over doddering or blind husbands. Like the protagonist of *JRN,* the *VD* Narrator is an old poet. In the winter of life, he suffers from melancholia and phlegm; the Greater Infortune Saturn is more appropriate to his state than bright-shining Venus. His continual indispositions reflect symbolic impotence, for it is by no means coincidental that, despite *Toute-belle's* repeated advances, she probably remains *virgo intacta* throughout *VD.* The Narrator is as inadequate as that other famous one-eyed lover, Polyphemus. Machaut tells the latter's story at length. We see an ugly, ridiculous personage, who, though he believes himself to be ravishingly handsome, cannot fool Galatea. Both the

---

[13] See Alexander J. Denomy, "*Jovens:* The Notion of Youth among the Troubadours, Its Meaning and Source," *Mediaeval Studies* 11 (1949): 1-22; cf. with René Nelli, *L'Erotique des Troubadours* (Toulouse, 1963), pp. 85, 111-14.

[14] Moshé Lazar, "Les éléments constitutifs de la 'cortezia' dans la lyrique des troubadours," *Studi Mediolatini e Volgari* 6-7 (1959): 67-96, esp. p. 81; reprinted in *Amour courtois et "fin'amors" dans la littérature du XII*e *siècle* (Paris, 1964), p. 33.

Narrator and Polyphemus fail in their amorous quests. The *VD* tells of an old poet who had renounced love but then is driven to folly by a young girl no wiser than he. It is the story of May and January, young and old, beautiful and ugly, two people totally mismatched in spite of themselves.

In his interpretation of the portrait of *Amour,* Machaut repeatedly tells us that a lover must be brave. He may be timid before his lady but must show courage to other men, be willing to earn her favor with love-service. However, although in this *aventùre* (p. 2) the Narrator is offered two occasions to test his prowess, he fails lamentably both times. Returning from *Toute-belle's* residence, he dreads an encounter with brigands. Real bandits do catch sight of him, but he is taken prisoner by an allegorical figure, a woman. *Esperance* is angry at him because he has neglected to mention her in *VD*; his ransom then is to compose a *lai* in her honor. Once he has been ransomed, the Narrator rides home and hides in his chamber. Machaut has created an amusing parody of courtly adventure. The episode is patently fictitious, an excuse for inserting in *VD* the poet's elegant, technically sophisticated *lai,* but it also tells us something about the Narrator's character, his inability to conform to Arthurian romance in a post-Jean de Meun world. *Toute-belle* goes along with the joke. She pretends to be overjoyed that the Narrator survived these "aventures vous avés eu en chemin" (Letter **XXII,** p. 182). Her use of the term *aventure* indicates that she too is aware of the tradition which her lover can follow only in jest.

The second occasion occurs when the Narrator permits his secretary and others to dissuade him from visiting *Toute-belle.* The weather is bad, says the secretary, and bandits prowl the land. "If they hold you prisoner for three or four days in a tower, you will surely die, *Car vous estes un tenres homs*" (p. 285). The times are too harsh even for a young man, not to speak of one suffering from gout; in any case *Toute-belle* would not want her suitor to risk his life. Indeed she does not, but cannot help reproaching him for not having come to see her (Letter XLIII). For, as *Toute-belle* points out, the Narrator not only stayed at home in winter and when the *grandes compagnies* were ravaging the land but also in summertime when the roads were open and his health improved. In fact, from June 20, 1363, to the end of the story (May 1365) he makes no concerted effort at all to visit the Star of Day and the Flower of

Flowers. *Toute-belle* says that if she had been in his shoes, she would have acted differently. All this implies, of course, that, judged from a courtly perspective, he fails as a lover and as a man.

As in *DL* and *JRN,* Machaut's protagonist is measured against the traditional hero of romance. The romance hero receives a call to adventure and leaves his home to follow a road of trials to the Other World, where he is aided by his squire or a supernatural protective figure. He enters a fairy castle, meets a divine maiden or temptress, triumphs over Other World monsters, and wins a boon, perhaps treasure or the divine maiden's hand in marriage. Then he returns to his homeland to enjoy the fruits of victory. His story, which recounts a *rite de passage* from childhood to adult status, generally ends with his initiation into the community. In *VD,* on the other hand, the Narrator refuses the call to adventure or, when he does set out, the obstacles he faces are only wind and rain or a few bandits in the distance. His quest takes the form of a novena in Paris and a pilgrimage to Saint-Denis. His homeland is Reims, the divine maiden's castle her family estate in or near Paris. Her secretary acts as the Herald of Adventure. Supernatural aid is provided by Venus, *Esperance,* and the Narrator's secretary (a surrogate squire), who is indeed wiser than his master but sometimes impedes the quest. The Narrator attains no victory. He does not marry *Toute-belle;* for most of the story they are separated except for an endless correspondence; the only token he wins is a key to her "treasure" he never has an occasion to use. By comparing himself to Gawain, Lancelot, and Tristan, the Narrator only reveals how his conduct differs from theirs, that in fact he resembles more closely King Arthur and Mark. His only adventures are psychological, his ordeal merely to face a lady. Normally in the world of romance a youth desires a beautiful maiden but is separated from her by a husband or husband surrogate. The hero's victory implies defying the husband's will and winning the girl for himself. In *VD* no father or husband prevents the Narrator from loving *Toute-belle,* and the chief opposition he must overcome is not the plague, bandits, or cold weather, but his own fear. He himself is old enough to be her father or grandfather; he is the father figure and bears within himself the obstacle to fulfillment.

The atmosphere of *VD* is more sensuous than in any other of Machaut's tales. *Toute-belle* allows the Narrator to kiss her in the garden, then gives him the *pax* in church. At Saint-Denis she suggests he join her in bed and, upon awakening, she makes him embrace her. Later, she asks him to visit her in her chamber at daybreak. He looks in by the open window, sees her nude, and enjoys some sort of possession (see below, pp. 189-91).

I have already said that sex is by no means absent from *fin' amor*. However, scaling the *gradus amoris* is a long, torturous process. At each stage the lover must prove himself worthy of his lady's favors, which she bestows only after lengthy debate. The erotic theme in *VD* resembles instead the noncourtly tribute of a Colin Muset to his *touzette*, the free, easy amours in pastoral, or the epic and romance hero's temptation by a passionate Saracen princess, an Other World fay, or simply a *femme fatale* married to someone else. The *VD* flatly contradicts the dictum that a lady must under no circumstances be the first to declare her love (cf. Lavine in *Enéas*, Soredamors in *Cligès*, and Brunissens in *Jaufré*). *Toute-belle* makes the advances, and it is the Narrator who recoils from physical contact. The very essence of *fin' amor* is turned into derision.

Both lovers recognize the importance of discretion. The Narrator takes care not to be seen too often alone with *Toute-belle*. She warns him to conceal part of their relationship from her brother and not to let him see her portrait over the Narrator's bed. We are also told it was necessary for Venus to descend in a cloud, covering the lovers from public view, before they indulged in physical intimacies. The Narrator protests often that his duties as a courtly lover include preserving *Toute-belle*'s reputation and honor. It is obvious, however, that he is more concerned with the former than the latter. And, cloud or no cloud, *Toute-belle* tosses aside all reserve. She insists that the Narrator tell the whole story of their liaison, suppressing nothing, not even the physical details, and takes pride that at court her name is on everyone's lips. She even writes the Narrator that she will be disgraced if their affair is publicly broken off, not because people will discover she loved an old poet socially her inferior but because they may assume that it was her fault. For *Toute-belle,* honor has ceased to reside in chastity or the reputation of chastity. It derives instead from the fame of a notorious relationship. A lover, seeking desperately but ineffectually to adhere to the old code, is set off against a lady who repudiates the code with effrontery and imposes upon him a totally different scale of values.

The Narrator shows no mercy to the traditional enemy of *fin' amor*, the *losengier*. He adheres to courtly tradition by castigating false lovers, braggarts, talebearers, and *jaloux:* they are like venomous serpents, he says, and should be transformed into boars, trees, and rocks. The Ovidian story of Coronis of Larissa is retold as a warning against them. Upon a closer reading of *VD,* however, we discover that the *losengiers* who speak against *Toute-belle* are a noble lord, another friend, the secretary, the Duke of Normandy, and the Narrator himself. These are worthy, respected people, whose statements are not to be rejected out of hand. Is Machaut telling us that *losengiers* tell the truth and courtly lovers are fools? Furthermore, unlike the conventional talebearer of lyric and romance, these *losengiers* do not slander the lover to his lady, nor both young people to her husband. They undermine the lady in her lover's eyes, and he, who ought never to dream of doubting her, half believes the tattle.

Away from the court, *fin' amor* is inconceivable. Courtly society exists to sanction love; love is society's ethos, and love-service a formal social rite. In *JRB, RF, JRN,* and *FA* Machaut in no way deviates from the traditional perspective. And in *VD,* whether because people have discovered the Narrator's new liaison or for her own inherent good qualities, *Toute-belle* becomes an object of praise in society (Letter XXV, p. 191). The Narrator's trips to court and his pilgrimage to Saint-Denis establish an atmosphere of bustle, play, gallantry, and spectacle. Love flowers in a social situation, symbolically part of a spring festival.

On the other hand, although this love takes place in society, society seems to disapprove of it. The Noble Lord praises *Toute-belle* but ridicules the Narrator for loving her in a passionate, all-consuming way; and his other friends attack *Toute-belle* to his face. Machaut's plebeian suitor adheres to courtly doctrine, while aristocrats act like anticourtly *losengiers*. Perhaps the Narrator's passion is unseemly in a low-born, overage rhymester, in which case it is not courtly love in the abstract but only this one *amour* that is undermined. Or perhaps Machaut tells us how ridiculous the conventions of *fin' amor* appear outside the world of books, even to the class which gave it birth. In any event, at the end of the poem the Narrator does not return to the court. With or without *Toute-belle,* he is not integrated into courtly society; both he and his beloved are condemned to solitude. Since the Narrator makes the mistake of taking a game (The King Who Never Lies; *Fin' amor*) seriously, his excesses are reproved by the community.

An ideal courtly lover is patient, submissive, and well disciplined, the epitome of *mezura,* ever faithful to his lady even though she mistreats him. The *VD* Narrator does conform to the stereotype, at least in part: his *Complainte* (pp. 252-56) and *Le Lay d'Esperance* (pp. 172-80) would not be out of place in the most orthodox courtly circles. He declares that if all the women in the world offered themselves, he would refuse them for love of *Toute-belle*; on the contrary, he will serve ladies and sing their praises entirely out of respect for her.

However, such declarations are juxtaposed to episodes where the Narrator acts in an uncourtly manner. In *Toute-belle*'s presence he either bursts into tears without provocation or remains silent in the face of her most charming advances. Admittedly, an *amant couart* can neither maintain control over himself nor live up to the highest ideal of *mezura.* However, the Narrator goes too far. His temper tantrums, inappropriate to a young lover, are ridiculous in a man three or four times *Toute-belle*'s age.

More damaging still are his fits of jealousy. Because he has heard that *Toute-belle*'s sentiments toward him have changed, without making any further investigation the Narrator curses his eyes, the day he was born, *Toute-belle*'s beauty, Fortune, and Loyalty, and then takes out his wrath on the beloved's portrait by locking it in a chest. Although the Narrator does not wholeheartedly sub-scribe to his friends' insinuations against *Toute-belle* and with a fine show of prudence decides not to condemn her in haste, he does withdraw into himself, finds that artistic inspiration has abandoned him, and debates whether or not he should leave her. His lukewarm response, the way he mulls over the *losengiers'* slanders, are an insult to *Toute-belle* and to *fin' amor.* He even descends to anti-feminism: this poet, who proclaimed he would sing the praises of all ladies in *Toute-belle*'s name, tells how falcons are trained and draws the lesson that lovers should train their ladies in the same way (cf. *DA*). A man should love a woman if she responds well to training but cast her off if she does not. Then he compares *Toute-belle* to Dame Fortune, accusing his beloved of indifference, blind-ness, and deception.

The old Narrator attacks ladies in general, and *Toute-belle* in particular, with the same verve as in *JRB, DA,* and *JRN.* He too is as much a disciple of Jean de Meun as of Guillaume de Lorris. Yet, unlike the witty, sophisticated defendant in *JRN,* he mocks ladies from weakness not strength. He is a cowardly, suspicious lover who flaunts his failure, who berates *Toute-belle* for what he imagines rather than for what she has done. Nor can he be consistent even in error, for he vacillates between jealousy and confidence, reproaches and humble submission. *Toute-belle's* priest points out that Dame Fortune resembles the Narrator, not *Toute-belle*; he acts like a woman, blindly credits tattle, and falls into melancholia over a trifle. In every respect he is totally ill equipped to enter into a meaningful relationship with his beautiful young admirer.

He adores *Toute-belle* as a goddess. He sends her a verse epistle in which every two or three lines appears the refrain, "Mon cuer, ma suer, ma douce amour" (pp. 184-85); in a poem of only fifty-one lines the refrain recurs twenty-four times, thus creating an effect not unlike the mock litanies in Baudelaire and Verlaine. [15] Twice the Narrator proclaims that *Toute-belle* has cured his illness. Saints perform miracles to heal people, he has been told, but he has never seen one nor witnessed any so great as reviving a dispirited lover. The Narrator also adores the poems, letters, and love-tokens *Toute-belle* sends him; he kneels before her portrait as an icon; and we are told that the image heals him and appears in his dreams. It is obvious that *Toute-belle* has been assimilated to Mary and that the Narrator venerates her as he would the Holy Virgin. This does not prevent our clerical hero from worshiping Venus too, nor from transforming *Toute-belle* herself into a pagan deity, higher in station than Pallas, Juno, and Venus, who after she dies will become a star to illumine the world.

The Narrator's immediate ecclesiastical superior would probably be more concerned to discover that his canon undertakes a novena as an excuse to visit *Toute-belle,* and every day in church thinks only of her; that he reads the Hours while waiting for her at a rendezvous or, worse still, composes lyrics in her honor instead of performing his devotions. They go on a pilgrimage to Saint-Denis,

---

[15] See Gustave Cohen, "Le *Voir Dit* de Guillaume de Machaut (vers 1365)," *Lettres Romanes* 1 (1947): 99-111, esp. pp. 109-10.

where the Narrator meditates only on her, and they snuggle in bed. Of course, the Narrator is not *Toute-belle*'s only contact with Holy Church. One of her confidants is a priest, who, after *Toute-belle* tells him of her love in the confessional, discloses all to the lover in question. The lover commends *Toute-belle* for confiding in this ecclesiastic and at no time does he rebuke the man's conduct.

We can readily agree with Paulin Paris when he writes: "Peut-être serons-nous aujourd'hui scandalisés de cette sorte d'accord entre l'amour divin et l'amour profane; mais le quatorzième siècle n'avait ni les mêmes scrupules ni la même délicatesse" (p. xxxiii). However, although Machaut's contemporaries would not have been shocked by his narrative, they could have responded to it as comedy. Unlike Lancelot, Guilhem de Nevers, and other heroes of romance, the *VD* Narrator is not a knight parodying or temporarily masquerading as a cleric, but the contrary: a cleric aping a knight. Profane love is ennobled by contact with the divine in the *Lancelot-Grail Cycle* and in Dante. In *VD* the opposite takes place: *Toute-belle* and Venus replace the Virgin, and flesh triumphs over spirit. The Narrator, a man of the cloth, is successfully tempted from the true path and consciously, willfully whores after strange gods. A scholar and poet, he takes himself seriously as a lover, abandons Reason for Love, and fails miserably. We discover that the knight-lover and poet-scholar are distinct entities. Any effort to play both roles at the same time results in disaster.

In *VD* the roles of lover and beloved, knight and lady, are reversed. The Narrator manifests cowardice, prudishness, vacillation, and a quick temper, and is compared to Dame Fortune. *Toute-belle,* on the contrary, makes the advances and gives evidence of pluck and courage. For all her innocence, she appears more experienced in the code of *fin' amor* than the Narrator himself. He teaches her poetry and music, but she instructs him in love. Wisdom is to be found in the girl, a *puella senex,* not in the distinguished poet who, despite his advanced years, acts like a child. The Narrator functions as a woman, while *Toute-belle* assumes the man's role; their attributes have been exchanged or, at least, merged.

The reversal of roles and a series of contrasts in the love-relationship (young-old, beautiful-ugly, natural-artificial, profane-sacred) give rise to humor. Certain episodes are frankly comic, such as the Narrator's encounter with *Esperance* in the guise of a bandit, his timidity with *Toute-belle* in bed, and an earlier rendezvous when the Narrator's secretary acts as go-between, urging his timid master to kiss a leaf he has placed on the lips of *Toute-belle,* who pretends to be asleep. Of course, at the decisive moment the secretary withdraws the leaf, and *Toute-belle* feigns anger, to the Narrator's exaggerated consternation. The Narrator has only, while dreaming, to see *Toute-belle's* portrait wear green (the color of change and renovation) instead of blue (the color of loyalty), to run in panic to the King Who Never Lies, but, despite his haste, he loses valuable time giving a lesson in princely conduct to the "monarch" whose advice he seeks and interrupts his own love-plaint to discourse on high taxes and the war. Meanwhile, the King chaffs the Narrator: "A real example of metamorphosis, such as Ovid or Josephus recounts, would terrify you far more than what has happened to *Toute-belle's* portrait; furthermore, all the sages of Antiquity cannot help you in erotic matters. You shouldn't attack Love or your Lady. And in any case you have talked too much." A general burst of laughter sets a dog barking, whereupon the Narrator wakes up to see *Toute-belle's* portrait also laughing at him. Later in the story, when his secretary urges him not to visit *Toute-belle* in winter, the Narrator rejects his advice, accusing him in turn of having spoken too much. This does not prevent him, however, from believing the secretary *in petto* and postponing his trip indefinitely. He does so because a noble friend also counsels him not to go. "You are besotted by love and won't listen to me," he says. "I don't say anything against *Toute-belle;* she is splendid. But you have degraded yourself by becoming love's slave. Ah! I knew you wouldn't listen to me; my time is wasted." The scene's irony lies in the fact that the friend does indeed attack *Toute-belle,* accusing her of infidelity, and that, in spite of himself, the Narrator does cease to trust his beloved.

In Bergsonian terms the Narrator is guilty of rigidity. His cowardice, jealousy, and prudishness become obsessions and render him ridiculous. The realities of life—his age and social status as a cleric—interfere with his desire to be an ideal courtly lover. He is directed from without, as a puppet: by his dreams, by the hearsay of others, by what he suspects to be a change of tone in *Toute-belle's* letters. And, whatever manifestations his obsessions take—tears, sickness, anger, reproaches—they occur again and again, repeated in almost identical fashion. Additional humor is created by this element of repetition, central to Bergson's notion of *raideur mécanique*. Furthermore, the Narrator is the victim of what Bergson calls the snowballing technique. On the one hand, assuming his amorous life is in peril, he complains to kings, merely on the strength of an admittedly unreliable dream or of hearsay from equally unreliable sources. On the other hand, when evidence does pile up against *Toute-belle,* whether it be valid or not, Machaut's helpless suitor does nothing to confirm his suspicions one way or the other. Thus great causes give rise to disproportionately tiny effects, and earth-shattering forces are unleashed by insignificant events.

As in *JRN,* Machaut's undermining his own *persona* becomes perhaps the major theme of *VD.* Although this is a peculiarly modern phenomenon, Jean de Meun, Machaut, Chaucer, Gower, and Juan Ruiz laid the groundwork. The total effect is a corrosion of romance by what may be called the ironic vision. The lyrics contribute a courtly tone, a representation of love in the abstract, which is then belied by rhyming couplets that tell of a liaison between two people in the world. The exalted language of the *ballade* and *complainte* does not fit the day-to-day existence of *Toute-belle* and her suitor. Sentimental rhetoric is deflated when characters who try to live up to the romance ideal are forced into a situation where their code proves worthless. The public discovers that people cannot live up to the ideal, and that the ideal itself is invalid when it no longer relates to everyday reality.

The plot line of *VD* is subject to more than one ambiguity. When the Narrator comes to say good-bye to *Toute-belle* (pp. 153-63), we do not know whether their love is consummated or not. Since in the course of the poem the two will never meet again, the question is of some importance. After gazing upon a nude *Toute-belle,* the Narrator prays to Venus for *hardement.* The Goddess of Love then descends in a cloud of *manne* and *fin baume,* which permits the Narrator to satisfy his desires hidden from public gaze:

p. 157   Que de joie fui raemplis
            Et mes desirs fu acomplis:
            Si bien que plus ne demandoie
            Ne riens plus je ne desiroie [.]
f. 255 r° (b)   Car a la deësse plaisoit
            Par miracles qu'elle faisoit.

Some scholars assume that, having given herself to the Narrator, from that moment *Toute-belle* ceased to be a maiden. However, the Narrator protests at length that *Toute-belle*'s honor has not been sullied and that only people with dirty minds will accuse them of sin. Perhaps Machaut believes that the last of the *quinque lineae amoris* is praiseworthy or that *Toute-belle*'s honor will be preserved if talebearers do not catch them in the act, that her reputation remains untarnished regardless of the state of her virtue. Or perhaps the Narrator's paean of satisfied desire should not be taken as literally as in a contemporary novel. He says that his soul became satiated by *Toute-belle*'s fruit (p. 159), but we are then informed that *Pité* plucked this fruit from *Toute-belle*'s "colored" face. The fruit may then be nothing more than a silent avowal of passion (*Toute-belle*'s blushing countenance), rather than more concrete sexual favors.

I propose a solution to this problem based on the fact that just after the bed scene and before the Narrator leaves, *Toute-belle* gives him the key to her treasure:

> p. 162 ..."Ceste clef porterez,
> Amis, et bien la garderez,
> Car c'est la clef de mon tresor.
> Je vous en fais seigneur des or,
> Et desseur tous en serez mestre.
> Et si l'aim plus que mon oeil destre,
> Car c'est m'onneur, c'est ma richesse,
> Et ce dont puis faire largesse.
> Par vos dis ne me puet descroistre,
> Ainsois ne fait tousdis qu'acroistre."

La clé du cœur is a standard motif in Chrétien de Troyes, *Claris et Laris,* and *Le Roman de la Rose. Toute-belle* explains that the key represents her honor. If we interpret "honor" as "reputation," then we can assume that *Toute-belle* lost her virginity and the Narrator has become temporary master of her person and permanent master of her good name. Only if he remains discreet will her honor be preserved. His power over her is symbolized by the key. However, we may also interpret the key, coffer, and treasure as sexual images, in accordance both with Freudian dream-theory and traditional literary erotic metaphor. Jupiter visited Danae as a shower of gold (cf. *FA*); in *VD* also the Narrator comes into *Toute-belle*'s room by the window, but he is in quest of treasure. However, although

later in the poem both lover and beloved look forward to the day
when he will return to unlock her coffer, since they never have an
occasion to do so and since *Toute-belle* gave him the key but he
has yet to use it (the Narrator compares himself to Tantalus dying
from thirst or to Midas who cannot enjoy his inexhaustible treasure),
I conclude that she did not lose her virginity. Presumably the Narrator was able to satisfy his desires without defloration having taken
place. [16]

In Letter **XLV** the Narrator blames *Toute-belle* for having sent
him a jewel from her treasure (his secretary served as go-between).
He begs her never again to send such a gift in that manner, "pour
ce que trop grant familiarité engendre haine" (p. 362). He prefers
to wait twenty years before relying on an intermediary. Paulin Paris
(p. 361, n. 1) comments on the Narrator's exquisite tact and prudence.
But how can the Narrator object to his secretary's bringing him the
jewel since the latter knows all his master's secrets and has served
as his *internuntium* from the beginning? I ask, may not the jewel
from *Toute-belle*'s treasure be a sexual favor, perhaps a kiss? *Toute-
belle* would have given the secretary a kiss, asking him to deliver
it to the recipient, but the latter fails to appreciate her tact (or her
unpleasant joke) and begs her to cease such familiarities. *Toute-belle*
accedes to his request, declaring (tongue in cheek) that she would
never have done so had she divined the Narrator's reaction; she

---

[16] Cf. with Paris, *Le Livre du Voir-Dit*, p. 160, n. 1, and Poirion, *Le
Poète et le Prince*, pp. 529-30, and *Le Moyen Age: II. 1300-1480* (Paris, 1971),
p. 193. Note that in *Le Dit de la fleur de lis et de la Marguerite* Machaut
compares the daisy's green stalk, white petals, red corona, and yellow pollen
to a lady's youth, joy, modesty, and "treasure":

> 231   Une greinne a toute jaunette
>   Qui est si plaisant et si nette
>   Qu'il semble qu'elle soit dorée,
>   Einsi Nature l'a formée.
>   Mais c'est mervilleuse chose,
>   Quar quant la marguerite est close,
>   En ses fueilles enseveli,
>   Ha son tresor aveques li—
>   C'est sa greinne qui samble or fin.
>   Et croy qu'elle le fait a fin
>   Que sa greinne ne soit gastée,
>   Ravie, tollue, ou emblée.

According to Machaut, the daisy closes *at night* to protect her treasure, then
opens *in the morning* to the sun (243-50).

swears that she has never yielded any portion of her treasure except that one precious stone she just sent him (Letter XLVI), further proof that Machaut speaks of kisses, not rubies. If my interpretation of these passages is correct, Machaut intentionally veils the telling of what went on in *Toute-belle*'s room and of her relations with the secretary, much as in the story Venus veils the physical act.

No less a subject for misinterpretation is the ending to *VD*. The majority of scholars have assumed that, in the closing pages, the lovers agree to separate forever, probably because of *Toute-belle*'s forthcoming marriage, and that the Narrator returns her key. A careful reading of the text, however, proves the above interpretation to be without foundation. Nowhere in *VD* is *Toute-belle*'s hypothetical marriage alluded to in any way. In Letter XLV (pp. 360-63) the Narrator swears he believes in her fidelity. No one can now convince him of the contrary. When he says that all things done, said, and written between them will be forgiven and forgotten, he simply echoes *Toute-belle*'s similar request in Letter XLIII (p. 345). He is making up a quarrel, not ending their relationship (as claims Eichelberg, pp. 121-22), and asks that their disagreements, not their love, be terminated. And he continues: "Si menrons bonne vie, douce, plaisante et amoureuse" (p. 362). The Narrator also declares not that he will send back her key but that he will bring it as soon as he can, "pour veoir les graces, les gloires et les richesces de cest amoureus tresor" (p. 362). Then he declares that he and *Toute-belle* are joined forever by Venus (p. 366). In Letter XLVI (pp. 367-69), the last in the book, *Toute-belle,* her sorrow gone forever, exults in the defeat of Fortune. She once again invites the Narrator to visit her, and her warning to beware of bandits differs in no way from similar ones in the course of the story. And in a passage, most of which was deleted by Paris, the Narrator embroiders on the theme of reconciliation and harmony:

p. 370   Ainsi fusmes nous racordé,
              Com je vous ay ci recordé [,]
f. 305 v° (d)   Par tresamïable concorde.
              Grant joie ay quant je m'en recorde,
              Et grant bien est dou recorder,
              Quant on voit gens bien acorder,
              Et plus grant bien de mettre acort
              Entre gens ou il a descort,
              Et, pour ce, encor recorderay

Briefment ce qu'a recorder ay:
Comment Toute-bele encorda
Mon cuer, quant a moy s'acorda...

Far from closing out the love affair, these last letters open up possibilities for a lasting relationship.

How could such a gross misinterpretation of the text have arisen? It was natural, indeed inevitable, that Tarbé should have assumed *VD* ended with *Toute-belle*'s marriage, because he identified her with the historical Countess Agnès de Navarre, who married Gaston de Foix in 1349. When Paris refuted Tarbé's identification and "proved" *Toute-belle*'s historical prototype to be Peronne d'Unchair, dame d'Armentières, he still maintained the marriage-hypothesis (pp. xxiv and 363, note 2), even though we have no evidence that the historical Peronnelle ever married. Perhaps Paris was so imbued with Tarbé's version of the story that he allowed it to twist his own reading; perhaps, like Tarbé, he believed the poems attributed to *Toute-belle* in *VD*, and Machaut's other lyrics where the speaker is feminine, to have been written not by Machaut but by his inamorata: Agnès-Peronne. Therefore, when a *ballade* and a *complainte* treat explicitly the traditional courtly liaison between a bachelor lover and a married lady (Chichmaref, 1:208 and 249-50), Paris, like Tarbé, assumed they refer to details of Machaut's own life, that is, his continued relationship to Agnès-Peronne shortly after her marriage (pp. 406-8). However, the marriage-hypothesis crumbles when we remember that neither Agnès nor Peronne nor anyone else but Guillaume de Machaut wrote the *VD* lyrics, whether ascribed to the fictional Narrator or to his fictional mistress, and all other lyrics in the Chichmaref, Ludwig, Schrade, and Wilkins editions, whether the presumed speaker is male or female. Because they have confused fiction with reality, and art with history, scholars not only have falsified the "composition" of *VD* but even the details of the plot.

Paris and his successors may also have imagined *Toute-belle*'s marriage to explain the estrangement that develops between her and the Narrator in the second half of *VD*, because they sympathize with the Narrator and believe his suspicions to be justified. These are generally the same men who condemn *Toute-belle* as a person, claiming she is less sincere than the Narrator, that she took up with him only out of caprice or to make a reputation—that she never really loved him at all. I agree that there must be some physical or psychological reason to explain why the lovers, so close to consummation (or already there), do not meet again for over two years. But should we ascribe their estrangement to *Toute-belle*'s fickleness or to the Narrator's cowardice and jealousy? Who is "in the right," *Toute-belle* or the Narrator?

On the one hand, a certain number of people persuade the Narrator of *Toute-belle*'s infidelity. Some are notables at the court, and their word is not to be treated with contempt. Perhaps *Toute-belle* does urge her suitor not to visit her a trifle too often. On several occasions she appears overly concerned with her personal glory. And although *Toute-belle*'s portrait recounts the story of Coronis of Larissa to prove that tattling is folly, the myth also tells against *Toute-belle*, since, according to Ovid, Coronis was indeed guilty of deceiving Apollo and Pallas did have something shameful to hide.

It is also true that *Toute-belle* never ceases protesting that she adores the Narrator and no one else. She points out that although he claims to be in love, he causes her nothing but pain. Her portrait says that the Narrator will lose *Toute-belle* if his doubts persist; yet, tormented by jealousy, he ceases writing to her and avoids visiting her even in good weather, even though it is his role, as the male, to bestir himself. In the end, he half believes the stories told against her. And one character of at least as much integrity as the Narrator's friends bears witness to *Toute-belle*'s honor: a distinguished ecclesiastic who himself confessed her.

Ascertaining the truth is rendered difficult by space and time. The story begins at summer's end, 1362, when *Toute-belle* first sends a *rondeau* to the Narrator, and ends with the forty-sixth letter, which can be dated after May 1, 1365. It covers almost three years, a longer duration than for any of Machaut's previous tales, with the possible exception of *DA*. We are made aware of the passing of time, of the change of seasons, of a lover's frustration without word from the beloved. People evolve over so long a period, and their sentiments change too. The Narrator insists too much on the theme of metamorphosis in Ovid and the Bible not to be conscious of metamorphosis in his own life. But he is never certain of who and what have been transformed at any particular moment, whether at a given instant *Toute-belle* does indeed love him or, on the contrary, his suspicions are justified.

He would have little difficulty in discovering *Toute-belle*'s true feelings but for the fact that communication between them is precarious. He and *Toute-belle* are separated for almost the entire *dit*. Much of the external décor of *VD,* and secondary characters too —bandits, storms, winter, the plague, allegorical figures such as *Malebouche* and *Dangier*—serve one function only: to keep the lovers apart. Although the Narrator sets forth more than once to find his beloved, his quest is never realized; the lovers attain neither permanence nor total commitment. Space stands between them, preventing understanding. Each lover remains in solitude or surrounded by people who cannot help him, unaware of or hostile to his love.

They are eager to see each other, for sight nourishes love and truth. *Toute-belle*'s eyes possess curative powers; even in a dream, she heals the Narrator by gazing at him. On the other hand, he dreads appearing in *Toute-belle*'s presence, lest his physical unattractiveness should dampen her ardor. Dazzled from afar by her beauty, he doubts whether he can dazzle her in return. The first time they lie together in bed he cannot see her, for they are in the dark: he touches her gropingly, is paralyzed by fear, and she must make the advances. The second time he enters through an open window (phallic imagery) and contemplates her in the nude. Venus's cloud covers them from the gaze of outsiders while their passion triumphs; they see each other without being seen. Yet the Narrator's victory is short-lived, since he is not permitted to behold *Toute-belle* again. How well did he ever see her, this one-eyed old man? The bad lover, Polyphemus, also one-eyed, never discovered the truth about Galatea; he was later blinded by Odysseus, as perhaps the Narrator has been all along by the God of Love.

Toute-belle and the Narrator do communicate by mail, although their correspondence is hindered by a variety of material considerations and *Toute-belle*'s limited freedom of action as an unmarried young lady of the gentry. A person's letters are an artificial, semiliterary projection of himself, not necessarily more authentic than if he were writing a novel. The Narrator can never be certain that *Toute-belle*'s letters are sincere, nor can she count on his. In fact, he informs us that in one epistle he intentionally tampers with the truth (p. 313). Furthermore, by the time one of them reads the other's letter, it no longer necessarily reflects the writer's sentiments or how their situation has evolved in the interval. The lovers also communicate in their dreams, but the Narrator does not believe dreaming to be an infallible source of truth, for he declares: "Car clerement vi que mon songe / N'avoit riens de vray fors mensonge" (p. 233). Dreams, letters, lyric poetry, even the portrait, are mediators; they help the lovers to come together but, objects or external happenings, they contain no guarantee of validity. The Narrator and *Toute-belle* each is aware of his own sentiments but can never "prehend" the other's. And the reader cannot arrive at objective truth either.

Machaut tells his story in the first person, through a narrator who (as in *DV, RF,* and *DA*) is also the protagonist and a lover. Except for the letters and poems ascribed to *Toute-belle, VD* is filtered through the Narrator's consciousness, whether he recounts events as participant or observer. His is the central focus; the action is seen almost uniquely through his prism. Although an I-narrator will often elicit from the reader sympathy and a heightened emotional reaction, he cannot create the illusion of omniscience we find in most third person narratives. Machaut is himself aware that the reader places limits on how much an "I" can reasonably be expected to know outside his own purview: hence the Narrator's explanations that he was informed of certain events by *Toute-belle*'s confidante or by *Toute-belle* herself.

For the first time in Machaut's fiction the Narrator's limited perspective has an important function in the plot. If we accept his truth-claim, relate to his norms, and allow his point of view and ours to coincide, then we must agree with his version of the story. However, the "I" is not necessarily reliable nor are we obliged to accept without question his interpretation of the events he recounts. We have the right to disagree with him. We know the Narrator's interpretation of events but not that of Guillaume de Machaut the poet, for whom the "I" is a literary character the same as *Toute-belle*. Earlier scholars unconsciously sensed a dichotomy between poet and narrator when they criticized *Toute-belle* as a person, in spite of her suitor's praise. This blurring of focus is the key to the tale's structure. Narrative omniscience is totally out of place in a story which reveals the Narrator-hero's lack of omniscience. Ironically, in *VD,* The True Story, neither protagonist knows the truth, nor do we, the readers.

Does *Toute-belle* love the Narrator for himself or for his reputation? Is she moved primarily by love's ecstasy or by the desire to acquire worldly fame? Who sees farther, the wise man (the Narrator's friends, his secretary) or the fool (the Narrator himself)? If these aristocratic friends fail to tell the truth or, in telling it, undermine *fin' amor* and a lady's honor, can they be truly noble? And are they real friends? The Narrator's dream proclaims *Toute-belle's* infidelity, yet the dream may be pure illusion. The King Who Never Lies, who defends *Amour's* interests, may be telling the truth or lying, yet he too appears in the same dream. Who interprets correctly the allegorical portrait of *Fortune,* the Narrator or *Toute-belle's* priest? Illusion is taken for reality, and reality for illusion. Truth is perhaps revealed through illusion (a dream), or perhaps a lie is told in seemingly truthful terms and given the authenticity of a dream-vision. Neither the Narrator nor the reader ever succeeds in unraveling the *VD* mystery.

One thing is certain, however: knowing no more than the Narrator, we perceive his weakness and vacillation. In the course of the story he unconsciously reveals his own failings. We do not see the reality behind *Toute-belle's* mask (her portrait, letters, and dream appearances), but we do recognize it is a mask, and that the Narrator is incapable of distinguishing between it and reality. Regardless of the true state of affairs, the Narrator demonstrates a crushing lack of trust. His tragedy lies not in the Other but in himself, and the ultimate truth of The True Story concerns not his external relations to another (over which he agonizes) but his inner self, of which he is almost totally oblivious. In this sense surely the reader discovers a "truth" the Narrator never dreamed of and arrives at a point of knowledge far beyond the Narrator's.

The *Toute-belle* perceived by the Narrator, in part a product of his imagination, inevitably differs from the real *Toute-belle,* whom neither he nor the public ever gets to know. She is his inspiration, his Muse, but as such takes on a universal, not a particular, aura. He conceives of her as the *domna* of tradition, not a living fourteenth-century girl less than twenty years old. He writes his best poetry when they are separated, perhaps unconsciously seeks obstacles to keep them apart, for the reality of *Toute-belle's* presence

cannot but interfere with his idealized picture of her and silence
him. Significantly, in the second half of *VD Toute-belle*'s portrait
comes to replace the real girl. Just as *Toute-belle* is dehumanized
in the relationship, so too in the Narrator's mind she is metamorphosed into an object (the portrait) and a phantom (who comes
to him when he dreams), on whom he projects fantasies at will.

As we have seen, one mode of communication in *VD* is the written word, embodied in lyric poetry, prose letters, and the book
itself, a True Story, which the Narrator is supposed to be writing.
The theme of art is more fully developed in *VD* than in any of
Machaut's other narratives. In spite of his age, ill health, and loss
of an eye, the Narrator attracts *Toute-belle* because of his reputation
as a poet. Throughout the story she sends to him for lyrics, declares
she adores reading them and will learn them by heart, song and
verse. As critics have pointed out, she takes pride in winning the
love of a celebrity. The Narrator goes along with her pretensions
by composing lyrics uniquely in her praise. He also agrees, though
with misgivings, to transcribe the whole of their affair in his book.
Toute-belle sacrifices her honor and defies convention for the sake
of fame. And, it cannot be denied, she succeeds in her objective.
Within the context of the narrative, she becomes known in society
as the Narrator's muse. And, in a larger sense, she has won a degree
of immortality comparable to Dante's Beatrice, Petrarch's Laura,
and Ronsard's Cassandre, Marie, and Hélène. She is known even
today only because she was a character in a poem by France's leading writer of the fourteenth century.

A second reason for *Toute-belle*'s paying court to the Narrator
centers on her own artistic ambitions. Although she demonstrates
commendable modesty ("et se il y a aucune chose à amender, si le
vueilliés faire, car vous le sarés mieus faire que je ne fais; j'ay
trop petit engien pour bien faire une tele besongne, et aussi n'eus-je
onques qui rien m'en aprenist.... Car je en apenroie plus de vous
en un jour que je ne feroie d'un autre en .i. an," Letter V, p. 48),
she does engage in a poetic correspondence with the master and
requests that he correct her poems and set them to music. It can
be said that the Narrator's letters are as much those of a professor
as a wooer, that he and *Toute-belle* discuss poetry almost as often as
they speak of love.

The Narrator is a lover and a poet, a lover because he is a poet and vice versa. In *Floris et Lyriope, Cléomadès, La Divina Commedia, Il Filocolo,* and *VD,* a book causes two people to meditate on love and on each other. Poems, letters, and the tale itself, viewed as the lovers' story in the making, bring the Narrator and his beloved together; they are mediators, perhaps the only mediators, in a love situation which would never otherwise have come into being and which is kept alive only by poetry.

The Narrator of course does ultimately fail as a lover. Machaut laughs at the melancholic, decrepit old rhymester who dares assume the role of *chevalier-servant.* The Narrator is ripe in years, but a lover must partake of *jovens.* As a poet, he depends for inspiration on books weighing down much of his tale, especially the second half, with mythological or allegorical lore. He tells stories and draws conclusions but does not act to win his lady, as a young suitor must. Although the Ancients teach him that love brings in its wake suffering and death (the *exempla* of Polyphemus and Coronis), he should be oblivious to everything in the universe that does not emanate from his lady. A bookish man, the Narrator is afraid to experience the world directly, yet without concrete activity he cannot succeed in love. The *VD* is a tale of language—speech, poetry, prose correspondence—in which words and the poetic art impede rather than encourage physical action. An educated poet is as much a fool as other men *sub specie Veneris,* and all his knowledge turns out to be useless. The Narrator would never have had a chance with *Toute-belle* if he were not a great poet, but the absence of concrete human experience implicit in the clerical life also condemns him to failure.

However, whatever his success or failure as a lover, the Narrator's status as an artist is never left in doubt. He takes pride in his work, is conscious of his preeminence as a poet, and on more than one occasion brings off a tour de force: answering *Toute-belle*'s or Thomas Payen's poems in their own rhyme scheme, writing a technically sophisticated *lai* and *complainte,* and composing impromptu *rondeaux, ballades,* and *virelais* which illustrate intense emotional states as they occur, the most extraordinary being the *virelai* he composes at the very moment he enjoys *Toute-belle* in bed.

Likewise, *Toute-belle,* said to be an excellent singer even before she met the Narrator (p. 4), develops into a fine poetess herself. She learns to answer the Narrator's poems following his rhyme scheme and, like him, to compose *rondeaux* spontaneously in moments of intense emotion. It can be said that *Toute-belle* turns out better as a poet than the Narrator as a lover. She improves in the one realm, while he falters in the other, and, to give him his due, he is a more successful professor of literature than she is an instructress in the ways of love.

The two protagonists collaborate on their story, which will become *VD;* the writing of *VD* becomes the subject of *VD.* This book is purportedly written by the Narrator pretty much as the story takes place, from July 1363 to May 1365. *Toute-belle* declares that her greatest pleasure lies in reading parts of it as it comes into being; surely her love is nourished by the book and her own role in its elaboration. Then, at the end of the narrative, although the Narrator's passion has not been consummated and the future of his relationship with *Toute-belle* remains uncertain, he has the book to fall back on: he will complete the story of their love. It exists, when all else proves to be illusion. [17] In a sense, this man, who loves his craft more than his lady, sublimates an impossible yearning for *Toute-belle* by creating *VD.* As Apollo kills Coronis but their son, Aesculapius, is saved, so too the Narrator's love eventually dies, but his creation, the Book, will live on. The poet becomes truly educated by experiencing life and by creating out of his failure in life a successful poem. Ultimately, art triumphs over life because life itself, as Machaut's protagonists live it, has no meaning or permanence apart from art. It is not coincidental that whereas in Machaut's other tales Lady Fortune, the Lion, the Trial, the Allerion, or the Fountain appear in the title, in *VD* the book itself is the archimage that dominates a poem which refers to and is justified only by itself.

The *VD* is less obviously structured than Machaut's other tales; the absence of a tight pattern of correspondences and antitheses explains in part why scholars have been willing to assume that the

---

[17] For the symbolism of the book in the Middle Ages, see Curtius, *Europäische Literatur und lateinisches Mittelalter,* chapt. 16.

story is autobiography not fiction. Nonetheless, certain themes, motifs, or episodes repeated in the course of the poem do create a rhythm of recurrence: letters, poems, love-tokens, visits, pilgrimages, bedroom scenes, and dreams. Especially in the first half, these increments are shaped to form a progression or gradation leading to a climax; the resultant pattern corresponds to the *quinque lineae amoris* or to Andreas Capellanus's hierarchy of the stages of love: "Ab antiquo quatuor sunt gradus in amore constituti distincti. Primus in spei datione consistit, secundus in osculi exhibitione, tertius in amplexus fruitione, quartus in totius personae concessione finitur," p. 38). We follow the Narrator's slow, uncertain, but tangible progress in the conquest of his lady. They communicate by letter; he beholds her face, first in a portrait, then when they meet at her house; they speak; he kisses her hand at their first rendezvous, her lips at the second and when she visits him in church; they embrace at Saint-Denis and later enjoy something approximating *totius personae concessio.* The high points in the affair are concentrated into two bed scenes. In the first, chaperones are present, *Toute-belle* is the aggressor, and nothing much happens; in the second, the lovers are alone (but for Venus and her cloud), the Narrator takes the initiative, and his desires are satisfied.

In the second half of *VD* artistic "composition" is less overt. Scholars have claimed that Machaut lost interest in the story once the Narrator entered *Toute-belle*'s bed or that other literary concerns caught his fancy, and that Part 2 contains mostly "fill-material" of a mythological or allegorical nature inserted to keep the tale from dying. [18] In my opinion, on the contrary, Machaut has sought to portray what happens in a love affair after the happy ending. Influenced by the conventions of romance, people believed that love crystallizes according to more or less fixed patterns of physical conquest, but the tradition seldom if ever dealt with the dissolution of an affair. Machaut examines in a truly "realistic" manner how easy it is in the first flush of passion to adhere to the precepts of *fin' amor,* to play at love according to the rules, but in time lovers must find their way on their own. And their failings as human

---

[18] Hanf, "Ueber Guillaume de Machauts Voir Dit," pp. 195-96; B. J. Whiting, "Froissart as Poet," *Mediaeval Studies* 8 (1946): 189-216, esp. p. 200.

beings—*Toute-belle*'s fickleness, the Narrator's jealousy and cowardice—are revealed to the public and to each other. The protagonists seek to follow the code and indeed succeed in creating beautiful words, but they do not communicate, and in the process love, understanding, and human values disappear.

The *VD* is the most complex of Machaut's tales. His ending especially is ambiguous because, although the lovers do reconcile, we are never made aware of the exact relationship between them and to what extent either one loves the other or is capable of a mature relationship. The Narrator believes in their reconciliation, but he and the reader are ignorant of *Toute-belle*'s sentiments in the matter. Whether he ever will unlock the maiden's coffer is open to question. This incomplete ending gives the poem an aura of truth, for tensions are left unresolved as is so often the case in real life. The plot is open, not closed; the characters live on, and their problems persist, not to be resolved by a fortuitous marriage or death. Machaut anticipates contemporary fiction by creating the illusion that his book takes shape as the characters live it, that they create their own story, and that the work of art itself becomes a living organism, free from convention and an author's will. Yet, as we know, such is not the case in Machaut's world any more than in Gide's and Sartre's. An author does shape his characters; he adheres to or rebels against literary conventions; he constructs a narrative. The contrast between the reality of artistic creation and the illusion of realism, as well as between the ideal of *fin' amor* and the reality of two people living on our planet, is central to the ironic vision of Machaut's True Story.

10. *LA PRISE D'ALEXANDRIE*

Machaut tells the story of Peter de Lusignan (1329-1369), king of Cyprus. From his very earliest days Peter lives only for the Crusade. Upon his accession to the throne in 1359, he seizes two strongpoints in Asia Minor, Gorhigos and Adalia, then recruits for the Holy War in Western Europe. The combined allied forces achieve a great victory in 1365 with the storming of Alexandria. For the next few years Peter negotiates fruitlessly with the Saracen Emir, Yalbugha al-Khassiki, and his successors, wins several minor victories, including the defense of Gorhigos and the sack of Tripoli, and refutes accusations leveled at him by one of his barons, Florimond de Lesparre. In 1368 the Lusignan again seeks reinforcements in Europe and is offered the Crown of Armenia, but the following year he is assassinated in his own palace by his own people.

GUILLAUME DE MACHAUT WROTE *VD* both to attain verisimilitude in fictional narrative and to come to grips with some aspects of contemporary reality. His next long poem, *La Prise d'Alexandrie,* [1]

---

[1] 8,886 lines, plus three interspersed epistles in prose; ed. L. de Mas Latrie (Geneva, 1877): 8,887 lines, according to Mas Latrie, but an error in numeration occurs on p. 31 (cited hereafter as *PA*). For historical background, see Aziz Suryal Atiya, *The Crusade in the Later Middle Ages* (London, 1938); Frederick J. Boehlke, Jr., *Pierre de Thomas: Scholar, Diplomat, and Crusader* (Philadelphia, 1966); Eugene L. Cox, *The Green Count of Savoy: Amadeus VI and Transalpine Savoy in the Fourteenth Century* (Princeton, N.J., 1967); Sir George Hill, *A History of Cyprus* (Cambridge, Eng., 1948), vols. 2 and 3; N. Jorga, *Philippe de Mézières, 1327-1405, et la croisade au XIVe siècle* (Paris, 1896); Philippe de Mézières, *The Life of Saint Peter Thomas,* ed. Joachim Smet (Rome, 1954), and *Le Songe du Vieil Pelerin,* ed. G. W.

represents an even greater stride in this direction. For the first time in his career, at the age of seventy, Machaut tries his hand at history: *PA* is a chronicle or biography of a contemporary historical figure: Peter I de Lusignan, king of Cyprus, the most illustrious crusader of his day.

Machaut takes seriously his duties as chronicler. Before recounting Peter's death, he declares that he will tell the facts to the best of his ability, as they were told to him; he acts neither out of jealousy, hatred, family interest, and personal advantage nor for promises or money, but in the interest of truth (7976-95). On another occasion, Machaut again proclaims that he will not hide the truth, for neither love, hatred, nor friendship can make him turn truth into falsehood (8382-87).

As in *VD, PA* contains prose epistles as documentation. There are two letters from Florimond de Lesparre to King Peter, dated August 3 and 4, 1367, the one setting forth Lesparre's recriminations against his lord, the other challenging Peter to a duel, followed by the latter's acceptance of the challenge, dated September 15 of that same year. We have reason to believe these letters are indeed authentic (L. de Mas Latrie, p. xxi).

When documentation is not available, Machaut relies upon informants, veterans of Peter's campaigns. Two are mentioned: Jean de Reims, an eyewitness to the defense of Gorhigos and the seizure of Alexandria and Tripoli, who also joined one of the negotiating teams to Egypt; and Gautier de Conflans, Machaut's source for Peter's assassination. It turns out that Jean's information was largely correct and that Gautier's was not. However, since Machaut had to rely on these purported eyewitnesses, his good faith cannot be called into question.

According to Mas Latrie, *PA* has considerable historical interest and must be considered "un monument de premier ordre pour l'histoire de l'île de Chypre et de l'Orient latin" (p. viii). Aside from romanticized accounts of the hero's mythological birth and of his death, *PA* is a major source for King Peter's life and times, especially the Alexandria and Gorhigos campaigns. Modern historians such as Aziz Suryal Atiya or Sir George Hill cite Machaut as frequently

---

Coopland, 2 vols. (Cambridge, Eng., 1969); Steven Runciman, *A History of the Crusades* (Cambridge, Eng., 1954), vol. 3.

as they do the other chroniclers of the period (Makhairas, Strambaldi, Amadi, Philippe de Mézières, and the Egyptian al-Nuwairī).

Scholars have found *PA* full of information on fourteenth-century manners, politics, military and naval affairs, tournaments, and music, and have praised the impression of authenticity Machaut gives to battle descriptions, negotiations, quarrels, and the final conspiracy.[2] Would a courtly romance or love allegory recount how the protagonist vomits from *mal de mer* or that his illness postpones the war twice in the same year? We are told that a Scotsman tried to set on fire one gate at Alexandria but was killed by a falling rock, that a sailor and squire-at-arms were the first to enter through an opening in the walls. Two years later, of the six galleys which set out for the defense of Gorhigos, four arrive before the others; they transported in all 600 men-at-arms and 300 archers. The Christians suffered from heat and a lack of doctors and arbalesters. A first losing battle was unleashed by a row between Cypriot sailors and some enemy footsoldiers. Finally, we are not spared the grisly details of Peter's assassination: the number of wounds Peter receives, who strikes him and where, down to the clothes he was buried in. Machaut also gives precise dates which, even when false, nonetheless contribute to the aura of credibility emanating from his work.

He lists the countries to which the Emperor Charles IV brought peace, Peter's itinerary in Central Europe and Italy, musical instruments played at receptions for him, and the kinds of ships which took part in the Alexandria campaign. He names one by one the knights and squires who made up each of the six Gorhigos galleys and even informs us that one of the compaigners was a lady's man and another disliked cold weather. He later draws up comparable though less extensive data for the assault on Tripoli. Although the modern reader may reproach Machaut for pedantry and lack of imagination, the effect in his own day must have been quite different. Such lists presumably convinced the public of his own expert knowledge of the crusade and probably helped maintain their suspension of disbelief.

---

[2] For example, Gröber and Hofer, *Geschichte der mittelfranzösischen Literatur,* 1: 21.

A chronicle of the crusades permits evoking Oriental local color. Machaut describes minutely the topography of Gorhigos and the odors of Tripoli. We discover that Saracen horses are accoutered in an exotic manner, that the Egyptian ambassadors are amazed by tournaments in Cyprus, for they have no such spectacles at home, that *cadis* is the word for cleric in their religion, and that they swear an oath by putting a finger to their teeth. Finally, Jean de Reims must have regaled the poet with anecdotes from his Egyptian travels, for Machaut includes material on the Nile, the architecture of the royal palace in Cairo, the dress and arms of the palace guards, Egyptian music, court etiquette, and the royal menagerie. Machaut is also aware of the communications gap between peoples of different nationalities. Yalbugha speaks to one of his lieutenants, the Christian renegade Nasr-ed-Din, in Arabic, *their Latin;* later in the story Nasr-ed-Din conducts the Cypriots to Cairo, acting also as interpreter, for he knows the languages of both camps.

In the early epics war is conceived as a pitched battle between immense armies, fought largely on horseback on an open plain. The outcome is determined, at least symbolically, by the success or failure of the leaders. This highly stylized representation of warfare has been modified, in later *chansons de geste* and *romans,* to conform more closely to the reality of medieval life. [3] The *PA* also adheres to a more realistic tradition. We are constantly reminded of the footsoldiers' dread and of dissention among their leaders. Peter refuses to announce the destination of his mission before the army puts to sea, and upon quitting Rhodes sails in the direction of Asia Minor, to keep spies off the right track. After having advised the Cypriots to attack the Old Port of Alexandria on a Friday (market day and the Muslim sabbath), Perceval of Coulonges then picks the weakest gate to assault. He had been a prisoner in Alexandria, we are told; but he acts as if he too were a spy. Indeed the Egyptians assumed a spy must have helped the Cypriots capture their city—according to legend, King Peter himself, disguised as a merchant! When the Crusaders land, Peter restrains his men from attacking until they have rested, the wounded are cared for, and horses have arrived. The invaders then storm the city; the walls

---

[3] Calin, *The Epic Quest,* pp. 41-45.

are battered in traditional fashion, while Saracens rain stones on the assault teams. After the fall of Alexandria. Peter would like to cut the Cairo bridge, lest the enemy bring up reinforcements. He cannot do so, however, because his army is occupied in sacking the defenseless city. And during the night Saracens sneak back inside the walls for an ambush the following morning. At Gorhigos too, although not always successful, the Cypriots plan their campaign on good tactical grounds. They hold off attacking until all their troops have arrived, then send their six galleys back to Famagusta for reinforcements, thus tricking the Saracens into believing that they have given up and left the area (the Trojan Horse ruse).

The speeches of the leaders, in council or to the troops, are based on carefully thought-out arguments, appropriate to the strategic or tactical considerations of the moment. An admiral has good reasons for urging Peter not to storm Alexandria: the city's thick walls, vast numbers of defenders, and the fact that the crusaders lack reinforcements and a strongpoint to cover their retreat or for refuge in case they are beaten. King Peter recognizes it is folly to persevere against the Cairo bridge, for his men are greatly outnumbered, and while outside Alexandria's walls, the enemy can kill his men, close the city gates on him, or return to attack the other Cypriots busy pillaging. Intelligent arguments are presented why the crusaders must finally abandon Alexandria: they are too few to hold their prize, they cannot expect reinforcements, they lack food to withstand a prolonged siege, and the Saracens are fanatics who will not accept ransom for prisoners. Nor should we ignore the role of negotiations as a tactic in war. Machaut is as aware as any modern historian that after the fall of Alexandria the Egyptians parleyed in bad faith. They could not defeat Peter on the spot but hoped that if they pretended a desire for peace, his European allies would go home, whereupon they could rearm at leisure and, when ready, overwhelm him.

Machaut gives quite an impression of historical accuracy in such areas as physical detail, geography, the personnel involved, exotic local color, and military strategy. Nevertheless, scholars have determined that his account of Peter's life contains a certain number of errors, especially in matters of chronology. Peter had a vision urging him to the crusade in the Church of the Holy Cross in Stavrovouni, not Famagusta as Machaut reports. The king left Venice on

June 27, 1365, not May as Machaut would have us believe, and his fleet left Rhodes on Sunday, October 4, 1365, not Monday, September 28. Machaut contradicts himself by claiming both that Peter sailed from Venice to Candia (1602) and that he sailed directly from Venice to Rhodes (1682-85). At Gorhigos he makes still another chronological error (Mas Latrie, p. 285, n. 44) and exaggerates the size of the Saracen armies, as he had done for the Alexandria campaign. Finally, Peter quarrels with the Giblet Family on January 8, 1369, not January 28, and was assassinated on January 17 of that year, not the sixteenth.

These are relatively minor lapses, imputable to any premodern historian. More serious are some of the following: the fact that early in his career King Peter did not seize Gorhigos from the Turks, as Machaut claims, but was given the fortress by King Leo V of Armenia (Lesser Armenia or Cilicia) in return for a promise of aid. Second, Machaut's report that Peter decided to attack Alexandria on the last-minute advice of a relatively obscure counselor, one Perceval of Coulonges, smacks of unfounded rumor (spread by Perceval or his friends) or the tradition of *chanson de geste,* where the monarch always makes last-minute decisions proposed by a Naimes or a Turpin. Perceval also receives too much credit for the victorious tactics at Alexandria; the Arabic source, al-Nuwairī's *al Ilmām,* gives a far more plausible account of how the Christians, after initial defeats and more than a little fumbling, fall upon the weak spot in Alexandria's defenses by chance (Atiya, pp. 359-60). We have reason to believe that *PA* devotes too much attention to the defense of Gorhigos, while it largely neglects a comparable Turkish threat to Adalia (Hill, 2:349, n. 2, and 3:1115). Although he recounts the quarrel between Florimond de Lesparre and the king accurately enough, Machaut apparently did not know that this quarrel originated in an earlier one between Peter and the Lord of Rochefort. Most of all, our poet grossly misinterprets the Lusignan's assassination. All modern historians agree that Peter was killed neither by enemies of the crusade, jealous kin, nor conspirators against the monarchical system but because he had become a tyrant. Machaut is unaware of a sordid quarrel between Peter's wife and his mistress which led up to the final events; he is equally mistaken in implicating the king's brothers and mother in the assassination plot. His account of how the martyr is surprised in bed, lying naked next to his beloved queen, is exaggerated, while that of his burial has been called an outrage to dignity as well as to historical truth (Mas Latrie, p. xxv).

It is difficult to answer the question: how good a historian is Guillaume de Machaut? He did his best, given his sources of information, to write accurately of the Alexandrian crusade. For that alone, regardless of the degree to which he succeeded, he does anticipate certain tendencies in modern historiography and, from our perspective, deserves commendation. On the other hand, as with Froissart, his genial successor who also relied heavily upon eye-witnesses, it would be absurd to judge him by the same criteria we apply to Atiya and Hill, or, for that matter, Marc Bloch and Georges Duby. Furthermore, the twentieth-century imperatives of objectivity, impartiality, absolute concern for accuracy, and interest in socio-economic factors, reflect as much a *prise de position,* a philosophical commitment, as the presuppositions of medieval historiography. Machaut's chronicle, for all its errors, prejudices, and downright falsehoods, reflects better the spirit of the Middle Ages than many a modern account of the same period.

The *PA* is a poem of the crusade. We are told that religion played an important role in Peter's education and that all his thoughts turn to God. At the Church of the Holy Cross he hears a Voice ordering the crusade. Shortly thereafter, still a youth, Peter creates the military Order of the Sword. Machaut explains the Order's heraldry (which contains a cross) allegorically and praises the miracles that have been vouchsafed to famous saints who cross themselves. When Peter's father dies, the young prince can bring his dreams of crusade to fruition. He travels to the West, seeking recruits, especially from Emperor Charles IV, himself a founder of churches (1003), and is welcomed by religious processions, the singing of hymns and re-sponses, and the ringing of church bells. Peter uses biblical imagery in speeches; we are told that the fall of Alexandria entails the greatest slaughter since the time of the Pharaoh; on several oc-casions Machaut refers to Saint Louis's crusade and compares Peter to Godfrey of Bouillon. After the Alexandria campaign, Peter per-sists in the good fight for another four years until his death. He does not relish a peace treaty but, when brought to heel, will accept one if it relieves Christian pilgrims of tribute to the Sultan and guarantees for himself holy relics. He also returns to the West a second time, seeking contingents for still more Holy Wars. Then this figure of Christ the Warrior is transformed into Christ the Martyr; for Peter's immolation, perhaps inspired by heroes of *geste,* Vivien, Garin le Lorrain, and Bègues, is also patterned after Our Lord's Passion. He is cut down naked, betrayed by his own brothers, who give him Judas's kiss. It is proper that the Lusignan, who had faith in the divinity throughout his life, should pass away with a prayer to the Virgin on his lips (8762-68). Although, when Machaut says that King Peter is buried in rags, his face covered, with a parchment crown, scepter, and orb, he twists the truth historically (as Mas Latrie complained), artistically he maintains to the end his conception of a monarch assimilated to the King of the Jews, the Warrior who harrowed Hell, who at his crucifixion wore a loincloth and a crown of thorns.

Peter does not stand alone against the Saracens. He is aided by Pope Urban V, one of the Cypriot's strongest partisans, who apparently believed in good faith that Peter's coming to power meant a return to the Golden Age of crusading. Machaut passes lightly over the pope's activity in the early 1360s. But he emphasizes Urban's role as mediator in the quarrel between Peter and Florimond de Lesparre. The pope delivers two appeals for reconciliation (7656-7711, 7819-47) during Holy Week 1368. He stands unequivocally on Peter's side but reminds the Lusignan that he must not commit the sin of hatred. Because the pope asks his indulgence, because of Holy Week, when Christ pardoned his betrayers, and in order to promote unity for the crusade, Peter does forgive Lesparre.

When Machaut recounts how Peter and King John II of France take the cross together at Avignon, he lavishes praise on Pierre Talleyrand of Périgord, whom Urban V named legate to the crusade. Machaut then laments his death, which occurred on January 17, 1364, in the same breath with King John's. However, Talleyrand's protégé since 1345 and successor as legate plays a more important role in the narrative. I refer to Peter Thomas, Procurator General of the Carmelite Order (1345), ambassador to Stephen Dušan, king of Serbia, and bishop of Patti and Lipari (1354), nuncio to Venice, Hungary, and Constantinople (1356), bishop of Coron in Greece and papal legate to the East (1359), archbishop of Crete and vice-regent of Bologna (1363), Latin Patriarch of Constantinople and crusade legate (1364). This man, one of the most extraordinary figures of the late Middle Ages, made his mark as educator, diplomat, and enthusiastic promulgator of the Holy War. Machaut was not informed of the legate's personal heroism during the landing at Alexandria, but he does recount in detail Peter Thomas's loyal support of the Lusignan's proposal to hold on to the captured city. The legate delivers a magnificent speech on this occasion. He was one of the very few to follow an intransigent line to the end. Truly a Turpin figure, he is the ideal second to King Peter and representative of the Church Militant.

One other "character" plays an important role in the narrative: the Divinity. Guillaume de Machaut tells us that God caused old King Hugh to weep over his son's imprisonment and pardon him. He receives credit for the Cypriots' triumph at Alexandria. He spares Peter from a tempest on the return trip and hastens his convalescence during the winter of 1366. At Gorhigos the Christian army is hot, tired, and weighted down by heavy armor, but God helps them climb a mountain where the Turks are encamped. Victory is due to God's grace, not the Cypriots' natural strength or skill in tactics. And God protects Cypriot ambassadors from a furious populace in Cairo. As in Racine's *Athalie,* although the Divinity never appears directly on the scene, much of the action takes place under his direction and according to his plan. Machaut's narrative does not possess the carefully shaped, coherent structure of seventeenth-century tragedy, but this omnipresent higher power does contribute a focus to both works: in Racine's case the divine plan for world history manifested in the Tree of Jesse; in Machaut's, the desirability of Holy War.

Guillaume de Machaut, known to posterity as a secular poet and musician, spent approximately thirty-seven years of his life as a canon in Reims. He wrote a series of Latin religious motets and the first complete setting by one man for the Ordinary of the Mass. His faith also manifests itself in *lais* 15 and 16 and in *CA*. He urges young lovers to win their knightly laurels on a crusade (*DL*, *CA*), and ever honors his patron, King John of Bohemia, who in his Prussian campaigns was considered a crusader against the heathen Lithuanians. Indeed, Machaut praises John in terms that were generally used for the Knights of the Teutonic Order, for John's honor, generosity, and abnegation are crusading virtues *par excellence.* [4] It is doubly significant then that in *PA* Machaut compares Peter of Cyprus to John of Bohemia and heaps special praise on John's son, Emperor Charles IV.

We have reason to believe that Machaut actually served King Peter in the 1360s and that they met on the occasion of Charles V's coronation at Reims (May 19, 1364). He wrote for the Lusignan *Le Dit de la Marguerite, Complainte* 6 "Mon cuer, m'amour, ma dame souvereinne," and other lyrics, as well as *PA.* [5] It need scarcely surprise us that Peter showed an interest in Machaut's work. According to Villani (but his story may be false), the Lusignan "judged" a poetry and music contest at Venice in 1364, Petrarch being a member of the jury; a laurel crown was awarded to Francesco Landini the greatest Italian musician of the century and the only man in all of Europe capable of rivaling Machaut.

Machaut also may have been presented to Peter Thomas, the legate, to the latter's friend and disciple, Philippe de Mézières, Chancellor of Cyprus, or to Perceval of Coulonges. Humbert II de Viennois, who led an ineffectual crusade in 1345-1347, abandoned his heritage to the king of France on July 16, 1349, in order to become a Dominican friar. He was subsequently named Latin Patriarch of Alexandria in 1351, and in 1352 Administrator of the Archbishopric of Reims, where Machaut held a canonate. Contact between these men and the author of *PA* is strictly conjectural. We know for a fact, however, that Machaut did have relations with Amadeus VI of Savoy: in 1371 the Green Count rewarded the poet upon receipt of a manuscript of his works. Amadeus, a famous crusader in his own right, had fallen under the king of Cyprus's influence. Eager to join Peter, after the fall of Alexandria he was diverted to Constantinople, where he succeeded in capturing Gallipoli and two minor fortresses and liberating Emperor John V Paleologus from the Bulgarians. Amadeus, who had close ties with the French royal family, married Bonne de Bourbon, sister-in-law to the future Charles V

---

[4] A. Prioult, "Un poète voyageur: Guillaume de Machaut et la *Reise* de Jean l'Aveugle, roi de Bohême, en 1328-1329," *Lettres Romanes* 4 (1950): 3-29.

[5] Poirion, *Le Poète et le Prince,* p. 195, and James I. Wimsatt, *The Marguerite Poetry of Guillaume de Machaut* (Chapel Hill, N.C., 1970). See below, pp. 229-31.

in 1355, and his son married Jean de Berri's daughter Bonne in 1377. Machaut may well have made Amadeus's acquaintance during one of the latter's rare trips to the Valois court.

Under whatever circumstances the poet knew King Peter and these other personages, one thing is certain: Guillaume de Machaut displays the most intense personal admiration for his protagonist. Instead of *La Prise d'Alexandrie*, his poem could have been more aptly named *Le Livre des faicts du bon roi de Chypre* or a variation therein. As Machaut tells it, the sun, moon, stars, and zodiac convene a parliament to discuss King Peter's birth. Jupiter creates the infant; Venus and Mars are designated his official patrons; Vesta and Saturn speak on his behalf. Hebe, Minerva, Juno, and Venus, who symbolize respectively youth, wisdom, riches, and love, contribute to his upbringing. His arms are provided by Vulcan. At various points in the chronicle Machaut claims that the Lusignan deserves a place among the Nine Worthies, in fact could well be the tenth, or that a new one is needed to replace the Nine, who have disappeared, and Peter is that man. The poet also laments Peter's death in a beautiful *planctus* (8834-73) and excoriates his murderers. Machaut, who yearns nostalgically for a bygone Golden Age, exalts Peter by saying that in his own decadent times only one man embodies those virtues that made the past so great. That man is the subject of his poem.

King Peter manifests unusual prowess in war. The Saracens themselves consider the fall of Alexandria to be their greatest disaster since the time of Pharaoh. The king of Cyprus, who personally joins the landing operations, kills thirty of the enemy and, after an appropriate exchange of insult, fells a Saracen emir, an act that causes the enemy to panic. Then, after Perceval's assault fails, he joins the Hospitallers in storming the city gates, ax in hand, and succeeds in breaking into the city. Later on in the day he kills another 100 and the following morning, with only fifty or sixty men behind him, puts to the sword 10,000 Saracens who sneaked into Alexandria during the night. Although Peter's prowess in Egypt marks a high point in his career, we should not forget his other feats: the capture or sack of Gorhigos, Adalia, Tripoli, Tortosa, Laodicea, Valania, and the town, though not the citadel, of Lajazzo. Even during his cavalcade across Christian Europe, this redoubtable warrior wins first prizes in tournaments. These victories over Europeans are less

bloody than those in the Orient but are surely as meaningful a
tribute to his honor.

Unlike many a hero of *geste,* Peter's *fortitudo* does not exclude
sapientia. I have already discussed his mastery of strategy. In contrast to the clumsy, inept, or hasty maneuvering of the Saracens at
Alexandria or of Florimond de Lesparre (a man who will become
Peter's enemy) at Gorhigos, the king of Cyprus always makes the
right move at the right time and, for all his crusading zeal, does
not hesitate to beat a retreat if tactical considerations render it
imperative. He does not lose his temper when challenged by Lesparre nor upon discovering that the Saracens parley only to stall for
time. Peter himself negotiates in good faith (according to Machaut;
modern historians judge the Cypriot more harshly in this regard),
honestly seeking a just peace, but, aware of Saracen treachery,
forbids most of his knights from joining the embassy to Cairo. The
second half of *PA* devotes as much attention to negotiations as to
battles; the Lusignan is presented as an ideal king, at war and at
the council table.

Peter is surrounded by wise, valiant comrades, who support him
in battle and give counsel in peacetime. Their function in the narrative is to enhance the hero's honor. His greatness is reflected in the
men who serve him. We have already spoken of Pope Urban V and
the legate, Peter Thomas, the latter an obvious Turpin figure.
Among the barons temporal, two stand out: Bremond de la Voulte
and Perceval de Coulonges. Compared to Gawain in the Arthurian
cycle, Bremond appears on Peter's left hand during the Alexandrian
landing, battle-ax in hand, like a castle on a rock. He performs great
feats in this campaign, leads one wing of the army at Gorhigos, and
participates valiantly in the capture of Tripoli. Still greater, however,
is the enigmatic Perceval (his name also recalls Arthurian romance),
who suggests to Peter the assault on Alexandria and devises tactics
to enter the city. This man stands on Peter's right at the debarcation.
After the Tripoli expedition, he goes to Paris to arrange for Peter's
expected duel with Florimond de Lesparre. Even a character we
know historically to have been Peter's enemy, the Prince of Galilee,
is portrayed in Machaut's chronicle as a loyal vassal, who seconds
his master valiantly in his major campaigns.

However, as in the Old French epic, King Peter is surrounded
by bad councillors as well as good, or by good councillors who,

lacking the prince's sterling virtues, deteriorate in the course of the story. One of his bravest followers, William Roger, Vicount of Turenne, is the chief spokesman for abandoning Alexandria. For all his apparent common sense, he proffers bad advice, which, even though refuted by Peter, does convince the others. Florimond de Lesparre, a professional soldier of fortune, serves Peter well, especially at Gorhigos. But then he turns against the king and challenges him to a duel. Finally, Peter's brother, the Prince of Antioch, although he directs the Gorhigos expedition competently, is implicated in his brother's assassination.

Prince John betrays his brother for reasons best known to himself—greed, ambition, perhaps the quality of evil inherent in a Ganelon and Judas. But the other characters, including King Peter, act principally for the sake of honor, the same concern for glory that motivated Roland, Raoul de Cambrai, and Girard de Roussillon. Lesparre, a mercenary, no doubt resents his low wages, but above all he cannot tolerate having been left out of the Tripoli campaign. This is a direct affront to the feudal baron *qua* baron and therefore unforgivable. The Giblets, father and son, also quarrel with Peter over a point of honor: that Peter's son, the Count of Tripoli, seized their hunting dogs. As for the protagonist, he runs from home seeking honor; he claims that he will be dishonored if the Christians leave Alexandria or if Lesparre's challenge is not answered; he will forgive Lesparre only after the recalcitrant baron swears publicly that Peter is an honorable man; and he takes revenge on the Giblets because, when his son is insulted, his own honor has been sullied:

> 8336 Quant li roys oy la nouvelle,
> Il dist: "Ma doleur renouvelle,
> Quant je voy qu'on me tient si vil,
> Qu'on dit villenie à mon fil!
> Biaus dous Dieux, que t'ai je meffait?
> Ne sera pugnis ce meffait?
> J'ay perdu honneur et loange
> En ce monde, se ne m'en vange."

Feudal honor is often dependent on the family. Lesparre's relatives, if any, play no role in the story. But Jacques de Giblet insults the Count of Tripoli because his son Henri's dogs were stolen, and

King Peter imprisons both father and son because his own son did the stealing. Then Peter humiliates, imprisons, and tortures Marie de Giblet simply because she is Jacques's daughter and Henri's sister. Behind the orderly façade of rule by law, private passions reign. Each man, including the king, takes the law unto himself. One minor, imprudent act unleashes a feud between two headstrong families, which recalls the private wars in *Garin le Lorrain,* for example, or *La Chevalerie Ogier.* As in the legend of Ogier, children begin the quarreling, but their fathers, the great heroes, are soon dragged in and must take on their shoulders the duty of upholding the clan's honor.

Medieval society functions upon the assumption of mutual obligations. The feudal barons owe aid, counsel, and loyalty to their lord the king; he owes them fidelity, protection, and justice in return. Florimond de Lesparre claims that he and Peter are equals, since both belong to the aristocracy, the only difference between them being that Peter wears a crown. Lesparre goes on to say that Peter does so under false pretenses, for no one both evil and given to lying deserves to reign over others. This rebel figure indicts the kingship and an individual king's rights more than any of the great protagonists of the Old French epic of revolt. And, to the extent that Peter does indulge in fits of temper, especially against ladies, he is partly responsible for his own destruction. Nevertheless, as in the epic of revolt, he is at the center of the political system, the head of the body politic, consecrated by God. Machaut claims it is wrong to challenge a king, even for good reasons. Peter possesses a special royal virtue which places him above customary standards of right and wrong, before which the Lesparres and the Giblets must yield. Even when they are in the right (and Machaut denies such is the case), it behooves them to act as if they were wrong and beg pardon —in order that society function in its proper way. [6]

Historically speaking, the struggle between Peter and his barons is but one manifestation of a European phenomenon: a confrontation between the rising near-absolute monarchy of the late Middle Ages and an older feudal tradition of baronial rights. Cyprus was one of the most conservative backwaters in the Mediterranean world. Legal-

---

[6] Calin, *The Old French Epic of Revolt,* chapt. 3.

ly, government resided only in the Haute Cour, and after Peter's death the barons sought to prevent further royal encroachment. They had no intention of giving up their prerogatives without a fight. However, Peter's reign also meant a return to old values of chivalry and the crusade (a "closed society"), resented by subjects committed to an Italianized lay culture based on trade, profit, and the good life (an "open society"). Machaut reduces a complex situation to its simplest possible terms. He considers the Cyprus court strictly from a Western perspective, colored by a long literary tradition. Peter and the barons are portrayed as if they were Charlemagne and Ganelon or Christ and Judas. The story of Peter's martyrdom creates a fine aesthetic effect, but in the telling much complexity in the human condition is sacrificed.

Peter and his friends consciously seek to maintain an atmosphere of pomp and elegance, to live up to the highest ideals of romance found in books. His entrance into Prague follows a pattern: the emperor heads a magnificent welcome procession; hymns and responses are sung; the procession returns to the capital for a feast preceded by a concert. After dinner Peter makes a formal request for aid; he receives an equally formal reply. Then a tourney is held and gifts are exchanged, after which Peter proceeds to the next stop. Later in the narrative Lesparre sends formal letters of challenge, to which King Peter replies in kind. Peter accuses Lesparre of acting *villeinement* and *orguilleusement,* of committing *folie* and *grans outrages* so as to diminish his *vasselages* (7563-74). Against the advice of wiser heads Peter insists upon entering into single combat with his enemy. Peace is restored only after, in a formal, stylized ceremony, on Holy Saturday in Rome, Lesparre kneels to beg forgiveness, sighing and weeping, seconded by a sighing, weeping populace. Following this spectacle, Lesparre serves Peter at table; the king then has a record made of the whole affair. Peter's duel, which does not take place but gives him a symbolic victory anyway, is the last in a series of triumphant feats of arms. His string of first prizes in tournaments recalls similar achievements in romance by Lancelot, Gawain, Partonopeus de Blois, Amadas, Gliglois, Guilhem de Nevers, the Châtelain de Couci, and others. And a triumph on a point of law is a salient feature of French belles lettres in the Middle Ages generally.

Courtly life without the graces of love is inconceivable. The erotic does not particularly belong to the crusade ethos, but Guillaume de Machaut, the greatest French love-poet of his century, could no more banish it from *PA* or *CA* than could Froissart from the *Chroniques*. We are told that Venus played a major role in Peter's conception and the makeup of his character. Of the four deities charged with his education, she is the most important. At the age of nine he manifests a precocious interest in the fair sex:

> 267 Toutes ses inclinations
>   Et ses ymaginations,
>   Tuit si penser, tuit si desir
>   Furent en faire le plaisir
>   De dames et de damoiselles.

During his European *Reise* Peter is so well received by ladies that he imagines himself in paradise; especially the Duchess of Austria makes much of him *tres amoureusement*. We are also told that one soldier likes to court the ladies and another has a pretty girl friend.

The author of *PA* revels in displays of pomp and descriptions redolent with color and sheen. Chivalry has become an aesthetic ideal, a game for courtiers; it is played out in the tournament, declarations of vows, the creation of an Order, artificial love conventions, and the crusade. Even vengeance is taken according to a prescribed, formal pattern. Manifestations of sentiment are public and stylized. This is the sublime life, believed in so intensely that it became real for the late medieval aristocracy and has remained ever since a hallmark of their age. [7]

Like *DL, PA* to some extent follows the pattern of quest-romance. The protagonist desperately seeks to leave home in search of adventure. A first attempt in 1349, while old King Hugh is still alive, proves abortive. Later, however, Peter crosses the threshold three times: his first European voyage, the storming of Alexandria, and a second trip to Europe. Of much less importance are the Gorhigos, Tripoli, and Ajazzo campaigns as well as a series of negotiations held alternately in Cyprus and Egypt.

Peter's goal is to capture cities. He seizes or sacks Gorhigos, Adalia, Tripoli, Ajazzo, Tortosa, Laodicea, and Valania and wends

---

[7] See Huizinga, *The Waning of the Middle Ages,* chapts. 2-7.

his way peacefully to Rome. But the end of his quest, the center
of the Other World, is of course Egypt: first Alexandria, then Cairo.
Cairo and Babylon *(Le Vieux Caire)* are each said to be twice as
large and contain twice the population of Paris. Machaut describes
the splendiferous palace of the Sultans, replete with a menagerie,
and the riches of Alexander's city, which gives its name to Peter's
story and is surely the most important single image contained in it.
The historical reasons why Alexandria was chosen for attack—its
military and commercial importance, the fact that Sultan Sha'ban
was only eleven years old and his emir, Yalbugha al-Khassiki, hated
by the populace—pale before mythical ones. Throughout this part
of the narrative the city is considered an object of luxury, the final
goal of the quest-hero, indeed something resembling a bride to be
ravished. [8] Perceval discovers the weakest point in the city's defenses;
the Cypriots break through a narrow opening in the walls and
penetrate within, sword and ax in hand. Outside, the seawater is red
from flowing blood. Within, the crusaders march through lab-
yrinthian streets to seize or defend other gates and cut bridges to the
interior. Alexandria and Babylon stand as demonic antitypes to
Rome and Jerusalem. As Christ the Warrior harrowed Hell, so his
disciple, a Christ figure, harrows the earthly Hell of Egypt's queen
city. However, the Lusignan's capture of Alexandria is also portrayed
as an initiation rite. Peter was never associated with his own cities
in Cyprus: Nicosia, Famagusta, Limassol. But once he has seized
Alexandria, even though he must give it up at once, it becomes his
and is forever associated with his destiny—as Guillaume with Orange,
Girard with Roussillon, and Renaud with Montauban.

After the city has been captured, King Peter crosses the return
threshold to the Christian world, where he possesses a kingdom,
and where later in the story he will be offered the crown of Armenia.
Peter comes into the world by a miraculous birth and leaves it, after
losing favor in his own land, with something approaching a miraculous end. An ideal hero of romance, superior in degree to other
men, he is limited only by death, and only an act of treason can
defeat him. As with Roland, Vivien, Lancelot, and Arthur, death

---

[8] For a similar configuration in chansons de geste, see Calin, *The Epic
Quest,* chapt. 1.

calls forth admiration as well as pity. Three moments highlight his struggle for the Christian faith: birth, initiation, and death.

Except for the first Alexandria expedition, Peter never attains quick, easy victories. On returning from Alexandria, his fleet is almost destroyed by tempest. Later, bad weather cuts short two other campaigns, by Bremond de la Voulte (winter 1365-1366) and Peter himself (1366-1367). The ocean proves a formidable barrier to the symbolic Other World, one which the Cypriots find increasingly difficult to overcome.

Further obstacles are provided by the pagan hosts and within Peter's own camp. Although the enemy exist as hordes to be cut down, they do manifest qualities of guile and treason. They sneak back into Alexandria at night to ambush Peter's men, and their leaders negotiate in bad faith. On one occasion, Egyptians welcome Cypriot ambassadors civilly, then propose to have them assassinated, but their plot is not carried through to fruition.

Even after the successful landing at Alexandria, Peter's men are for the most part afraid to fight and skeptical of victory. Then, inside the city, they are too busy pillaging to be of military use. Ignorant sailors are responsible for an imprudent, counterproductive melee at Gorhigos. His army also contains knights from Europe come for booty, who prefer peace to war. When the Vicount of Turenne suggests abandoning Alexandria, these weaklings are responsible for the city's loss:

> 3378   Avec ce tuit li estrangier,
> En tout, sans muer ne changier,
> L'avouerent et l'ensuirent,
> Et au roy tout en haut deïrent
> Qu'il n'en convenoit plus parler,
> Car il s'en voloient raler,
> Et que sans doubte il ne porroient
> Tenir la cité, ne voloient.

Guillaume de Machaut makes a distinction between the various contingents, however. More aware of contemporary politics than at any other time in his career, he has nothing but praise for the French troops. He singles out for adulation a squire from the South-West who preferred exile to becoming vassal to the king of England (4608-19), and he lists the knights and squires from France, especially those known for their exploits in the Hundred Years War. On the other hand, William Roger, Vicount of Turenne, who counsels retreat, is a vassal of the English. So is Florimond de Lesparre, a Gascon: Lesparre would like to have his quarrel with Peter judged before king Edward or the Black Prince, but Peter chooses King Charles of France. John Visconte reveals the assassination plot to the king, along with a scandalous report about Peter's wife, Queen Eleanor. The Cypriot barons urge Peter not to accept John's testimony because, among other things, he is a dishonored Englishman, false, wicked, a perjurer and traitor, who lies in his teeth (8125-32). Yet the Cypriots later murder their king, reproaching him for being too friendly to the French, and their vengeance includes expressions of Gallophobia:

> 8748 "Or va, va, si fay tes armées
> En France et tes grans assamblées;
> Va en Prusse, va en Surie;
> Pren nos filles, si les marie;
> Et meine nos femmes, très chier,
> Avec les Fransois qu'as très chier.
> Apris t'avons une autre dance
> Que ne sont les dances de France!"

To believe Machaut, King Peter won his battles almost in spite of the foreign mercenaries. He makes an exception only for the French contingent: from his point of view, the Lusignans were a French House. He or his informants undoubtedly projected onto Cypriot affairs their own concerns with the Hundred Years War. Their world is portrayed in terms of good versus evil: good, represented by the Valois Fleurs de lis, evil by Cypriot rebels and the Lions rampant of the Plantagenets.

Before setting out on the crusade, Peter must overcome his father's opposition. King Hugh IV of Cyprus, although subject to gratuitous fits of cruelty, was for most of his long reign (1324-1359) a quiet, peace-loving man, interested in studies (Boccaccio dedicated to him the *Geneologia Deorum*) and the chase, not crusading. Machaut does not go into these matters. But he does recount at some length young Peter's desire to sign up recruits for his Order of the Sword and to leave Cyprus in search of adventure. King Hugh opposes both ventures. And when Peter finally escapes the island in

1349, Machaut tells how the old monarch has his son captured and imprisoned. For two months and nine days Peter remains incarcerated—"Là petit but et po menja" (573). Finally, God, our Father in Heaven, causes Peter's father to weep loving, paternal tears and release the young prince. Although the two men are reconciled, Peter keeps his inmost thoughts to himself until he inherits the crown. For the author of *PA,* the historical father represents an obstacle to his son's development as a Christian warrior. In epic tradition also, even the greatest crusaders, Guillaume and Charlemagne, upon aging impede their ardent young nephews (in *La Chanson de Gillaume, Aspremont,* and *Gui de Bourgogne,* among others). These greybeards, who no longer possess enthusiasm, purity, and commitment, have to give way before a *puer senex,* who, because he is committed to Holy War, possesses truer wisdom than his elders. A similar generation gap occurred historically in the late fourteenth century, as evidenced by the opposition of old and young knights on the Barbary and Nicopolis Crusades. The old king must die before a new one can take his place and restore a decayed society to its pristine glory. To help him do so, in a scene reminiscent of *CA,* our only true Father mollifies the old man's heart and restores his son to favor.

The Saracen world presents a comparable situation. Sultan Sha'ban is only eleven years old, helpless in the grip of the emir, Yalbugha, and the latter's councillor, the renegade Nasr-ed-Din. Yalbugha is a wily old plotter, hated by his people and, along with the renegade, despised by the Cypriots and by Machaut. Significantly, whereas Peter, with God's help, escapes from prison, replaces his father, and proceeds with the crusade, the Sultan of Egypt is never liberated from the wicked father figures and ax-wielding guards who protect him. He never reigns, never really exists in the narrative at all. One young man fails because he is what he is—an infidel; the other succeeds because he is a *puer senex,* invested with the *sapientia* of God's grace. He triumphs over King Hugh and Yalbugha.

Peter replaces his father and defeats Yalbugha, who later is cut down by his subjects. But the war does not cease; the Saracens are neither converted nor wiped out. In the end, Peter of Cyprus, like the Egyptian emir, is massacred by his own people. King Hugh imprisons Peter; Yalbugha imprisons Perceval of Coulonges and, after the fall of Alexandria, all Christians who dwell in his realm. Peter also takes prisoners but willingly returns those he can as a gesture toward peace. At the end of the chronicle, however, he seizes Henri, Jacques, and Marie de Giblet. Jacques, his legs in irons, labors on the moat of the Margarita Tower; jailers twist Marie's soft flesh on the rack and force her to swallow quantities of warm water mixed with olive oil. Thus Peter, who at birth was the darling of Venus, at the age of nine thought only of love-games, and in the early 1360s was welcomed by the finest damsels of Europe, later plays the role of *gilos* and *marits*. Stories are told about Queen Eleanor having deceived him, and he tries to force Marie de Giblet into a heinous marriage against her will. The Lusignan has become a father figure in turn, a harsh, cruel man who defies the rules of *fin' amor*, persecutes the widow, and imprisons as he has been imprisoned. His blasphemy against the code of chivalry, condemned by Machaut, may well explain why, according to principles of immanent justice, he had to be deposed.

We have seen that the structure of *PA* parallels to some extent that of romance. Peter's major concern, early in the chronicle, is to break away from his island. He makes an abortive trip to Europe, then captures Gorhigos and Adalia and makes a second, this time successful, European *Reise*. From words the story shifts to deeds, from victories in jousting to an assault upon a real city. The storming of Alexandria crowns Peter's career, the fulfillment of a vow made when he first heard voices in the Church of the Holy Cross at Stavravouni.

However, Machaut's protagonist is not granted an apocalypse at this or any other time. After the fall of Alexandria, he must retreat from the Cairo bridge, defend against infiltrators, and finally give up the prize altogether. His story, called *La Prise d'Alexandrie*, does not end with the capture of the city; Machaut tells of his entire life, from birth to death. The second part of the chronicle recounts a series of battles and parleys less exciting than the events narrated in Part 1. Part 2 tells of confusion in the aftermath of a seemingly great victory and a series of campaigns which simply do not succeed. The Cypriots are held back by the elements and by their own physical ailments; they destroy an enemy fleet but fail to capture Alaya, are compelled to defend Gorhigos, win a victory at Tripoli and a semivictory at Ajazzo. The great battle of Part 2, Gorhigos, corresponds to the storming of Alexandria in Part 1. Although Machaut describes the Gorhigos compaign in glowing terms, it is evident that the Cypriots are now far from the Holy Land or the centers of Saracen power, and Peter himself is not present at the victory. Formerly the aggressors, they now are forced on the defensive; used to great triumphs, they must be content with half-successes and minor skirmishes. Then too the crusade is impeded by negotiations which lead to no good end. Cypriots, who formerly stormed Alexandria, now visit Cairo only as impotent guests, again in the king's absence. Part 2 is made up of two narrative lines joined by the process of *entrelacement:* the war and the negotiations. The Christians' tenuous position is accurately reflected in this more diffuse, complex, indecisive pattern.

Then, after better times seem to have returned (victory at Tripoli, Lesparre confounded) and Peter has attained a simulacrum of apocalypse (his accolade in Rome, his acceptance of the Kingdom of Armenia), he is cut down by his own people. Part 3, which recounts the events leading up to his death, marks a return to the simple, straightforward style of Part 1. In the course of *PA* King Peter suffers from acts of felony: by Yalbugha, an enemy; by Lesparre, a friend; and by the Lusignan's own brothers. Only this final, most terrible act of treachery destroys him. The high points of the narrative, aside from King Peter's birth, are the fall of Alexandria and his assassination. Peter's great military triumph coincides with his greatest moment of mobility and freedom, while death finds him immobile, trapped in a bed, in a room, in a castle in Nicosia. These two moments set limits to his mortality.

From a twentieth-century perspective, crusading in the late Middle Ages was all but a complete failure. Although from time to time Christendom went on the offensive, her efforts were crowned with a few ephemeral successes at best: the capture of Rhodes in 1310, Smyrna in 1344, Adalia in 1361, Alexandria in 1365, and Gallipoli in 1366. Far more important, however, were the almost uninterrupted series of Turkish victories in the Balkans, as the frontier between Christendom and Islam moved progressively westward. The Turks seized Nicaea (1329) and Nicomedia (1337). Invited into Europe by one of the principals in a Byzantine civil war, they took Gallipoli (1354) and Andrianople (1357) and routed the Serbs on the Maritza (1371) and at Kossovo (1389). Meanwhile, the Armenian Kingdom of Cilicia fell in 1375, and the West's great counterattack, the Nicopolis Crusade of 1396, was a total failure, as disastrous to French chivalry as Crécy and Poitiers. Tamerlane gave the West respite when he overwhelmed Bajazet in 1402, but Turkish victories at Varna (1444) and Kossovo (1448) and the fall of Constantinople (1453) crowned a period in history beginning with the fall of Acre that Atiya has quite properly labeled "The Counter-Crusade."

Peter of Lusignan's compaigns must be judged in this larger context. Politically and militarily, the Alexandria expedition was fruitless. It failed to achieve a permanent beachhead in Palestine or Egypt and to inflict a serious defeat on the Saracens. The immediate results were wanton destruction of a great city, the enrichment of a few adventurers, a temporary disruption in trade between East and West, and rage against Cyprus on the part of Egypt and the Italian city states who depended on good economic relations with Islam for survival. They were not to forgive or forget. The Egyptians, waiting for better days, wreaked immediate vengeance on the native Copt population and closed the Holy Sepulchre to pilgrims for three years. Venice and Genoa had been quarreling over commercial privileges in Cyprus ever since the first privileges were granted to the Genoese in 1218. At the coronation of Peter II in 1372 the two went at it again. The Cypriot populace took sides against the Genoese in a violent manner; the latter retaliated by sending an army, which burned Limassol, sacked Nicosia, and occupied Famagusta permanently. After 1374 the Lusignans found themselves the impotent rulers of an impoverished, ravaged island. But it was the Egyptian invasions of 1424, 1425, and 1426 (with the Genoese at Famagusta as collaborators), culminating in the battle of Khirokitia, which finally ended Cyprus's existence as an independent state. Like the Byzantine Empire *(mutatis mutandis),* Cyprus was first assaulted by Latin Christians, then finished off by the Hordes of Islam. And it happened within two generations of Peter I's reign.

This "reality" of the fourteenth century was not understood by Peter, Machaut, and their contemporaries. In the West Peter was considered one of the great paladins of all time, and the Storming of Alexandria the central event of his reign, perhaps of the entire century. This, the grandest *passagium* since Richard of England and Philip Augustus, caught men's fancies. The pope was overjoyed; Du Guesclin and Amadeus VI of Savoy took the cross; even Charles V promised to go. People ascribed the failure to hold

Alexandria and subsequent defeats to vacillation on the part of Peter's followers: the *Athleta Christi* himself could do no wrong. When the Lusignan was assassinated, all the major authorities (Mézières, Froissart, Cuvelier, Christine de Pisan, Aeneas Silvius) exonerated Peter and castigated his murderers. In fact, the later tragic events in Cypriot history were presumed by many to be God's vengeance on a dissolute people of rebels and traitors.

Thus Machaut's Tenth Worthy soon became as much a creature of legend as the other Nine. The poet did not want Peter's story to be forgotten; no doubt *PA* contributed more than a little to its survival. Chaucer's mention of Peter's death in *The Monk's Tale* (VII 2371-78) was influenced by Machaut; and as for his Knight, "At Alisaundre he was whan it was wonne" (I [A] 51). Villon's reference to "Le roy de Chippre de renon" in the *Ballade des seigneurs du temps jadis (Le Testament,* 369) can refer only to the greatest of the Lusignans. [9] And it is perhaps not inappropriate that the last great baron to defend the Central Marches, the Duc de Guermantes, who in his own way fought a losing battle for a generation against an open society, claims direct descent from the Lusignans, kings of Cyprus, and is proud of his family's connection with the Knights of Malta.

Guillaume de Machaut, who, through so much of his career, displays ambivalence toward heroism and romance, in his last work propagates a new myth to equal those of the past. The artist creates a vision of grandeur. From the *Song of Roland* and Godfrey of Bouillon to the time of Aragon, Emmanuel, and De Gaulle, this too is part of the French tradition.

---

[9] John L. La Monte, "The 'Roy de Chippre' in François Villon's 'Ballade des Seigneurs du Temps Jadis,'" *Romanic Review* 23 (1932): 48-53.

EXCURSUS: MACHAUT'S SHORT *DITS*

IN THE 1360s, a period which saw the composition of his two longest works, *VD* and *PA*, Guillaume de Machaut also wrote a series of shorter *dits*, which I shall discuss briefly here.

Le Dit de la Harpe. [1] The Speaker says he will compare his Lady to a harp. He lauds the harp and proclaims his desire to learn how to play it, in order to sing the Ladys' praises. He then names the harp's twenty-five allegorical strings (*Bonté, Loyauté, Debonnaireté,* etc.) and relates these endowments to his Lady, who possesses them all.

With this poem Machaut reverts to the allegorical style of *DA*. The medievals were no doubt impressed by his striking comparison of a lady to a musical instrument and by his skill in finding traits to correspond to that instrument's strings. However, from the perspective of modern criticism, it is hard to imagine a less vital or witty poetic conception than to list abstract virtues belonging to the harp, divide them into families (*Debonnaireté* and *Humilité, Honnesté* and *Verité, Juenesse, Deduit,* and *Leësse* form three distinct groups of sisters), and then re-list all of them with reference to the Lady. Although Karl Young alludes correctly to Machaut's "agreeable versatility and fluency" (p. 20), to the "pleasant fancy of a graceful versifier" (p. 13), in my opinion this highly tedious poem must surely be considered one of Machaut's least successful efforts.

The medievals divided instruments into two classes, the *haut* (loud) and the *bas* (soft). In the second category, soft instruments

---

[1] 354 lines; ed. Karl Young, "The *Dit de la Harpe* of Guillaume de Machaut," in *Essays in Honor of Albert Feuillerat,* ed. Henri M. Peyre (New Haven, Conn., 1943), pp. 1-20 (cited hereafter as *DH*).

played indoors, King David's harp was held in the highest esteem. Only aristocrats play it in the *Prose Tristan,* and Tristan himself wins fame as a harpist. For the harpist is no vulgar entertainer, but a minstrel and storyteller in his own right. [2] This may explain why, in *DH,* Machaut expresses such contempt for the masses (251-62). *Raison* urges people not to carry the harp into taverns, lest its honor diminish; only fine knights, clerics, and ladies with soft, lovely hands ought to listen to the harp, "Non pas villein ne garson ne merdaille" (259). No doubt, harps were played in the marketplace and the tavern as well as in the ducal hall. The Speaker insists that his is a fine noble instrument, not a low-class one, and thus worthy of serving as an allegory for his Lady.

Because the harp is assimilated to the Lady, it is exalted as she is. Five of her endowments (*Avis, Congnoissance, Grace, Maintieng,* and *Maniere,* 233-40) qualify her to play the harp (Young, p. 18) or make her, a harp, worthy of being played. In any case, harp allegory gives Machaut an opportunity to laud a musical instrument and, by extension, music and poetry in general. His speaker-lover is a potential musician, who wishes to play the harp and sing praises of the Lady on it. To back his claim that the harp is the finest of instruments, he cites the three greatest harpists of myth: Orpheus, who conquered Hell and brought Eurydice back from beyond the grave with his playing (cf. *PA*); Phoebus, who preferred the harp to all other instruments (cf. *VD*); and David, who with a harp calmed the wrath of God. Machaut probably was aware of mythological speculation on the origins of musical instruments (as was the author of *l'Ovide moralisé*), of biblical exegesis that interpreted plucked stringed instruments in Christian terms, and that, in *l'Ovide moralisé* as throughout the Middle Ages, Orpheus appears as a Christ figure, the Good Shepherd, who plays to his flocks and harrows Hell. Machaut will treat aesthetic problems more explicitly in *Le Prologue.* However, in *DH,* written approximately at the same time as *VD,* he

---

[2] Edmund A. Bowles, "Haut and Bas: The Grouping of Musical Instruments in the Middle Ages," *Musica Disciplina* 8 (1954): 115-40. Also Curt Sachs, *The History of Musical Instruments* (New York, 1940); Karl Geiringer, *Musical Instruments* (London, 1943); Jean Maillard, *Evolution et esthétique du lai lyrique, Des origines à la fin du XIVème siècle* (Paris, 1952-1961); Roslyn Rensch, *The Harp: Its History, Technique and Repertoire* (New York-Washington, 1969).

already borrows from classical and Christian sources to exalt the harp and, indirectly, the world of art in general.

Le Dit de la Marguerite [3] and *Le Dit de la fleur de lis et de la Marguerite.* [4]

The *DM* sings the praises of a flower, the daisy, and of the Speaker's Lady, assimilated to the daisy. In *FLM* the Speaker lauds the daisy and the lily, compares his Lady to both flowers, but in the end decides that he will serve the daisy as long as he lives.

In his edition of *FLM*, James Wimsatt speculates that Machaut's *Complainte* 6 "Mon cuer, m'amour, ma dame souvereinne" was written for King Peter I of Cyprus, the protagonist of *PA*, shortly after Charles V's coronation at Reims (May 19, 1364). According to Wimsatt, the poem, in Peter's voice, lauds Margaret of Flanders for political reasons. Machaut then would have composed *DM* in 1366, after the storming of Alexandria, also for Peter and Margaret and also in Peter's voice, and *FLM* for Margaret's wedding to Philip of Burgundy in 1369.

These two poems are of the same kind as *DH*: extended allegories in praise of the Speaker's Lady. Both *dits* contain clichés of *fin' amor*. In both, the Speaker is devoted to his Lady, absolutely subservient and ecstatic with the joy of love. Without a doubt, the Lady towers over all other women. The theme of separation is elaborated with unusual skill. In strophe 12 of *DM* the Lady is compared to the sun, moon, North Star, lifeboat, captain, oar, mast, sail, hardtack, and sweet water that guide and sustain the Speaker:

> p. 128 C'est li solaus qui esclaire et qui luist;
> C'est la lune qui fait la clère nuit;
> C'est l'estoile qui par mer me conduist;
> C'est la nasselle
> Forte, seüre et plainne de déduit;
> C'est li patrons qui me gouverne et duit;
> C'est l'aviron qui de mer fent le bruit
> Par sa cautelle,

---

[3] 208 lines; ed. P. Tarbé, *Les Œuvres de Guillaume de Machault*, pp. 123-29 (cited hereafter as *DM*).

[4] 416 lines; ed. James I. Wimsatt, *The Marguerite Poetry of Guillaume de Machaut* (cited hereafter as *FLM*).

> C'est le fort maht qui pour vent ne chancelle;
> C'est li voiles qui en ma nef ventelle,
> Qui la maine sauvement et ostelle;
>   C'est le bescuit
> De quoy je vis; c'est l'yaue douce et belle
> Qui me freschit et qui me renouvelle
> Et toudis est sainne, clère et nouvelle:
>   Ainssi le cuid.

Appropriately, King Peter the crusader, who sailed to Europe, then to Alexandria, is depicted as a distant pilgrim on the sea, his way lit by a star. In *FLM* we are also reminded that the Marguerite is a pearl, that Saint Margaret dwells in Paradise, and that Margaret, the prettiest of names, was created before all others:

> 269   Et aussi chascuns aperçoit
>   Que c'est li plus biaus no[m]s qui soit;
>   Et je croy tout certeinnement
>   Que cils noms fu premierement
>   Que ne furent les autres noms,
>   Pour ce en est signés li renoms.

Machaut probably refers to a line of distinguished Margarets, daughters of the House of France, that stretches back to the time of Louis IX. It is equally significant that the third-century Saint Margaret dwelt in Antioch, a city which formed part of the Lusignans' lost holdings in Palestine; that, like King Peter, she had a special faith in the Cross and defeated a dragon through the Sign of the Cross (cf. *PA*, 453-54); that Cyprus was an island especially rich in pearls; and that one of Peter's daughters, one of his mules, and a tower he built, were all named Margarita. [5]

Machaut tells us that the daisy opens her petals in the morning and, after inclining to the sun whatever way it goes all day, closes them at night. This indicates humility, piety, and knowledge of God's power. The daisy's green stalk, white petals, red corona, and yellow pollen represent respectively the Lady's youth, joy, modesty, and "treasure" (cf. *VD*). The roots of the lily symbolize faith, from which sprouts the gift of grace, that is, love of Our Lord; the stalk symbolizes *fermeté, vertu, force,* and *estableté* (133-34); the white

---

[5] Wimsatt discusses at some length Marguerite (pearl-daisy) symbolism, particularly as it may be connected with Peter of Cyprus.

petals, purity and chastity; and the stamens with yellow pollen, good speech, good deeds, and prayer. Machaut claims to know that the pollen of the daisy can revive the dead or, if his source is incorrect, that it is good for the eyes, helps heal wounds and broken bones, and contributes to potions, plasters, and baths. He also claims that a fluid colder than ice, manufactured from the lily, cures men of fever or at least reduces the pain. Needless to say, these medicinal powers are compared *ad nauseam* to the Lady's ability to cure *maus d'amours* with a tear or one glance of her eyes; Machaut no doubt also refers to King Peter's successful recovery from illness in 1366.

The assimilation of woman to flower and flower to woman we know to be one of the oldest, richest archetypes in world literature. *Le Roman de la Rose* and many other rose poems (Jean Renart's *Roman de la Rose,* the *Carmen de Rosa, Le Lai de la Rose,* Baudouin de Condé's *Conte de la Rose*) testify to its vogue in the medieval period. [6] Machaut's tales contain *loci amoeni* with flowers. In most of them and in many of his lyrics, the lady herself is compared to a flower. *Lai* 21, a typical love-plaint, is called *Le Lay de la Rose,* even though neither the rose nor any other flower is named therein. Also in the 1360s he wrote a *Dit de la Rose.* The vitality of the archetype no doubt contributed to the success of Machaut's *DM* and *FLM.* These two poems, by singling out for praise the daisy instead of the rose, then launched a subgenre, the Marguerite poem, that influenced Froissart, Deschamps, and Chaucer. In fact, Machaut originated most of the Marguerite imagery cultivated by his successors. For all their historical importance, however, *DM* and *FLM* are relatively static, uninspired pieces, and, although not as artificial as *DH,* like *DH* they display more wit than imagination, more learning than poetry.

Le Dit de la Rose. [7]

On a lovely spring day the Narrator strolls into a beautiful garden. He then traverses a region of rocks and thickets, where he perceives a rose surrounded

---

[6] See Lommatzsch, "Blumen und Früchte im altfranzösischen Schrifttum."

[7] 108 lines; ed. Tarbé, *Les Œuvres de Guillaume de Machault,* pp. 65-67 (cited hereafter as *DR*). Without informing the reader, Tarbé omits fragments which add up to twenty-eight lines. Therefore, I have consulted Ms 1584, fond français, of the Bibliothèque Nationale and will quote from it when appropriate.

by thorns. He would like to pluck the rose but does not have a knife, sword, or glove. Finally, he rips open the bush with his bare hands and, although scratched in more than sixty places, plucks the flower. Then, to the Narrator's surprise, each of his wounds heals immediately upon contact with the precious rose.

The *DH* and *DM* are panegyrics which recall Machaut's long allegory, *DA*. The *DR*, on the other hand, resembles *DL*. As in the case of *DL*, Machaut does not spell out the poem's allegorical meaning: certain questions are left unanswered, and each reader must interpret *DR* in his own way.

The rose itself refers undoubtedly to the Narrator's Lady or to her love; no other meaning is possible in a disciple of Guillaume de Lorris, who also wrote *DM* and *FLM*, poems in praise of a flower and a lady. In *Lai* 6 Machaut proclaims that his Lady's beauty and goodness surpass all beauty and good in the world and that, in honor and sweetness, she is to other women as a rose is to thorns. In *FLM*, paraphrasing scripture, he declares that his Lady is superior to all other prudent, chaste maidens like a lily among thorns (43-58), then interprets these thorns as the misery, sadness, talebearing, temptation, tribulation, and trickery that surround but do not tarnish her honor. Perhaps then the thorns in *DR* refer to the Lady's handmaidens, confidantes, and friends, who, in addition, may speak ill of him and of her, too. Nicole de Margival states in *La Panthère d'Amours* (a poem Machaut used as a source for *DL*) that brambles symbolize *losengiers'* evil talk, but he also interprets nettles and thorns as the lover's amorous thoughts and his desire. In *DL* too the Narrator and the Lion must traverse a thorny region which corresponds to the pain they suffer, while *losengiers* are represented by wild beasts.

We will never know whether Machaut meant the *DR* thorns to represent *losengiers* (male or female) or the Narrator's suffering as a true lover. In the economy of the poem, they symbolize equally well one or the other or both at the same time. In any case, the knife or glove which the Narrator could have used to pluck the rose without hurting himself probably refers to erotic gambits employed by bad lovers: fancy talking, a cold, calculating heart, and social dexterity. These are techniques which Machaut consistently attacked throughout his career. By touching the rose with his bare hand, the Narrator demonstrates that he sincerely deserves to win her love.

At first the Narrator is repelled by the thorns which protect his rose. He dares not touch it. After this first failure (and a strategically placed *encomium rosae*), he risks his bare hand and succeeds. In a first moment of victory the rose is his; then in a second triumph it heals the wounds he endured in winning it. On the one hand, *DR* proclaims the value of suffering, declares that only through suffering can man hope to enjoy *fin' amor*. Yet Machaut also says that happy love will nullify the pain. As in *RF, DL,* and *DA,* a true courtly suitor alone is capable of enjoying love, for, whether or not he succeeds in the love-quest, he will be content; and because he is worthy of his Lady, he must succeed.

The *DR* garden partakes of the best tradition of the *dit amoreus.* In a few lines, but with extraordinary grace, Machaut places the Narrator in one of the prettiest *loci amoeni* of the late Middle Ages. Tarbé, who apparently was less impressed than I am by these descriptive passages, left out verses treating the song of birds, the sweetness of the morning, and the rose's odor, such as the following:

> 365 vº (c)   Quant je fui ens, moult mesjoÿ
> Pour les oisillons que j'oÿ,
> Qui si tresdoucement chantoient
> Et de chanter si s'efforçoient
> Que tous li lieus retentissoit
> Dou bruit qui de leur bec issoit,
> Et si estoit la matinee
> Si douce et si bien ordenee,
> Qu'onques mais si douce ne vi,
> Ne lieu si tresbien assevi.

Immediately after describing the garden, Machaut places us in a totally different landscape, with rocks, shrubs, clumps of trees, thick hedges, brambles, and thorns. He contrasts these two *loci,* as he does the Narrator's bare hand and his glove or sword, or his sixty scratches and the rose that heals them. The two landscapes, manifestations of pathetic fallacy, symbolize the Narrator's inner state as a lover. He goes through both of them before coming to the rose. I see his progress in space indicative of a comparable progress in life and the ways of love. Then comes a more exacting task. After a preliminary failure, the Narrator tries again and succeeds as if spurred on by the meditation on the rose's beauty Machaut interposes between the two attempts and by his own very deep commitment to ideal love.

For a poem that presents only one animate character in only 108 lines, *DR* tells a fine little drama. The Narrator has won the rose and been initiated into love. He also has experienced the two extremes of life, joy and misery, desire and repulsion, roses and thorns. So many poets, including Ronsard, Goethe, Jouve, and Aragon, have also spoken of *Rosae inter vepres.* Machaut recognizes that roses cannot exist without thorns, that both are essential to the human condition. He expresses these concepts in a poem which tells a story and creates a mood of evanescent beauty, where symbolism stimulates the reader's fancy and joy.

Le Prologue. [8]

Nature comes to Guillaume de Machaut, offering him her children, *Scens, Retorique,* and *Musique,* to help him write new poems of love. *Amours* then offers him her offspring. *Dous Penser, Plaisance,* and *Esperance,* for the same purpose. Machaut thanks his benefactresses and promises to work hard, He discusses the gifts he has received, especially music, and the process of artistic cration, lists the literary genres he shall employ, and speaks in praise of ladies.

Machaut wrote these lines, which appear at the beginning of several important manuscripts and purport to introduce *DV,* toward the end of his career (c. 1371), as an introduction to his opus as a whole (Hoepffner, 1:lii-liv). In the octosyllabic commentary on the *ballades* we are told that the gifts of Nature and Love help the poet to compose narrative and lyrical works including those set to music. And in *Ballade* 2 he promises to write both long and short poems, some with music and some presumably without. He has a sense that his work forms a unified opus. Furthermore, as Hoepffner points out, *P* is an epitome or microcosm, containing the various elements which are elaborated in the *Œuvres complètes:* lyrical and narrative verse, allegory and classical myth, didacticism, a story, and an actively present, obtrusive, dramatized Narrator: the poet himself.

---

[8] Four *ballades,* containing 27, 27, 30, and 30 lines each, followed by a commentary of 184 lines; ed. Hoepffner, 1: 1-12 (cited hereafter as *P*).

For the first time, Machaut sets down his personal aesthetic. He lists the various genres (*dis, chansonnettes, hoquès, lais, motès, rondiaus, virelais, complaintes,* and *balades,* 11-16) and the kinds of rhyme (*serpentine, equivoque, leonine, croisie, retrograde, sonant, consonant,* 151-56) he employs. This strictly technical approach to the poet's craft anticipates the various *Arts de Seconde Rhetorique* that will proliferate in the following century and a half, beginning with the *Art de Dictier* by his disciple, Eustache Deschamps. Machaut also explains, in allegorical terms, how poetry is composed. The three gifts he receives directly from *Nature* deal with the formal aspect of poetry: *Scens* (inspiration? the faculty of reason which plans and controls artistic creation? the art of composition?), *Retorique* (the technical art of rhyme and rhythm), and *Musique* (song). *Amours*'s gifts—*Dous Penser, Plaisance,* and *Esperance*—refer to the matter of the poet's song and to the mental state he has to experience in order to create.

Nature supplies the form of Machaut's poetry, Love the content. This relationship between Love and Nature was a matter of concern to Machaut and his contemporaries, as it had been to Jean de Meun. [9] The fact that these two elements are presented symmetrically (in *Ballades* 1 and 3) gives the impression that they are of equal importance. Of course, Nature, who created everything in the world, appears in *P* ahead of Love. Love presents her three offspring because she has heard of Nature's gifts. Therefore, perhaps form precedes content (chronologically or dialectically), and the poet's skill as a craftsman antedates his falling in love or his desire to impart a particular poetic message.

On the other hand, Nature proclaims that she created Machaut especially to celebrate love. She presumably approves of love as much as of poetry, for the creative act serves a practical purpose: to exalt love and ladies—*La Louange des Dames. Amours,* who warns against *villenie,* prohibits the author from speaking badly of ladies. Machaut himself swears to defend the fair sex at all times and to write only for them. Indeed, since poetry and love derive from Nature, they both possess a legitimate place in the cosmos and are not to be thought a corruption of something finer.

---

[9] Poirion, *Le Moyen Age,* p. 50.

Machaut tells us that poetry is ineluctably bound to happiness. A young man in love, whose heart beats from joy, is capable of writing good poetry. But if he is in a bad mood or suffers from *villenie* or *mesdis,* he cannot create. Jealous, unhappy lovers are artistically sterile. Even if the matter to be treated is sad (frustrated love, separation, loneliness), the manner in which it is written ought to be joyful. The poet's joy comes from his state of mind, his total commitment to love, not from the creative act itself. But, when performed, the composition then brings joy to the beholder, Machaut's public. Joy appears at the beginning and end of the creative process; these states are linked by the work of art itself, created by a writer in love.

In the commentary on the *ballades,* sixty-two lines are devoted to music, only twenty-two to the other five gifts. Machaut tells again the stories of David and Orpheus. He claims that music is enjoyed in the world (it combats melancholia) and in heaven. We are reminded of Machaut's lists of instruments in *RF* and *PA* and his exaltation of the harp in *DH.* For the medievals, music was to be found in the harmony of the cosmos, in church, in the song of birds, in city streets, in the heart of the poet, and in Paradise. It was a proper medium for communicating with God and for understanding him. Machaut was one of the last masters to identify poetry with music, both derived from the joy of a universe governed according to principles of harmony. In conformity to the universe and God's will, the poet-musician goes about his task.

Finally, superhuman forces do not help just any poet-musician: *P* praises one artist above all others, Guillaume de Machaut himself. Nature, who created the entire world, says she formed Machaut *a part,* especially to write new love poems. She predicts that he will be famous as an artist and that good people will respect him. Significantly, the author of *VD* is promised success as a writer but not necessarily as a lover. And, as a writer looking back over his career, he ascribes to himself a special destiny. Like his great forerunners, Orpheus, Apollo, and David, he has been initiated into mysteries, and he will serve Nature, creating in the way a mortal can.

Although in his *dits* Guillaume de Machaut exhibits some false modesty, generally he exalts the work of art and his production as an artist. This is the man who inserts lyrics as models into *RF,* who appears as the protagonist of *JRN* because he is a poet, who is a teacher and friend to princes in *CA* and *FA*, and who in *VD* attains the joy of love uniquely because of his greatness as a poet. Machaut's position, though it does not approximate the arrogant claims of the Greeks and Romans (divine madness, the gift to grant immortality to oneself and others), nevertheless marks a departure from the modest, self-effacing attitude assumed by most of his predecessors in the vernacular. No doubt that Guillaume's pride in his work anticipates that of the Burgundian Rhétoriqueurs and the Pléiade. This contemporary of Petrarch and Boccaccio manifests more than one trait of the Renaissance. And his *P* is one of the first vernacular texts in the history of French poetics.

CONCLUSION

Spanning a career of some forty years, Machaut wrote, in addition to his lyrics, ten long narrative *dits* and several short ones. His narrative verse adds up to a total of close to 45,000 lines. Like those other masters of French literature who have produced much —Ronsard, Corneille, Balzac, Hugo, Zola, Aragon—Machaut manifests an extraordinary variety of theme, message, and tone. Scholars, who have total freedom in speculating on a writer's evolution, sometimes fail to take into account his ups and downs, the false starts, the repetitions—all that is unpredictable in the world of art. Rigid, neoclassical value judgments lead them to concentrate on only one aspect (albeit an important one) of a man's career and thus to neglect fascinating works which deviate from the norm: such as Ronsard's *Hymnes* and *Discours,* the early and late Corneille, Hugo's *La Fin de Satan* and *Dieu.* As a result, they oversimplify the complexity inherent in every rich creative talent. To make matters worse, we cannot even be sure of the order in which Machaut's *dits* were composed. Although Hoepffner's chronology is the most plausible, nonetheless any hypothesis concerning Machaut's development as an artist inevitably remains only that: a hypothesis.

At one time scholars posited for writers, as for literary genres, an evolution from immaturity to a moment of perfection (Corneille's *Le Cid, Horace, Cinna,* and *Polyeucte;* Hugo's *Les Contemplations, La Légende des Siècles*) followed by decay and disintegration. Today we recognize that seldom, if ever, does a master's career follow the precise curve traced for him in the Academy. An obvious case is Zola, who, along with masterpieces—*L'Assommoir, Nana, Germinal, La Terre, La Bête humaine, La Débâcle*—wrote such novels as *Une Page d'amour, Au Bonheur des Dames, La Joie de vivre,* and *Le Rêve.* In the case of Guillaume de Machaut, even if we accept Hoepffner's chronology, my aesthetic evaluation of his canon is necessarily subjective, as subjective as with Corneille or Zola. This said, in my opinion, his early period gives an impression of rapidly maturing powers. With *DV, JRB, RF,* and *DL,* each poem registers improvement over the preceding, a greater freedom and scope. From 1340 on I submit that Machaut's masterpieces are *DL, JRN, FA,* and *VD,* works of extraordinary subtlety and beauty. Yet, as with Zola, I find interspersed in the same period *DA, CA,* and *PA,* which, although they possess undeniable literary qualities, are not of the same caliber as the others. It would appear that, like the classical dramatist and the nineteenth-century novelist, a medieval poet's career too has its ups and downs, its periods of enthusiastic creation and of respite, which alternate according to a rhythm up to now beyond the critic's ken.

Religion plays a role in Guillaume de Machaut's life and work. Although he never took Holy Orders, Machaut earned a Master of Arts degree, probably at the University of Paris, and occupied for almost forty years a canonicate at Reims. His first datable composition, the motet *Bone Pastor Guillerme,* was written to commemorate the accession of Guillaume de Trie to the archbishopric of Reims in 1324. And the last twenty years of his active career, the time of his greatest artistic triumphs, saw the composition of two *dits* with strongly religious overtones—*CA* and *PA*—*Lais* 15 and 16, the majority of his sacred motets, the *Hoquetus David,* and the *Messe de Nostre Dame.* Perhaps in Machaut's case a concern for religion blossomed with the coming of old age. However, the immense majority of his compositions, musical, lyric, and narrative, treat of profane, not sacred, love and of man's cares in the secular world. In this respect, Machaut in no way deviates from Béroul, Thomas, Chrétien, Jean Renart, Gace Brulé, Thibaut de Champagne, Adam de la Halle, and Beaumanoir. Neither Machaut nor his public found it incongruous for a man to serve the Cathedral chapter of Reims and the king of Navarre, to sing of the Virgin Mary and of *Toute-belle.* For them, the world of art includes a place for *fin' amor* as well as for *Caritas.*

Not only did Machaut sing of profane love; he also consciously strove toward a more concrete literary representation of reality, that is, in the direction of realism. I have, from time to time in this book, objected to Hoepffner's prejudice in favor of realistic elements in Machaut and his condemnation of the more traditional courtly ones. I also refuse to assume that these elements of realism are necessarily autobiographical. This said, I cannot deny that Machaut introduces into several of his tales a sense of contemporary reality which includes but goes beyond ornament, amplification, and local color. He grounds some *dits* in a precise space-time continuum, refers to contemporary historical personages and events, describes *realia* with precision, treats nonheroic characters in stories lacking excessively supernatural or romance overtones, and concentrates on valid human psychological problems. Machaut's concern for realism increased in the course of his career. Of his last two important narratives, one, which he called The True Story, pretends to be strictly autobiographical, and with the second, for the first time in his life, he writes a chronicle. It is possible that Guillaume believed the *dit amoreus* no longer provided him with sufficient scope to recreate reality in the way he wished; in that case the poet had no choice but to cross the line from fiction to chronicle, to become a historian.

Machauts' greatest triumph as a realist, and as a narrative poet, may well be the new literary type he created or, at least, made his own: the inept, blundering narrator, who is also an inept, blundering lover. This pseudoautobiographical character is prone to cowardice, sloth, snobbery, misogyny, and pedantry. Guilty of excess, unable to cope with everyday social life, obsessed by his failings, he acts in a delightfully comic manner, in contrast to the elegant gentlemen and ladies of the court. For the first time in French literature the fool has become a protagonist of serious belles lettres. And Machaut's creation was to have a profound influence upon his most gifted successors, Froissart and Chaucer.

Sometimes in Machaut a lover recounts his experiences directly *(DV, RF, DA, VD);* sometimes they are told by a witness-narrator *(JRB, DL, FA).* The hero's story is thus either presented dramatically by the agent or filtered through another's consciousness. As with the great eighteenth-century novelists. Machaut's narrator may be an active participant in the story or withdraw from it; he can be reliable or unreliable, omniscient or in error. By playing with point of view and illusion-reality, Guillaume pioneered in the development of a more sophisticated narrative technique. These themes (point of view, illusion versus reality) enter into the fabric of three of his finest tales *(JRN, FA, VD)*, giving them a complexity seldom to be found in early fiction.

Halfway through his career, Machaut introduced *exempla* into his tales—first contemporary anecdotes *(DA, JRN)*, then stories from classical Antiquity *(JRN, CA, FA, VD)* and the Bible *(CA, VD)*. Although at first the *exempla* are inserted into the narrative clumsily and in a haphazard way, soon Machaut learned to have them contribute organically to the poem as a whole. His sophisticated treatment of Greco-Roman myth anticipates Scève and Ronsard. In certain *dits (RF, FA, VD, PA)* lyric poems and/or prose epistles are also integrated into the narrative. The *dit amoreus* becomes longer and more complex at the same time that the author seeks greater realism. As a result, some scholars have condemned him for failing to repeat the simple, more coherent structures of his early period.

For all the variety the ten major *dits* manifest, most of them are based upon a single narrative pattern. A Lover or a Narrator leaves courtly society to enter a closed space, generally a garden or an island. There he is aided by a guide (the lion, a secretary, Lady *Bonneürté,* the Narrator as witness) and encounters a male or female authority figure (the God of Love, Venus, *Esperence,* the kings of Bohemia or Navarre). Having been given instruction by the authority figure, he or his double receives some kind of boon, often the boon of knowledge. He grows in the course of his experience, is initiated into the secrets of life and love, and made fit to return to the court, where he is accepted as a full-fledged member of his community. A static situation gives way to a dynamic one. Integration into society marks a successful completion of the initiation-experience, for, just as the Lover or Narrator awakens after a dream, he conquers symbolic death and is reborn to a new, finer life. Obviously, this structure is based upon the typical quest-pattern of romance, adapted to the allegorical world of *Le Roman de la Rose.* In *DL* and *PA* Machaut retains some trappings of romance and in *JRN* and *VD,* as well as *DL,* parodies the quest-theme in the comic mode.

Those ten *dits* generally exhibit a two-part structure. In *JRB* and *RF* the Narrator first enters a garden of love, then a beautiful castle. The hero of *JRN* spends a winter isolated in his room before

setting out to enjoy himself in spring, whereupon he is taken before
the king of Navarre. He progresses from winter to spring, from
death to life, from solitude to the court. Although in *FA* the Lover
and the Narrator also move from darkness to light and from misery
to joy, the usual pattern is reversed, for the décor shifts from an
indoor scene, representing darkness, to the garden and fountain,
representing light. Finally, both *VD* and *PA* contain a first section,
in which the hero progresses naturally to his goal (loving *Toute-belle*
or capturing Alexandria), followed by a second, less tightly structured
section where disillusion sets in, the prize is lost, and the protagonist
settles for half-victories or defeat. Although realism and a more
complex vision of life win out over the relatively simplistic perspectives of the early *dits,* Machaut's protagonists still set out for, and
return from, a court, a city, or a garden. Withdrawal and return
form the dominant pattern that shapes his entire narrative opus.

All of Machaut's *dits,* even *PA,* are poems of consolation. Although Love is the principal subject of complaint, like the *fin' amor*
of the troubadours and trouvères, it is to be taken partly as a game,
for it is an *acte gratuit,* free from material concerns, unproductive,
and based on its own code. We see the casuistry of mock-debate and
mock-trial before the court *(JRB, JRN);* we see purportedly
tragic passion reduced to allegory and treated with *élégant badinage.*
A social game, *Le Roy qui ne ment,* functions in *RF* and *VD,*
poems where the Lady believes a preposterous story told by the
Narrator, indeed accepts both his story and his love as part of a
game. Whether we consider the Narrator's love affairs to be intensely serious states of the human condition or moves in a court
chess match, *sub specie ludi,* a guide or authority figure usually
helps him in his moment of need. Machaut's lovers appear to win
their ladies or are on the way to winning them in many of the
dits amoreus; in *DA* a happy ending is imposed on the story
artificially. We are told that the lover *(RF)* and the political prisoner
(CA) ought to resist the blows of Fortune, for, if they are good
lovers, good rulers, and believe in God, they will defeat Fortune
and attain their secular goals as well. Machaut proposes that man
avoid despair and the excesses of a bookish erotic code. Instead,
he should follow the dictates of experience, live in the world,
and, if his amours do not succeed, learn to live and love again.

Souffissance is the key word in a doctrine based on practical common sense. And it applies to the political as well as the erotic sphere. In the center of Machaut's world view is to be found the theme of education: the protagonist matures in the course of the narrative and is initiated into society. He evolves from childhood to the adult world, from ignorance to wisdom, from misery to some sort of joy. Joy is enhanced by patterns of imagery, which include the *locus amoenus,* birds, the fountain, the ring, light, warmth, gold, and treasure. Machaut's *dits* often end with a feast. Often he describes in loving terms games and reveling. Often his characters enjoy the play of gallantry and rhetoric at court. His works manifest the grace and decorum of a highly civilized society, the refined life Huizinga finds so typical of the late Middle Ages.

At the same time, however, Machaut's world remains more than a little ambiguous. Joy, revelry, games, and the notion of *souffissance* perhaps express his central vision of life but not his entire world view. *Fin' amor* contains martial imagery, and military conflict comes to dominate *PA.* Somewhat similar conflict is to be found in the mock-debates of *JRB, JRN,* and *VD.* Machaut writes of complaint as well as comfort. Although the lover finds consolation against the mutability of Fortune, that august dame remains one of the author's major preoccupations. She is a force to be reckoned with in *RF, CA, VD, La Louange des Dames* 188 and 227, *Lais* 10, 17, 20, and 24, *Motet* 8, and *Ballade Notée* 31. Machaut's world contains evil as well as good authority figures *(CA),* evil as well as good advisers *(CA, VD, PA).* Obstacles spring up between a lover and his lady. The lady may be unfaithful; the lover may suffer political exile; lover and lady may be separated by social status, age, or they may even belong to different species *(DL).* And one may die before the other. Communication breaks down: even when they speak or write to each other, Machaut's characters often participate in a *dialogue de sourds (JRB, JRN, VD).* We come to know the male suitor, but his lady remains an enigma, for him and for us. Left to himself, alone, the lover struggles to find happiness, to communicate with the Other. His struggle is all the more poignant, given his lady's impenetrability and the fact that whatever victory he obtains is precarious *(JRB, RF, DL, DA, VD)* or takes place by anticipation *(DV)* or in a dream *(FA).* Forces beyond a man's control compel him to love, to work his way slowly to happiness, but then he often must begin anew. Did Machaut become disillusioned with *fin' amor* in the latter decades of his life? Did he himself, growing old, become aware of the passing of time and the absurdity of an old man's quest for love and happiness? The disparity in years between the Narrator and *Toute-belle* is a major theme in *VD,* and Machaut's later tales generally cover longer time spans and give the reader a greater sense of duration and of man's transformation over the years. And throughout his career the poet of Reims is concerned with melancholia and madness, ailments caused by love, and with death, an important theme in his *dits* and several of the lyrics.

Joy and misery are equally precarious; in Machaut one gives way to the other readily. Life is made up of a series of changing states under the influence of Dame Fortune. Man is torn between illusion and reality, between dreams and waking existence, between fiction and the reality of pseudoautobiography. Ambiguities form an essential element in *JRN* and *VD.* Machaut's world contains, juxtaposed and in synthesis, romance, realism, lyricism, psychological analysis, pseudoconfession, satire on literature and on life, dream motifs, the fairy world, myth, parody, human comedy, and a wholesome acceptance of life, nature, and the senses.

In addition to his doctrine of *souffissance,* Machaut upholds the primacy of art. Unlike other fourteenth-century writers, he played an active role in supervising the publication of his own works, for he is the first poet in French to arrange his *Œuvres complètes* in manuscript form and to be conscious of his opus as a unity. In the *dits,* the lover wins his lady because he is a poet *(RF, VD,* perhaps *FA),* and the lady too learns to write *(VD).* Lyrics, inserted in the narrative, serve as a means of communication and as an arm in the war of seduction. Also for the first time in French literature, poetry and the craft of writing are the central themes of a long narrative, The True Story, which purports to be an immediate by-product of the events it describes. And in *VD* and *P,* Machaut gives voice to his aesthetic code — becomes a master of poetics as well as a poet.

It is well known that the Master of Reims enjoyed a prestigious reputation in his own day and over the next two or three generations. His patrons included some of the greatest princes of the age: kings of France, Bohemia, Navarre, and Cyprus; dukes of Normandy, Berry, and Bar; counts of Savoy and Flanders. The number of his extant manuscripts and their extension, in regions as distant as Spain, Italy, Czechoslovakia, Poland, and Sweden, testify to his fame, as does praise from Gilles li Muisis, Eustache Deschamps, Oton de Granson, Alain Chartier, Achille Caulier, Martin Le Franc, Ugolino of Orvieto, Santillana, King René d'Anjou, and the author of *Les Règles de seconde rhétorique*. [1] Yet Machaut's influence was greatest on three poets who read his corpus and imitated it with care yet never mentioned his name: Froissart, Christine de Pisan, and Chaucer. For example, sources for Chaucer's *Book of the Duchess* include *DV, JRB, RF, DL, JRN, FA, VD, Lai* 17, *Complainte* 1, *Motets* 3, 8, and 9, and *Ballade Notée* 38. [2] There can be no doubt that the major developments in late medieval verse narrative—the debate and judgment poem, the poem of complaint and comfort or of consolation against Fortune, the poem made up of *exempla* from classical Antiquity, the Marguerite poem, the tale told by a garrulous, elderly, inept, cowardly narrator, the juxtaposition of fiction and reality, of allegory and pseudoautobiography, the presence of a more credible dream-psychology, the woman's point of view, classical myths and traditional *fin' amor* played with as in a game, the pride and prestige of the artist—all these are due in part to Guillaume de Machaut. He set a pattern which lasted a good hundred years.

Be this as it may, for the reader of today a writer's importance does not derive primarily from his influence or contemporary fame, that is, his place in literary history. We have come to recognize that Bernart de Ventadorn is greater than Arnaut Daniel and Guiraut de Bornelh, although the latter are praised by Dante; that Sponde, D'Aubigné, and Saint-Amant are far greater than Malherbe, who anticipated classical taste and pleased Boileau; that the importance of Anatole France, Romain Rolland, and Pierre Loti in their own time provides no guarantee of the verdict of posterity. Only the

---

[1] See Hoepffner, I: i-x; Chichmaref, *Guillaume de Machaut*, 1: lxviii-lxxi; Ludwig, *Guillaume de Machaut*, 2: 7-44; Machabey, *Guillaume de Machault: La Vie et l'Œuvre musicale*, 2: 163-70; Siegmund Levarie, *Guillaume de Machaut* (New York, 1954), pp. 18-19; Schrade, *Polyphonic Music of the Fourteenth Century: Commentary to Volumes II & III*, pp. 24-54; Reaney, "Machaut's Influence on Late Medieval Music," *Monthly Musical Record* 88 (1958): 50-58, 96-101; Wilkins, "The Post-Machaut Generation of Poet-Musicians," *Nottingham Mediaeval Studies* 12 (1968): 40-84.

[2] For his influence on Chaucer, see the Bibliography in this study.

universal aesthetic qualities in a poet's work make him worthy of immortality.

It is true that Machaut was not destined to be one of those rare masters, a Jean de Meun, a Villon, a Jean Lemaire de Belges, whose fame survived the so-called Revival of Learning. The meager place his work occupies in student manuals and histories of medieval literature testifies to a very real neglect. Nonetheless, I am convinced that Machaut, as a musician and as a poet, is one of the great international masters of the fourteenth century. With the *dit amoreus,* as with the *lai, virelai,* motet, and polyphonic *ballade* and *rondeau,* he brought to perfection a genre which, after his death, fell into decline. (Other genres—particularly the nonmusical *ballade* and *rondeau*—were perfected by Charles d'Orléans, Villon, and Marot.) Machaut the master, often imitated, at his best was inimitable. And his best as a narrative poet—*DL, JRN, FA, VD*—deserve a place among the classics of medieval French literature.

Although a founder of *Ars nova,* a *modernus* and proud of it, in literature as in music Machaut is not a revolutionary. He adapts, renovates, amplifies, and extends the heritage of the past, and thus creates a synthesis of past and present. He writes for those courtiers, clerics, and wealthy burghers capable of appreciating his wit, participating in his game, and practicing his wisdom. During the last twenty-five years of his career France was ravaged by the beginnings of the most tragic war of her history. On the whole Machaut and his contemporaries paid little attention to the Hundred Years War, too little for the nationalistic sensitivities of some scholars. Yet culture, art, and the life of the court outlived the holocaust. Indeed, perhaps the only way to protest against barbarism and ensure the survival of culture was by writing civilized poetry such as the *dit amoreus.* Machaut's art does not manifest decadence but renewal, not sterility but incomparable richness. You will find his spirit in the poetry of one who also wrote for the House of Navarre, Clément Marot, and in the work of another Champenois, who spoke of rabbits, horses, and dogs as well as the meanderings of the human heart—La Fontaine. The theater from Marivaux to Anouilh also preserves their tradition of golden, ironic *préciosité,* of sparkling *répartie* on problems of life, love, and death. No Frenchman, with the possible exception of Charles d'Orléans, incarnates better than

Machaut "that golden spring of the late Middle Ages that is timeless, placeless, forever a part of man's dream of earthly perfection." [3] This is surely a worthy contribution to literature.

---

[3] James J. Wilhelm, *The Cruelest Month: Spring, Nature, and Love in Classical and Medieval Lyrics* (New Haven, Conn.—London, 1965), p. 233.

BIBLIOGRAPHY

I. Editions of the Works of Guillaume de Machaut

Chailley, Jacques, ed. *Guillaume de Machaut (1300-1377): Messe Notre-Dame dite du Sacre de Charles V (1364) à 4 voix égales*. Paris, 1948.

Chichmaref, V., ed. *Guillaume de Machaut: Poésies lyriques*. 2 vols. Paris, 1909.

Gennrich, Friedrich, ed. *Guillaume de Machaut: Messe de Nostre Dame*. Darmstadt, 1957.

Hoepffner, Ernest, ed. *Œuvres de Guillaume de Machaut*. 3 vols. Paris, 1908, 1911, 1921.

Hoppin, Richard H., ed. "An Unrecognized Polyphonic Lai of Machaut." *Musica Disciplina* 12 (1958): 93-104.

Hübsch, H., ed. *Guillaume de Machault: La Messe de Notre Dame*. Heidelberg, 1953.

Ludwig, Friedrich, ed. *Guillaume de Machaut: Musikalische Werke*. 4 vols. Leipzig, 1926, 1928, 1929; Wiesbaden, 1954.

Machabey, Armand, ed. *Messe Notre-Dame à quatre voix de Guillaume de Machault*. Liège, 1948.

Mas Latrie, L. de, ed. *La Prise d'Alexandrie ou Chronique du roi Pierre Ier de Lusignan par Guillaume de Machaut*. Geneva, 1877.

Michon, L.-A. Joseph, ed. *Documents inédits sur la Grande Peste de 1348*. Paris, 1860.

Monod, Bernard, ed. *Quinze Poésies inédites de Guillaume de Machault, poète champenois du XIVᵉ siècle*. Versailles, 1903.

Paris, Paulin, ed. *Le Livre du Voir-Dit de Guillaume de Machaut*. Paris, 1875.

Schrade, Leo, ed. *Polyphonic Music of the Fourteenth Century. Volumes II and III: The Works of Guillaume de Machaut*. Monaco, 1956.

———, ed. *Polyphonic Music of the Fourteenth Century: Commentary to Volumes II and III*. Monaco, 1956.

Tarbé, Prosper, ed. *Les Œuvres de Guillaume de Machault*. Reims-Paris, 1849.

———, ed. *Poésies d'Agnès de Navarre-Champagne, dame de Foix*. Paris-Reims, 1856.

Thomas, Antoine, ed. "Guillaume de Machaut et l'*Ovide moralisé*." *Romania* 41 (1912): 382-400.

Van, Guillaume de, ed. *Guglielmi de Mascaudio: Opera. I: La Messe de Nostre Dame*. Rome, 1949.

———, ed. *Les Monuments de l'Ars Nova. Double Hoquet. Guillaume de Machaut (XIVᵉ siècle)*. Paris, 1938.

Wilkins, Nigel, ed. *La Louange des Dames*. Edinburgh, 1972.

——, ed. *One Hundred Ballades, Rondeaux and Virelais from the Late Middle Ages*. Cambridge, Eng., 1969.

Wimsatt, James I., ed. *The Marguerite Poetry of Guillaume de Machaut*. Chapel Hill, N.C., 1970.

Young, Karl, ed. "The *Dit de la Harpe* of Guillaume de Machaut." In *Essays in Honor of Albert Feuillerat*, edited by Henri M. Peyre, pp. 1-20. New Haven, Conn., 1943.

Zwick, Gabriel, ed. "Deux motets inédits de Philippe de Vitry et de Guillaume de Machaut." *Revue de Musicologie* 27 (1948): 28-57.

II. Studies on the Life and Works of Guillaume de Machaut

Becker, Georges. "Guillaume de Machaut." In *Dictionnaire des Lettres françaises: Le Moyen Age*, pp. 353-58. Paris, 1964.

Boer, C. de. "Guillaume de Machaut et l'*Ovide moralisé*." *Romania* 43 (1914): 335-52.

Bossuat, Robert. *Le Moyen Age*. Paris, 1931.

Caylus, M. le Comte de. "Premier Mémoire sur Guillaume de Machaut, poëte et musicien dans le XIVᵉ siècle: Contenant des recherches sur sa vie, avec une notice de ses principaux ouvrages." *Mémoires de littérature, tirés des registres de l'Académie royale des Inscriptions et Belles-lettres* 20 (1753): 399-414.

——. "Second Mémoire sur les ouvrages de Guillaume de Machaut; Contenant l'histoire de la prise d'Alexandrie, et des principaux évènements de la vie de Pierre de Lusignan, roi de Chypre et de Jérusalem; tirée d'un poëme de cet Ecrivain." *Mémoires de littérature, tirés des registres de l'Académie royale des Inscriptions et Belles-lettres* 20 (1753): 415-39.

Chailley, Jacques. *Histoire musicale du Moyen Age*. Paris, 1950.

Cohen, Gustave. "Le *Voir Dit* de Guillaume de Machaut (vers 1365)." *Lettres Romanes* 1 (1947): 99-111.

Coville, Alfred. "Ecrits contemporains sur la Peste de 1348 à 1350." In *Histoire littéraire de la France* (Paris, 1938) 37: 325-90.

——. "Poèmes historiques de l'avènement de Philippe VI de Valois au traité de Calais (1328-1360)." In *Histoire littéraire de la France* (Paris, 1949) 38: 259-333.

Damerini, Adelmo. *Guglielmo de Machaut e l'"Ars Nova" italiana*. Florence, 1960.

Douce, André. *Guillaume de Machaut: Musicien et Poète Rémois*. Reims, 1948.

Eggebrecht, Hans Heinrich. "Machauts Motette Nr. 9." *Archiv für Musikwissenschaft* 19-20 (1962-1963): 281-93.

Eichelberg, Walther. *Dichtung und Wahrheit in Machauts "Voir Dit."* Frankfurt am Main, 1935.

Ficker, Rudolf. "Polyphonic Music of the Gothic Period." *Musical Quarterly* 15 (1929): 483-505.

Frank, Grace. "French Literature in the Fourteenth Century." In *The Forward Movement of the Fourteenth Century*, edited by Francis Lee Utley, pp. 61-77. Columbus, Ohio, 1961.

Frappier, Jean. "*La Chastelaine de Vergi*, Marguerite de Navarre et Bandello." In *Publications de la Faculté des Lettres de l'Université de Strasbourg, No. 105: Mélanges 1945. II. Etudes littéraires*, pp. 89-150. Paris, 1946.

Geiselhardt, Jakob. *Machaut und Froissart. Ihre literarischen Beziehungen.* Weida i. Th., 1914.

Gennrich, Friedrich. "Zur Machaut-Forschung." *Zeitschrift für romanische Philologie* 50 (1930): 351-57.

Gérold, Théodore. *Histoire de la musique des origines à la fin du XIVe siècle.* Paris, 1936.

———. *La musique au moyen âge.* Paris, 1932.

Gorcy, Gérard. "'Courtois' et 'courtoisie' d'après quelques textes du Moyen Français." *Bulletin des Jeunes Romanistes* 4 (1961): 15-25.

Gourmont, Rémy de. "Le roman de Guillaume de Machaut et de Peronne d'Armentières." In *Promenades Littéraires* (Paris, 1913), 5:7-37.

Grimm, Jürgen. *Die literarische Darstellung der Pest in der Antike und in der Romania.* Munich, 1965.

Gröber, Gustav. *Geschichte der mittelfranzösischen Literatur.* 2d ed., revised by Stefan Hofer. 2 vols. Berlin-Leipzig, 1933.

———, ed. *Grundriss der romanischen Philologie.* Volume 2, Part 1. Strasburg, 1902.

Günther, Ursula. "Chronologie und Stil der Kompositionen Guillaume de Machauts." *Acta Musicologica* 35 (1963): 96-114.

Hanf, Georg. "Ueber Guillaume de Machauts Voir Dit." *Zeitschrift für romanische Philologie* 22 (1898): 145-96.

Heger, Henrik. *Die Melancholie bei den französischen Lyrikern des Spätmittelalters.* Bonn, 1967.

Hoepffner, E. "Anagramme und Rätselgedichte bei Guillaume de Machaut." *Zeitschrift für romanische Philologie* 30 (1906): 401-13.

———. "Die Balladen des Dichters Jehan de le Mote." *Zeitschrift für romanische Philologie* 35 (1911): 153-66.

Jahiel, Edwin. "French and Provençal Poet-Musicians of the Middle Ages: A Biblio-Discography." *Romance Philology* 14 (1960-1961): 200-207.

Joukovsky-Micha, Françoise. "La notion de 'vaine gloire' de Simund de Freine à Martin Le Franc." *Romania* 89 (1968): 1-30, 210-39.

Knowlton, E. C. "Nature in Old French." *Modern Philology* 20 (1922-1923): 309-29.

La Monte, John L. "The 'Roy de Chippre' in François Villon's 'Ballade des Seigneurs du Temps Jadis.'" *Romanic Review* 23 (1932): 48-53.

Lebeuf, M. l'Abbé. "Notice sommaire de deux volumes de poësies françoises et latines. Conservés dans la bibliothèque des Carmes-Déchaux de Paris; Avec une indication du genre de musique qui s'y trouve." *Mémoires de littérature, tirés des registres de l'Académie royale des Inscriptions et Belles-lettres* 20 (1753): 377-98.

Lehoux, Françoise. *Jean de France, duc de Berri. Sa Vie. Son action politique* (1340-1416). Vols. 1 and 2. Paris, 1966.

Leube, Eberhard. *Fortuna in Karthago: Die Aeneas-Dido-Mythe Vergils in den romanischen Literaturen vom 14. bis zum 16. Jahrhundert.* Heidelberg, 1969.

Levarie, Siegmund. *Guillaume de Machaut.* New York, 1954.

Machabey, Armand. "Guillaume de Machault." *La Revue Musicale* 11 (1930): 425-52, and 12 (1931): 320-44, 402-16.

———. *Guillaume de Machault, 130?-1377: La Vie et l'Œuvre musicale.* 2 vols. Paris, 1955.

———. "Le manuscrit Weyen et Guillaume de Machault." *Romania* 76 (1955): 247-53.

Magnin. [A review article of Tarbé's *Les Œuvres de Guillaume de Machault*.] *Journal des Savants* (1851): 399-410, 475-91.

Maillard, Jean. "Chronologie sommaire des événements contemporains de Philippe de Vitry et Guillaume de Machaut." *L'Education musicale* 12, no. 36 (1957): 10-12.

———. *Evolution et esthétique du lai lyrique, Des origines à la fin du XIVe siècle*. Paris, 1952-1961.

Morel-Fatio, A. "Sur Guillaume de Machaut." *Romania* 22 (1893): 275-76.

Muscatine, Charles. *Chaucer and the French Tradition: A Study in Style and Meaning*. Berkeley-Los Angeles, 1957.

Paris, G. "Un poème inédit de Martin Le Franc." *Romania* 16 (1887): 383-437.

Patch, Howard Rollin. "Fortuna in Old French Literature." In *Smith College Studies in Modern Languages*, 4, no. 4 (July 1923).

———. *The Goddess Fortuna in Mediaeval Literature*. Cambridge, Mass., 1927.

———. *The Other World, according to Descriptions in Medieval Literature*. Cambridge, Mass., 1950.

Patterson, Warner Forrest. *Three Centuries of French Poetic Theory: A Critical History of the Chief Arts of Poetry in France (1328-1630)*. 2 vols. Ann Arbor, Mich., 1935.

Petit de Julleville, L., ed. *Histoire de la Langue et de la Littérature française des Origines à 1900*. Vol. 2. Paris, 1896.

———. "La poésie lyrique au XIVe siècle. Guillaume de Machaut." *Revue des Cours et Conférences* 1 (1892-1893): 194-200, 289-96, 330-37, 429-34.

Piaget, Arthur. "*Michaut* pour *Machaut*." *Romania* 21 (1892): 616-17.

Poirion, Daniel. *Le Moyen Age: II. 1300-1480*. Paris, 1971.

———. *Le Poète et le Prince: L'évolution du lyrisme courtois de Guillaume de Machaut à Charles d'Orléans*. Paris, 1965.

Prioult, A. "Un poète voyageur: Guillaume de Machaut et la *Reise* de Jean l'Aveugle, roi de Bohême, en 1328-1329." *Lettres Romanes* 4 (1950): 3-29.

Puymaigre, Comte de. "Jean l'Aveugle en France." *Revue des Questions Historiques* 52 (1892): 391-452.

———. "Une campagne de Jean de Luxembourg, roi de Bohême." *Revue des Questions Historiques* 42 (1887): 168-80.

Quittard, Henri. "Notes sur Guillaume de Machaut et son œuvre." *Revue de Musicologie* 1 (1917-1919): 91-105, 123-38.

Reaney, Gilbert. "*Ars Nova* in France." In *The New Oxford History of Music. III. Ars Nova and the Renaissance, 1300-1540*, pp. 1-30. London, 1960.

———. "A Chronology of the Ballades, Rondeaux and Virelais Set to Music by Guillaume de Machaut." *Musica Disciplina* 6 (1952): 33-38.

———. "The Development of the Rondeau, Virelai and Ballade Forms from Adam de la Hale to Guillaume de Machaut." In *Festschrift Karl Gustav Fellerer*, edited by Heinrich Hüschen, pp. 421-27. Regensburg, 1962.

———. *Guillaume de Machaut*. London-New York, 1971.

———. "Guillaume de Machaut: Lyric Poet." *Music and Letters* 39 (1958): 38-51.

———. "The *Lais* of Guillaume de Machaut and Their Background." *Proceedings of the Royal Musical Association* 82 (1955-1956): 15-32.

———. "Machaut's Influence on Late Medieval Music." *Monthly Musical Record* 88 (1958): 50-58, 96-101.

Reaney, Gilbert. "The Poetic Form of Machaut's Musical Works." *Musica Disciplina* 13 (1959): 25-41.

––––––. "Towards a Chronology of Machaut's Musical Works." *Musica Disciplina* 21 (1967): 87-96.

Reese, Gustave. *Music in the Middle Ages.* New York, 1940.

Rive, M. l'Abbé. "Notice d'un Manuscrit de la Bibliothèque de M. le Duc de la Vallière, contenant les Poésies de Guillaume de Machau, accompagnée de Recherches historiques et critiques, pour servir à la vie de ce Poète." In Jean-Benjamin de La Borde, *Essai sur la musique ancienne et moderne,* Vol. 4. Appendix. Paris, 1780.

Robertson, D. W., Jr. *A Preface to Chaucer: Studies in Medieval Perspectives.* Princeton, N.J., 1962.

Roquefort-Flaméricourt, B. de. *De l'état de la poésie françoise dans les XII*e *et XIII*e *siècles.* Paris, 1815.

Schilperoort, Johanna Catharina. *Guillaume de Machaut et Christine de Pisan (Etude comparative).* The Hague, 1936.

Schrade, Leo. "The Chronology of the Ars Nova in France." In *Les Colloques de Wégimont. II. 1955. L'Ars Nova: Recueil d'études sur la musique du XIV*e *siècle,* pp. 37-59. Paris, 1959.

––––––. "Guillaume de Machaut and the 'Roman de Fauvel.' " In *Miscelánea en homenaje a Monseñor Higinio Anglés,* 2:843-50. Barcelona, 1958-1961.

Suchier, Hermann. "Das Anagramm in Machauts Voir Dit." *Zeitschrift für romanische Philologie* 21 (1897): 541-45.

Suchier, Hermann, & Birch-Hirschfeld, Adolf. *Geschichte der Französischen Litteratur.* Leipzig-Vienna, 1900.

Thomas, Antoine. "Extraits des archives du Vatican pour servir à l'histoire littéraire. III. Guillaume de Machaut." *Romania* 10 (1881): 325-33.

Travers, Emile. *Les instruments de musique au XIV*e *siècle d'après Guillaume de Machaut.* Paris, 1882.

Vesce, Thomas E. "Love as Found in Machaut's *Dit dou Lion.*" *Romance Notes* 11 (1969): 174-80.

Whiting, B. J. "Froissart as Poet." *Mediaeval Studies* 8 (1946): 189-216.

Wilkins, Nigel. "The Post-Machaut Generation of Poet-Musicians." *Nottingham Mediaeval Studies* 12 (1968): 40-84.

Williams, Sarah Jane. "An Author's Role in Fourteenth Century Book Production: Guillaume de Machaut's 'livre où je met toutes mes choses.' " *Romania* 90 (1969): 433-54.

Wimsatt, James I. *Chaucer and the French Love Poets: The Literary Background of the Book of the Duchess.* Chapel Hill, N.C., 1968.

––––––. *The Marguerite Poetry of Guillaume de Machaut.* Chapel Hill, N.C., 1970.

Wooldridge, H. E. *The Oxford History of Music,* 2d ed. revised by Percy C. Buck. Vol. I. London, 1929.

III. *Studies on Guillaume de Machaut and Geoffrey Chaucer*

Braddy, Haldeen. "The Two Petros in the 'Monkes Tale.' " *PMLA* 50 (1935): 69-80.

Bryan, W. F., and Dempster, Germaine, ed. *Sources and Analogues of Chaucer's Canterbury Tales.* Chicago, 1941.

Estrich, Robert M. "Chaucer's Prologue to the *Legend of Good Women* and Machaut's *Le Jugement dou Roy de Navarre.*" *Studies in Philology* 36 (1939): 20-39.

Fabin, Madeleine. "On Chaucer's *Anelida and Arcite.*" *Modern Language Notes* 34 (1919): 266-72.

Harrison, Benjamin S. "Medieval Rhetoric in the *Book of the Duchesse.*" *PMLA* 49 (1934): 428-42.

Kitchel, Anna Theresa. "Chaucer and Machaut's *Dit de la Fontaine Amoureuse.*" In *Vassar Mediaeval Studies,* edited by Christabel Forsyth Fiske, pp. 217-31. New Haven, Conn., 1923.

Kittredge, G. L. "Chauceriana. I. The *Book of the Duchess* and Guillaume de Machaut." *Modern Philology* 7 (1909-1910): 465-71.

———. "Chauceriana. II. 'Make the metres of hem as thee leste.'" *Modern Philology* 7 (1909-1910): 471-74.

———. "Chaucer's *Troilus* and Guillaume de Machaut." *Modern Language Notes* 30 (1915): 69.

———. "Guillaume de Machaut and *The Book of the Duchess.*" *PMLA* 30 (1915): 1-24.

Langhans, Victor. "Chaucers Book of the Leoun." *Anglia* 52 (1928): 113-22.

Loomis, Roger Sherman. "Chaucer's Eight Years' Sickness." *Modern Language Notes* 59 (1944): 178-80.

Lowes, John L. "Chaucer and the *Ovide moralisé.*" *PMLA* 33 (1918): 302-25.

———. "The Prologue to the *Legend of Good Women* as Related to the French *Marguerite* Poems and the *Filostrato.*" *PMLA* 19 (1904): 593-683.

Meech, Sanford Brown. "Chaucer and the *Ovide Moralisé*: A Further Study." *PMLA* 46 (1931): 182-204.

Preston, Raymond. "Chaucer and the *Ballades Notées* of Guillaume de Machaut." *Speculum* 26 (1951): 615-23.

Robinson, F. N., ed. *The Poetical Works of Chaucer.* Cambridge, Mass., 1933.

Severs, J. Burke. "The Sources of 'The Book of the Duchess.'" *Mediaeval Studies* 25 (1963): 355-62.

Stillwell, Gardiner. "Analogues to Chaucer's *Manciple's Tale* in the *Ovide Moralisé* and Machaut's *Voir-Dit.*" *Philological Quarterly* 19 (1940): 133-38.

Wimsatt, James I. "The Apotheosis of Blanche in *The Book of the Duchess.*" *Journal of English and Germanic Philology* 66 (1967): 26-44.

———. *Chaucer and the French Love Poets: The Literary Background of the Book of the Duchess.* Chapel Hill, N.C., 1968.

———. *The Marguerite Poetry of Guillaume de Machaut.* Chapel Hill, N.C., 1970.

———. "The Sources of Chaucer's 'Seys and Alcyone.'" *Medium Aevum* 36 (1967): 231-41.

INDEX

Adam de la Halle, 177-78; *Jeu de Robin et Marion,* 67
Adenet le Roi, *Cléomadès,* 70, 199
Adler, Alfred, 84n
adventure, 80, 87-88, 121-23, 155, 181-82, 218
Aegidius Romanus, 131
Agnès de Navarre, Countess, 168, 170, 193
Alexandria, 203-9, 211, 213-15, 219-20, 223-26, 229-30
allegorical figures. *See Amour, Bonneürté, Esperence, Mesure, Raison*
allegory, 29, 34-37, 41, 46-47, 53, 58, 66-67, 72, 74-79, 83, 87, 93-103, 107, 113-15, 117, 119, 124, 178, 201, 209, 227-34, 242-43
allerion, 92-95, 97-99, 102-3, 107
Altercatio Phillidis et Florae, 39
Amadas et Ydoine, 26, 65
Amadeus VI, Count of Savoy, 203n, 212, 225
amor mixtus, 42
amor purus, 27, 42
Amour (character), 55-56, 60, 66, 98, 104, 106-8
Andreas Capellanus, 26-27, 41-43, 88, 113, 128, 147, 180, 201; *De Amore,* 27, 39, 42
Androcles, 83
anti-feminism, 44-45, 110-14, 116-17, 185-86
Apollinaire, Guillaume, 29
Aquinas, Thomas, 131
Aragon, Louis, 29, 226, 234
archetypes, 24, 29, 34, 37, 44, 49, 51-52, 63-65, 66, 68, 73-74, 79,
80-87, 123, 128, 143, 151-52, 182, 220, 231
Aristotle, 61, 147
Arnaud de Cervoles, archpriest of Vélines, 174
Ars amandi, 24, 56, 87, 93, 103, 152
Ars poetica, 70
art and the artist, 69-73, 128, 150-51, 165, 198-200, 245
Art de Dictier. See Deschamps, Eustache
Arts de Seconde Rhetorique, 235
Athalie. See Racine, Jean Baptiste
Atiya, Aziz Suryal, 203n, 204, 208-9
Aucassin et Nicolette, 122
Auerbach, Erich, 163, 172n, 177
Ausonius, Decimus Magnus, 29

Bachelard, Gaston, 81, 134, 148n
balade, 70, 72, 234, 236, 247
baladelle, 68-71
Ballade des seigneurs du temps jadis. See Villon, François
Bangert, Friedrich, 82n
Baudouin de Condé, *Conte de la Rose,* 231
Beatrice. *See* Dante
Beauvais, Pierre de, *Bestiaire,* 98
Becker, Georges, 20, 132n
Belle Dame Sans Merci, La. See Chartier, Alain
Benedict XII, Pope, 15
Bergson, Henri Louis, 37, 68, 119, 188-89
Bernart de Ventadorn, 27, 178
Béroul, 27; *Tristan,* 42, 49, 81
Bestiaires d'Amours, 82, 104
Bible, 83, 131-34, 143, 209

Bloch, Ralph Howard, 31n
Blois, Robert de, 131
Blomqvist, Åke, 94n
Bloomfield, Morton W., 82n
Boccaccio, Giovanni, 88, 124, 221, 237; *The Decameron*, 124; *Il Filocolo*, 199; *Geneologia Deorum*, 221
Bodkin, Maud, 79
Boehlke, Frederick J., 203n
Boethius, 57-59, 61, 73, 131, 135, 145; *De Consolatione Philosophiae*, 57, 60, 70, 131; *Philosophia* (character), 64
Bone Pastor Guillerme. *See* Machaut, Guillaume de
Bonneürté (character), 44, 110-13, 116-23, 125-28, 242
Book of the Duchess. *See* Chaucer, Geoffrey
Bormann, Ernst, 94n
Born, Lester Kruger, 131n
Bowles, Edmund A., 228n
Bray, René, 40n

Cahier, Charles, 82n
Calin, William, 29n, 80n, 172n, 206n, 216n, 219n
Campbell, Joseph, 80
Canterbury Tales. *See* Chaucer, Geoffrey
Carmen de Rosa, 231
Caylus, M. le Comte de, 168
Cent Ballades, Les, 28
Chailley, Jacques, 17
Chamard, Henri, 18, 19
chanson balade, 70, 72-73, 234, 247
chanson de geste, 20, 32, 43, 81-82, 96, 104-5, 177, 206, 208, 210, 214, 219n
Chanson de Roland, 32, 226
chanson roial, 69-71
Charles II, King of Navarre, 115, 130, 242
Charles IV, Holy Roman Emperor, 51, 205, 212, 225, 229
Charles V, King of France, 119-20, 124, 128, 145, 221; as Duke of Normandy, 174
Charon complex, 81

Chartier, Alain, 28, 36, 131; *La Belle Dame Sans Merci*, 28
Châtelain de Couci, Le, 27, 42, 70
Châtelaine de Vergi, La, 42, 49, 70, 111, 126
Chaucer, Geoffrey, 20, 36, 88, 156, 189, 246; *Book of the Duchess*, 50, 53, 158, 246; *Canterbury Tales*, 128; *Legend of Good Women*, 104, 128; *Parliament of Fowls*, 104
Chichmaref, Vladimir, 17, 173n, 177, 193, 246n
Chrétien de Troyes, 27, 87, 123, 177, 190; *Cligès*, 45, 96-97, 104, 183; *Erec et Enide*, 44, 84, 104, 122; *Lancelot*, 42, 44-45, 64, 81, 84; *Perceval*, 65; *Yvain*, 44, 65, 77, 81, 88, 97
Christine de Pisan, 36, 44, 131, 156, 226, 246
Cicero, Marcus Tullius, *De Amicitia*, 61
Cléomadès. *See* Adenet le Roi
Cohen, Gustave, 186n
comedy. *See* humor
Commentarii in Somnium Scipionis. *See* Macrobius, Ambrosius Aurelius Theodosius
complainte, 67, 70-71, 137, 150, 163, 169, 185, 193, 234, 236
Confort d'Ami, Le, 15-16, 58, 130-45, 211, 218, 222, 236, 240, 242-44; character development, 142-43; consolation, 130-31, 135-37; education, 142-43; *exempla*, 131-32, 142-43; fortune, 135-36; friends and enemies, 144-45; imagery, 134-35, 142-43; I-narrator, 143-45; justice and injustice, 132-34; kingship, 138-41; love, 137-38; mirror to princes, 130-31, 141; practical politics, 141; reification, 134, 137-40; religion, 136-37, 140
consolation, 50-53, 59-62, 130-32, 135-37, 243-44
Conte de la Rose. *See* Baudouin de Condé
Coopland, G. W., 204n
Cosman, Madeleine Pelner, 141
Courcelle, Pierre, 57n
court and courtly life, 51-53, 217-18

courtly love. *See* love
Coville, Alfred, 123n
Cox, Eugene L., 203n
Crusades, 206, 209-10, 224
Curry, Walter Clyde, 31n
Curtius, Ernst Robert, 29, 30, 142n, 144n, 200n

Dame à la licorne, La, 65, 70, 83
Daniel, 131-40, 143-44
Daniel, Arnaut, 178
Dante, 101, 177; Beatrice, 64; *Divine Comedy, The,* 101, 199; *Inferno,* 104; *Vita Nuova, La,* 30
De Amicitia, See Cicero, Marcus Tullius
death, 114, 126-28, 148, 220, 242
De Consolatione Philosophiae. See **Boethius**
Denomy, Alexander J., 180n
Deschamps, Eustache, 70; *Art de Dictier,* 235
didacticism, 24, 31, 45, 55, 73, 92-93, 130, 132
Dis dou cerf amoreus, Li, 122
dit amoreus, 19, 32, 46, 59, 69, 149, 155, 163, 233, 242-43, 247
Dit de la fleur de Lis et de la Marguerite, Le, 15, 18, 229-32
Dit de la Harpe, Le, 15, 18, 227-29, 232, 236
Dit de l'Alerion, Le, 15, 17, 34, 45, 92-109, 114, 130-31, 158, 186, 227, 240-44; allegory, 93-102; bird imagery, 104-5; didacticism, 92-93; education, 108-9; falconry, 93-100; *locus amoenus,* 103-4; love, 93-100, 106-7; narrative structure, 102-3, 108; reification, 106; time, 194
Dit de la Marguerite, Le, 15, 18, 212, 229-32
Dit de la Panthère d'Amours, Le. See Nicole de Margival
Dit de l'Arbre royal, Le, 30
Dit de la Rose, 15, 18, 231-34
Dit dou Lyon, Le, 15-16, 75-91, 93, 100-101, 105, 115, 121, 123, 132, 144, 147, 149, 157, 182, 211, 218, 232, 240-44, 246-47; allegory, 75-79, 87; education, 86; humor, 88-90; I-narrator, 88-89; lion, 77-78, 83, 89-90; *losengiers,* 75-77; love, 75-79, 87-88; obstacles, 81-82; Other World, 83-84, 86; romance quest pattern, 79-88
Dit dou Vergier, Le, 15-16, 23-38, 40, 47, 56, 62, 78, 86, 93, 105, 108, 130, 144, 234, 240-41, 244, 246; allegory, 34-37; dream-vision, 31-34; education, 24-25, 86; imagery, 28-31; imitating *Le Roman de la Rose,* 23-29; I-narrator, 36-38, 69; pattern, 55; reward, 27-28
Divine Comedy, The. See Dante
Dragonetti, Roger, 77
dreams, 23, 31-34, 148-52, 156-60, 196, 242, 244
dream theory (Freudian), 190
Dufournet, Jean, 19n
Durbuy Castle, 39, 46, 51-53
Durmart le Galois, 122

eagle, 92, 94, 97-98, 106
education, 24-25, 55, 62-63, 73, 86, 108-9, 142-43, 152-53, 242, 244
Egypt, 206, 225
Eichelberg, Walther, 170, 171, 178, 192
Enéas, 45, 96, 122, 156, 183
Enfances Guillaume, Les, 65
epic tradition, 213-17, 222, 226
Epîtres de l'Amant vert. See Jean Lemaire de Belges
Eracle. See Gautier d'Arras
Erec et Enide. See Chrétien de Troyes
Escoufle, L'. See Jean Renart
Esperence (character), 55-56, 58, 60-68, 71, 73, 85, 108, 130, 137, 179, 181-82, 187
Evans, Joan, 155n
Exempla, 92, 97, 102, 110-11, 121, 131-32, 138, 142-43, 158, 161, 165, 199, 242, 246

fabliaux, 177
falconry, 93-100
Faral, Edmond, 40n
Fauvel, 70
Filocolo. Il. See Boccaccio, Giovanni
fin' amor, 23n, 26-27, 35, 40-43, 45-46, 50, 56-58, 61, 75-76, 78, 92-

93, 95, 98, 104-5, 107-8, 112-13,
122, 126-28, 134, 147, 152, 164,
178, 183-85, 187, 197, 201-2, 223,
229, 233, 240, 243-46
Fisher King, 85
Flamenca, 42-45, 96, 142
Fletcher, Angus, 100n
Florence et Blancheflor, 39
Florimond de Lesparre, 204, 210,
214-17, 221, 224
Floris et Lyriope, 199
Fonteinne amoureuse, La, 15-16, 146-
66, 173, 184, 236, 240-47; archetypal women, 151-52; art and
the artist, 150-51, 165; dreams,
148-52, 156-60; education, 152-
53; illusion and reality, 158-60;
imagery, 148, 154-55; lyrics, 163-
65; myth, 161-63; n a r r a t i v e
structure, 160-61; spatial patterns,
154-55
fortune, 55, 57-62, 69, 135-36, 139,
185-87, 197, 243-46
Fourrier, Anthime, 172n
frame-story, 33, 69, 124, 176
Frank, Grace, 124n
Frappier, Jean, 49n
free will, 59, 135
Freud, Sigmund, 33
Friedman, Lionel J., 89
Froissart, Jean, 36, 51, 101, 158, 201,
226, 246
Frye, Northrop, 118, 134
Fyfe, Marjorie, 94n

Gace de la Buigne, 94n, 96
Garcilaso de la Vega, 29
Gautier d'Arras, *Eracle*, 43, 45
Gautier de Conflans, 204
Gawain, 81, 182, 217
Gaydon, 65
Geiringer, Karl, 228n
Geiselhardt, Jakob, 19
Gennrich, Friedrich, 17
Gerbert de Montreuil, *Le Roman de
la Violette*, 70
gerfalcon, 92, 94, 96, 98-99, 103, 106
Giblet family, 208, 215-16, 223
Gilbert of Tornai, 131
Gilles de Chin, 83
gilos, 43, 97, 223
Giraldus Cambrensis, 131

Girard de Roussillon, 65
Gliglois, 26
gluttony, 138
God as character, 136-37, 211, 222
Godfrey of Viterbo, 131
God of Love, 23-28, 30, 32, 34-38,
47, 63, 96-97, 99, 108, 112, 130,
179, 195, 242
Gorhigos, 203-8, 213-15, 218, 223
Gower, John, 189
Grigsby, John L., 57n
Grimm, Jürgen, 123n, 124
Gröber, Gustav, 93n, 205n
Guermantes, Duchesse de (Proust),
65; Duc de, 226
guide, 68, 83, 243; to Other World,
83
Gui de Warewic, 26
Guigemar. *See* Marie de France
Guillaume au faucon, 104
Guillaume de Deguileville, *Le Pèle-
rinage de la vie humaine*, 100
Guillaume de Dole. *See* Jean Renart
Guillaume de Lorris, 23-24, 27-29, 31,
35-36, 40, 51, 58, 90, 101, 125,
156, 163, 177, 186, 232. *See also
Roman de la Rose, Le*
Guinevere, 64
Gunn, Alan M. F., 34n, 40n
Günther, Ursula, 17n, 171n

Hanf, Georg, 19, 109, 173n, 201n
Heger, Henrik, 175n, 179n
Helinand de Froidmont, 131
Henry VII, Holy Roman Emperor,
51
Hieatt, Constance B., 31n
Hill, Sir George, 203n, 204, 209
Hoepffner, Ernest, 16, 18-19, 23,
39n, 40, 54n, 55n, 57n, 68, 75, 92,
93n, 110n, 111, 114, 123n, 130,
132, 138, 144, 147n, 159-60, 234,
239-41, 246n
Hofer, Stefan, 20, 93n, 205n
Holmer, Gustaf, 94n
Homer, 29, 139
Honig, Edwin, 100n, 102
honor, 28
Hoquetus David. *See* Machaut, Gui-
llaume de
Horace, 29
Hübsch, H., 17

Hueline et Aiglantine, 39
Hugh IV, King of Cyprus, 221-22
Huizinga, J., 89, 172n, 218n, 244
Humbert II de Viennois, 212
humor, 47, 49-50, 67-69, 88-90, 101, 116-23, 127, 149-51, 156, 187-89, 242
Hundred Years War, 83, 221, 247
hunting, 121-22
Huon de Bordeaux, 32, 81, 83

illusion and reality, 67, 158-60, 197
imagery, 28-31, 51, 134-35, 148, 154-55; 160, 244; animals, 73, 81-82; archetypal women, 63-65, 74, 151-52; biblical, 209; birds, 30-31, 93, 104-5; castle, 51-53; court, 74; demonic, 134-35; diamond, 154-55, 158; flame, 28, 160, 162; flowers, 29, 230-32, 234; fountain, 83, 154, 161, 165; gold and treasure, 73, 134, 154, 190-92; hunt, 121-22; key, 190-91; lion, 76-90 passim; prison, 134-35, 142-43, 147-48, 155-56; ring, 65-66; trees, 30, 126; war, 28-29, 206-7, 242. *See also* archetypes, dreams, *locus amoenus,* Other World, plague, quest theme. romance features
imagery, erotic, 28-31, 86-87, 105, 121
Imbs, Paul, 17
I-narrator, 36-38, 47-49, 56, 58, 62-63, 67-69, 74, 88-89, 115-18, 121, 129, 143-45, 149, 151, 171, 179, 186-87, 196-98, 241-42
Inferno. See Dante
insomnia, 149, 156-57, 159, 161, 164
irony, 50, 67, 88, 116-17, 124, 127, 179, 189

Jackson, W. T. H., 93n
Jagd, Die. See Laber, Hadamar von
Jaufré, 84, 96, 183
Jean de Condé, *La Messe des Oiseaux,* 30
Jean de Meun, 23, 28, 44-46, 57-59, 61, 64, 122, 124, 135, 145, 152, 163, 177, 186, 189, 235. *See also Roman de la Rose, Le*
Jean de Reims, 204, 206
Jean le Fèvre, 128

Jean Lemaire de Belges, *Les Epîtres de l'Amant vert,* 104, 247
Jeanne of Armagnac, 146n
Jean Renart, *L'Escoufle,* 44-45, 105; *Guillaume de Dole,* 44, 65, 70, 75, 122; *Le Lai de l'Ombre,* 65; *Le Roman de la Rose,* 231
Jehan Acart de Hesdin. *La Prise amoreuse,* 70, 122
Jehan et Blonde, 26-27, 96, 105
Jerome, Saint, 83
Jeu de Robin et Marion. See Adam de la Halle
jeu parti, 39, 43
John, Duke of Berry and Auvergne, 146, 147, 151, 161-63, 213
John II, King of France, 130, 133, 136, 146, 210
John V Paleologus, Emperor of Constantinople, 212
John XXII, Pope, 15
John of Luxembourg, King of Bohemia, 15, 39, 41, 43, 45-48, 51-52, 59, 107, 136-37, 139, 142-43, 150-51, 211-12, 242
John of Salisbury, 131
Jonas of Orléans, 131
Jonin, Pierre, 81, 172n
Jorga, N., 203n
Jouve, Pierre-Jean, 29
Juan Ruiz, 88, 128, 189
Jugement d'Amours, Le, 39
Jugement dou Roy de Behaingne, Le, 15-16, 39-54, 57-59, 62, 68-69, 77, 104-7, 110-12, 114-16, 121, 126, 128, 132, 136, 148-49, 173, 184, 186, 240-44, 246; allegory, 46-47; antecedents, 39-40; anti-feminism, 44-45; consolation, 50-53; court and courtly life, 51-53; humor, 49-50; I-narrator, 47-49; judgment reversed, 40-41; love, 41-46; spatial patterns, 50-53; trial-scene, 46-47
Jugement dou Roy de Navarre, Le, 15-17, 41, 44-45, 110-29, 130-32, 148, 163, 179n, 180, 182, 184, 186, 189, 236, 240, 242-47; anti-feminism, 110-14, 116-17; art and the artist, 128; death, 114, 126-128; humor, 116-23; hunt-motif, 121-22; I-narrator, 115-18; mel-

ancholia, 125-26; narrative structure, 123-29; plague, 123-25; reversal of judgment, 110-14; romance features, 121-23; trial, 120, 128-29
Julie (Rousseau), 64
justice and injustice, 132-33

"King Who Never Lies," 67, 175, 188, 243
Koenigsberg, Richard A., 65n
Köhler, Erich, 26, 30n, 84n
Kuhn, David, 19n

Laber, Hadamar von, *Die Jagd*, 122
Lai d'Aristote, Le, 70
Lai de l'Ombre, Le. See Jean Renart
Lakits, Pál, 49n
La Monte, John L., 226n
Lancelot, 81, 182, 217
Lancelot-Grail Prose Cycle, 64, 84; *La Mort Artu*, 75; *La Queste del Saint Graal*, 81
Landini, Francesco, 212
Langland, William, *Piers Plowman*, 100
Langlois, Ernest, 40n
Lanval. See Marie de France
lapdog, 49, 78, 90
Latini, Brunetto, *Li Livres dou Tresor*, 61, 143
lay, 67, 70-71, 73
Lay de Plour, Le. See Machaut, Guillaume de
Lazar, Moshé, 180n
Legend of Good Women. See Chaucer, Geoffrey
Levarie, Siegmund, 246n
Lewis, C. S., 34n., 97n, 163n.
Lion as adversary, 81; as guide, 83; as lapdog, 78, 90; as lover, 76-77, 89; as masculine figure, 83
Livres dou Tresor, Li. See Latini, Brunetto
locus amoenus, 29-30, 50, 56, 66, 75, 79, 83, 99, 103-4, 134, 154, 231, 233, 244
Lods, Jeanne, 172n
Lommatzsch, Erhard, 29n, 231n
losengiers, 74-77, 79, 82, 87, 97-98, 134, 167, 184-85, 232

Louange des Dames, La. See Machaut, Guillaume de
Louis IX, King of France, 96
love, 25-28, 41-46, 56-57, 63-65, 75-79, 87-88, 93-100, 106-7, 110-15, 126-28, 137-38, 146-49, 151-54, 179-89, 218, 223, 243-45. *See also fin' amor*
love casuistry, 39-40, 120, 123, 243
Ludwig, Friedrich, 17, 19, 63n, 246n
Lyons, Faith, 172n

McCulloch, Florence, 83n
Machabey, Armand, 16, 17, 19, 63n, 70n, 123n, 173n, 246n
Machaut, Guillaume de, bibliographical, 16-20, 249-54; biographical, 15-16, 52, 211-13, 240, 245-46; *Bone Pastor Guillerme*, 240; canon of Reims, 15, 19, 117, 128, 211, 240; chronology of works, 16-17, 234, 239; *Hoquetus David*, 240; influence and reputation, 245-47, 253-54; *Lay de Plour, Le*, 126, 128-29; *Louange des Dames, La*, 17, 146n, 235, 244; major poems. *See* under titles; *Messe de Nostre Dame, La*, 15, 17, 240; musical works, 16-17, 19, 63, 247
Machaut, Jean de, 52, 174
Macrobius, Ambrosius Aurelius Theodosius, 31, 33; *Commentarii in Somnium Scipionis*, 32
Maillard, Jean, 228n
Manekine, La, 65, 81
Marcabrun, 27
Marguerite poems, 20, 231, 246
Marie de France, 44; *Guigemar*, 81, 122; *Lanval*, 84; *Laüstic*, 104; *Milon*, 104; *Yonec*, 104
Mas Latrie, Louis de, 17, 203, 210
Mavrogordato, J. G., 94n
melancholia, 116, 125-26, 128, 149, 157, 164, 179-80
Meliacin, 70
Melior et Ydoine, 39
Mentz, Richard, 31n
Merlin, 85
Messe de Nostre Dame, La. See Machaut, Guillaume de
Messe des Oiseaux, La. See Jean de Condé

Mesure (character), 111-12, 114-15, 120
Meyer, P., 82n
Mézières, Philippe de, 203n, 212
Milon. See Marie de France
Molière, Jean Baptiste Poquelin, 45
Moller, Herbert, 65n
Montanhagol, 27
Mort Artu, La. See Lancelot-Grail Prose Cycle
Moses, 81
MS 1584 fond français of the Bibliothèque Nationale, 17-18, 167, 231n
Muscatine, Charles, 124n
Muset, Colin, 178
music, 73, 227-28, 236

narrative structure, 53, 71, 73, 79-88, 92-100, 102-3, 108, 123-31, 160-63, 176, 189, 200-202, 223, 242-43
Nasr-ed-Din, 206, 222
Nebuchadnezzar, 58, 131, 133-37, 139, 142, 144
Nelli, René, 180n
Nesson, Pierre de, 36
Newman, Francis Xavier, 31n
Nicole de Margival, *Le Dit de la Panthère d'Amours*, 70, 78-79, 104, 232

Octavien, 83
Oedipal situation, 87
Old Testament, 58. *See also* Bible
Orléans, Charles d', 28
Orpheus, 228, 236
Other World, 49, 51, 66, 80-81, 84, 86-87, 89, 123, 182, 220
Oulmont, Charles, 39n
Ovid, 26, 28-29, 156, 194
Ovide moralisé, L', 30, 104, 110, 122, 126-27, 131, 142, 159, 167n, 179, 228

Pannier, Léopold, 155n
Panthère d'Amours. See Nicole de Margival
Paris, Paulin, 17, 167n, 168, 171n, 176, 187, 191, 192-93
Parliament of Fowls. See Chaucer, Geoffrey

Partonopeus de Blois, 81, 122
Patch, Howard Rollin, 57n, 61, 80n
pathetic fallacy, 66, 125, 233
Pèlerinage de la vie humaine. See Guillaume de Deguileville
Perceforest, 70
Perceval. See Chrétien de Troyes
Perceval of Coulonges, 206, 208, 212, 219
Perlesvaus, 83
Peronne d'Unchair, 168, 170-71, 193
Perrault, William, 131
Peter de Lusignan, King of Cyprus, 203-26, 229-31
Petit de Julleville, Louis, 19
Petrarch, 26, 128, 212, 237
Pichois, Claude, 20
Piers Plowman. See Langland, William
plague, 110, 123-25, 127, 167, 174-75, 182
"poem of complaint and comfort," 59, 71, 163, 246
Poirion, Daniel, 19, 20, 70n, 72n, 124n, 142n, 164, 171n, 191, 212n, 235n
Poliziano, Angelo, 29
précieux, 44, 247
Prioult, A., 212n
Prise amoreuse, La. See Jehan Acart de Hesdin
Prise d'Alexandrie, La, 15-18, 63, 174, 203-26, 227-28, 236, 240, 242-44; as history, 203-9, 224-26; courtly life, 217-18; epic features, 213-17; love, 218, 223; medieval society, 216-17; religion, 209-11, 219; romance features, 217-20
prison, 28, 147-48, 155-56, 216, 222-23
Prologue, Le, 15, 234-37, 245
Prose Lancelot. See Lancelot-Grail Prose Cycle
Prose Tristan, 28, 70
psychology, 89, 175, 194
puella senex, 64, 85, 152, 187
puer senex, 222
Pyramus et Tisbé, 42

Queste del Saint Graal, La. See Lancelot-Grail Prose Cycle
quest theme, 79-88, 122, 218-19, 242

Racine, Jean Baptiste, *Athalie,* 136, 211

Raglan, Lord, 80

Raison (character), 41-43, 47-47, 59-61, 64, 107-8, 111-12, 114-15, 120, 228

realism, 124, 159, 161, 172-78, 201, 203-5, 240-41, 243

Reaney, Gilbert, 16, 171n, 246n

regimen principum, 130, 141

reification, 106, 134, 137-40

Reinsch, Robert, 82n

religion, 131-32, 136-37, 186-87, 209-11, 219, 228-30, 240

Remede de Fortune, 15-16, 55-74, 76-78, 105, 115-16, 130-31, 135-36, 144, 173, 184, 236, 240-46; archetypal women, 63-65; art and the artist, 69-73; consolation, 59-62; death and rebirth, 66; education, 55-56, 62-63, 73, 86; fortune, 57-62; humor, 67-69; illusion and reality, 67; I-narrator, 56, 62-63, 67-69; love, 56-57, 63-65; lyrics, 70-73; ring imagery, 65-66; temporal patterns, 63

Remy, Paul, 40n

Rênal, Mme de (Stendhal), 65

Renart le Nouvel, 70

Renaud de Montauban, 32

Rensch, Roslyn, 228n

Ribard, Jacques, 19n

Richard de Fournival, *Bestiaire d'Amour,* 98

Robertson, D. W., 19-20, 105n, 121n

Röder, Josef, 131n

romance features, 79-88, 121-23, 181-82, 217-20

Roman de la Poire, Le, 30, 70, 104

Roman de la Rose, Le, 23-30, 32, 34n, 35-36, 39, 45-46, 56, 58, 61, 66, 78-79, 86, 94, 97, 100-101, 122, 145, 154, 163, 190, 231, 242. *See also* Guillaume de Lorris; Jean de Meun

Roman de la Violette, Le. See Gerbert de Montreuil

Romaricimontis Concilium, 39

rondelet, 70, 72

Ronsard, Pierre de, 29, 234

Roques, Mario, 57n

Rougemont, Denis de, 127n

Rousset, Paul, 89n

Rudel, Jaufré, 27

Runciman, Steven, 204n

Russo, Vittorio, 142n

Rutebeuf, 178

Sachs, Curt, 228n

Schilperoort, Johanna, 19

Schrade, Leo, 16, 17, 19, 246

Schutz, Alexander Herman, 94n

Segre, Cesare, 82n

sermo gravis, sermo humilis, sermo mediocris, 177

setting, 50, 62-63, 78-79, 83-84, 86, 99-100, 103, 109, 154. *See also locus amoenus*

Sha'ban, Sultan, 219, 222

sloth, 139

Smet, Joachim, 203n

Song of Songs, 29

souffissance, 59, 137, 243-45

sovereignty, 139

sparrow hawk, 92, 94-96, 98-99, 102-6

spatial patterns, 50-53, 154-55, 173, 194-95

Spitzer, Leo, 38n

Steinmeyer, Karl-Josef, 31n

Studer, Paul, 155n

Suchier, Walther, 31n

Sutherland, D. R., 178n

Taillevent, Michault, 131

Tarbé, Prosper, 18-19, 168, 193, 229n, 231n, 233

Tavani, Giuseppe, 40n

temporal patterns, 63, 173, 194-95

Theseus, 81

Thomas, Antoine, 17, 52n, 57n, 167n

Thomas, Peter, 203n, 210-12, 214

Thordstein, Arvid, 82n

Tilander, Gunnar, 94n

Tjerneld, Håkan, 94n

tragedy, 135

trial, 46-47, 120, 123, 128-29

Tripoli, 203-6, 213-15, 218, 223-24

Tristan, 43, 75, 81, 97

Tuve, Rosemond, 34n, 100n, 102

universe upside-down, 124-25

Urban V, Pope, 210, 214

Van, Guillaume de, 17

Vàrvaro, Alberto, 142n

Vengeance Raguidel, La, 81

Venus, 146, 150-55, 158, 160-63, 166, 186, 189, 195, 218, 242

Vidal, Peire, 178

Villon, François, *Ballade des seigneurs du temps jadis,* 226, 247

Vincent of Beauvais, 131

virelay. See chanson baladée

Virgil, 29, 147

Vita Nuova, La. See Dante

Voir-Dit, Le, 15-18, 158, 167-202, 203-4, 227-28, 236, 240-47; ambiguities, 189-98, 201-2; anti-romance, 178-89; art and the artist, 198-200; autobiography or fiction, 166-72; class and moral problems, 174-75; humor, 187-89; illusion and reality, 197; I-narrator, 196-98; love, 179-89; psychology, 175; realism, 172-78; religion, 186-87; space and time, 173, 194-95; style, 177; youth and age, 175, 179-81

Voulte, Bremond de la, 214-220

Vries, Jan de, 80

Walberg, Emmanuel, 82n

Waste Land, 75, 83

Watriquet de Couvin, 131

Whiting, B. J., 201n

Wilhelm, James J., 248n

Wilkins, Nigel, 17, 19, 246n

William Longsword, 96, 102, 106

William of Aquitaine, 27-28

William Roger, Vicount of Turenne, 215, 220-21

Williams, Sarah Jane, 17n, 147n, 171n, 175

Wimsatt, James, 18-20, 59, 117n, 212n, 229, 230n

wish fulfillment, 33, 65, 87, 157

Wood, Casey A., 94n

Woodford, Michael, 94n

Wüster, Gustaf, 82n

Yalbugha al-Khassiki, 203, 222, 224

Yonec. See Marie de France

Young, Karl, 18, 227

Yvain. See Chrétien de Troyes

Zola, Emile, 239